Palgrave Studies

Series Editors
Steven Maras
Media and Communication
The University of Western Australia
Perth, WA, Australia

J. J. Murphy
Department of Communication Arts
University of Wisconsin-Madison
Madison, WI, USA

Eva Novrup Redvall
Department of Communication
University of Copenhagen
København S, Denmark

Palgrave Studies in Screenwriting is the first book series committed to the academic study of screenwriting. It seeks to promote an informed and critical account of screenwriting and of the screenplay with a view to understanding more about the diversity of screenwriting practice and the texts produced. The scope of the series encompasses a range of approaches and topics from the creation and recording of the screen idea, to the processes of production, to the structure that form and inform those processes, to the agents and their discourses that create those texts.

More information about this series at
http://www.palgrave.com/gp/series/14590

Adam Ganz · Steven Price

Robert De Niro at Work

From Screenplay to Screen Performance

palgrave
macmillan

Adam Ganz
Royal Holloway University of London
Surrey, UK

Steven Price
School of English Literature
Bangor University
Bangor, UK

Palgrave Studies in Screenwriting
ISBN 978-3-030-47959-6   ISBN 978-3-030-47960-2   (eBook)
https://doi.org/10.1007/978-3-030-47960-2

Cover image: Photo by kind permission of Robert De Niro and the Harry Ransom Center, The University of Texas at Austin
Cover design by eStudioCalamar

This Palgrave Macmillan imprint is published by the registered company Springer Nature Switzerland AG
The registered company address is: Gewerbestrasse 11, 6330 Cham, Switzerland

Note on the Text

We have consistently presented Robert De Niro's handwritten annotations in italics and inside quotation marks, to distinguish between his comments and the screenplay typescript.

ACKNOWLEDGMENTS: ROBERT DE NIRO AT WORK

We wish first of all to thank Robert De Niro for donating his magnificent archive for scholars to study, and for permission to reproduce the images in the book.

We thank our editor, J. J. Murphy, for his wise and supportive advice and suggestions throughout the process, and series editors Steven Maras and Eva Novrup Redvall for their thoughtful responses to an earlier draft and their many helpful suggestions thereafter. Lilly Markaki's assistance was invaluable in preparing the manuscript and checking references; any remaining errors are ours. We would also like to thank the team at Palgrave, especially our commissioning editor Lina Aboujieb, and Emily Wood for so ably shepherding the book through publication.

We also thank all the wonderful staff at the Harry Ransom Center at the University of Texas at Austin, and in particular Steve Wilson, Curator of Film for his support and unparalleled knowledge of the collection, and Eric Colleary for advice on Stella Adler. Adam thanks the Robert De Niro Endowed Fund Fellowship for supporting his study at the Harry Ransom Center, and Steven is similarly indebted to the Ransom Center Fellowship Program. We both received invaluable practical assistance from Fellowship Co-ordinator Kate Hayes.

Our students and colleagues at Royal Holloway and at Bangor University have offered much helpful feedback, as have colleagues and friends at the London Screenwriting Seminar and the Screenwriting Research Network. David Bordwell has been inspirational in his support for research in this area. We would also like to thank all the archivists who have responded to our many queries during lockdown.

In Austin, Adam would like to thank Michael Gilmore for his help and sharing memories of first watching *Mean Streets*, Janet Staiger for guidance and collegiate cups of coffee, and Louis Black for hospitality and insights about Robert Thom. Kathryn Millard has been enormously helpful in shaping some of these ideas over long Skype conversations. James Bennett gave invaluable help with the book proposal. I'd also like to thank Mandy Merck, Olga Goriunova, Jen Parker-Starbuck (for advice on New York theatre), and the many others who have shared thoughts and feedback. Thanks also for support from Royal Holloway in research time and funding. May subsequent researchers be so lucky!

Thanks too to all those friends who have heard me endlessly talk about De Niro and offered suggestions and ideas, especially John Roberts, Marc Isaacs, Joe Ahearne, Simon McBurney, and Anamaria Marinca who helped formulate ideas about performance and intertextuality.

I'd also like to thank my colleagues at StoryFutures Academy and especially Jon Wardle—for getting me that Film Festival ticket. To Steven Price for being such a great collaborator and to Ulla Maibaum for watching all those films with me again. Yes, we were looking at him.

Contents

ABBREVIATIONS

HRC The Harry Ransom Center, University of Texas at Austin
RDN Robert De Niro Papers, The Harry Ransom Center, University of Texas at Austin

LIST OF FIGURES

CHAPTER 1

Introduction

This book started to become thinkable in 2006, when after some forty years of work on over seventy films Robert De Niro gifted his working papers to the Harry Ransom Center (HRC) at the University of Texas at Austin. De Niro is indisputably one of the greatest film actors of the second half of the twentieth and twenty-first centuries, and his archive, which was opened to researchers in April 2009 after the extraordinary quantity of materials had been catalogued and indexed, opened up new, more fully informed ways of thinking about how screenplays are written and worked with, how the film text is created, and the role of the actor as writer—not only in directly devising the lines, and as a co-creator of the film text, but also as somebody who literally leaves traces of themselves on the film; indeed, these traces *are* the film, or are at least large parts of it.

These multiple ways in which an actor writes a film have not been studied enough: partly because prior to De Niro's generous donation there were no such archival materials available of remotely comparable significance, partly because De Niro is unique in the range, ways and extent to which he participates in these processes, but also because film studies has tended to think of the film actor as something passive, as something to be looked at, or as a star or celebrity, rather than as somebody who is actively making conscious decisions at every moment about what will appear on film. It is notable, for example, that the first edition of Richard Dyer's *Stars* (1979), the most widely cited academic study of

© The Author(s) 2020
A. Ganz and S. Price, *Robert De Niro at Work*,
Palgrave Studies in Screenwriting,
https://doi.org/10.1007/978-3-030-47960-2_1

1

film stars, makes no mention of De Niro; perhaps not surprisingly, since the three parts of the study look at 'Stars as a Social Phenomenon', 'Stars as Images' and 'Stars as Signs'. The second edition (1998) contains a single reference to him in a supplementary chapter by Paul McDonald, under the resonantly suggestive subtitle 'Stardom as Labour'—but only to dismiss (quite rightly) the 'incoherence' or inadequacy of remarks by other commentators to the effect that De Niro and Al Pacino are 'the finest actors of their generation', or that 'film acting is very complex and psychological, and that people like Pacino and De Niro work in complex and psychological ways'.[1]

The problem with such simplistic constructions is not merely their excessive generalisation, but that they work at the level of affect: De Niro's work appears complex and psychological, therefore he must be working in complex and psychological ways, but we don't know what these are and so we can say no more. Consequently, in journalistic accounts of the actor there is a tendency to fall back on oft-repeated anecdotes about the lengths to which he would go in, for example, transforming his body while preparing to play the older Jake LaMotta in *Raging Bull*. The archive can help to change all this, because in its most straightforward sense it represents De Niro's decision to archive his process. It allows the researcher to look at this process in all its complexity, and how it developed and changed as he worked with different screen-writers and directors, beginning with his first feature film *The Wedding Party*, filmed in 1963 and directed by Brian De Palma. Since then he has worked with many of the world's finest directors: apart from his close relationship with Martin Scorsese, with whom he has made eight films—the latest, *The Irishman* (2019), being released as this book was being completed—he has worked with an astonishing variety of other directors, including Elia Kazan, Roger Corman, Quentin Tarantino, Bernardo Bertolucci, Sergio Leone, Barry Levinson, Ron Howard, Penny Marshall and Harold Ramis.

The screenwriters he has worked with are equally illustrious, including Paul Schrader, Harold Pinter and David Mamet. The screenplays of almost all of his films are held in the archive, frequently accompanied by correspondence with directors, writers and other collaborators. The archive also retains many of his costumes and props—the material traces

---

[1] Paul McDonald, 'Supplementary Chapter: Reconceptualising Stardom', in Richard Dyer, *Stars*, 2nd ed. (London: BFI, 1998), p. 195.

of an actor's performance. We are able to see his reading lists and look at his notes on original source material and the various forms of annotation he makes on the screenplays themselves, all of which reveal his understanding of character and process. We can see how he develops that working process and how he learns and changes from film to film as he works with different directors and screenwriters on different roles.

The archive raises questions about the nature of the screenplay text and the film text, and the actor's work. It deals with what is or appears 'authentic', 'real' or 'natural', and the work that a performer does to ensure that what they do on screen, or what the audience sees on screen, has the maximum dramatic and emotional effect on its audience. Actors do not only *interpret* a screenplay text and translate it to the screen: in an important sense they embody that text and *become* it as it transmogrifies into a different medium; they leave traces of themselves behind. The means by which De Niro prepares for this may sometimes be improvisational, but they are never accidental. They include the ability to write dialogue; to think about the way dialogue is stressed or spoken; to think about what other actors might be working with, and how; and to undertake different forms of textual analysis, often at a very intense theoretical level. As long ago as 1988, when the archive was unavailable to scholars and this aspect of the actor's work was almost entirely hidden from view, James Naremore could accurately describe De Niro as 'a sophisticated theorist, a man who seems drawn to self-reflexive performances'.[2] The archive makes this aspect of his work newly visible: he analyses texts with the same level of sophistication as a literary critic or a film theorist, but he is also a historian and researcher, using many kinds of primary and secondary materials to find ways he can as an actor interpret, embody and articulate the text.

We write as scholars of the screenplay rather than performance. We are looking at how De Niro interprets a script and realises it in a different medium. And this has suggested useful analogies, such as translation studies or microhistory, on which screenplay studies can draw and through which it can be extended. We are looking at the screenplay not so much as a concept or a 'screen idea'[3] but as a material object, with a

[2] James Naremore, *Acting in the Cinema* (Berkeley: University of California Press, 1988), p. 267.

[3] Ian Macdonald, *Screenwriting Poetics and the Screen Idea* (Basingstoke: Palgrave Macmillan, 2013).

history and a purpose that was used by one person to realise their role in the film.

At the same time as De Niro's archive was going through the process of painstaking cataloguing to prepare it for the use of researchers, a disparate group of scholars was beginning to question the marginalisation of the screenplay in both film and literary studies. Between 2007 and 2010 this group, in addition to publishing their own monographs and articles, established the Screenwriting Research Network, organised an ongoing series of annual international conferences, founded the *Journal of Screenwriting*, and a little later set up the Palgrave 'Studies in Screenwriting' book series in which the present volume appears. The authors of this book have both been extensively involved with these various activities, but one of the things that struck us most forcibly when researching De Niro's archive at the HRC is that there has been remarkably little discussion about what happens to the screenplay for the *actors*: the people who in some cases (certainly De Niro's case) work on it most, whose reading of the screenplay can often determine whether or not the film gets made at all, and certainly will help to determine *how* it is made. The archive is a manifesto that allows us to look at what one particular actor has done in order to make the performances he has made, and it asks important questions about how films come to be, and about how we understand them. In this book we would like to pick up that manifesto, and work with it.

These two contemporaneous developments—the establishment of the De Niro archive and the emergence of screenwriting studies as a new field of research—form the foundations on which the present book is built. In Chapter 2 we look at various theoretical approaches to the screenplay, including as a 'boundary object'—a flexibly heuristic device for thinking about the multiple uses of screenplays and the many different kinds of practitioner who may use the 'same' screenplay for their own particular reasons. Not only screenplays, but also the actor and the archive, can all be thought of as boundary objects, intersecting productively with multiple users and for multiple purposes. We also look at the implications the existence of the archive presents for the study of De Niro as an actor, and for screenwriting studies, with a renewed focus on the materiality of the text and the role of the actor in embodying it and translating it from page to screen. In Chapter 3 we look at De Niro's formation as an actor, and how his approach to both acting and the use of screenplays was influenced by his formative artistic and intellectual experiences.

In these two chapters, we use examples from many different archived screenplays to illustrate particular points; in the remaining chapters we examine De Niro's annotations of particular screenplays in greater detail, with our criteria for inclusion being simply the most interesting texts, or those that exemplify the most interesting questions. Archives are to some extent processes of chance and contingency: things are discovered in there, and the scenes we have chosen to discuss in detail are either exemplary or distinctive. We aim to reveal the development and refinement of De Niro's practice; and if we accept practice as research, in the manner of current emphases in academic research in the humanities, then De Niro is the most profound kind of researcher into the nature of film narrative as it is expressed through his performances.

Our selection is guided by the view that with *Taxi Driver* (1976—Chapter 4) De Niro is finally in a position to do his very best work, bringing together all of the different things he has learned by that point. It is the first time when he is the first writer of the character. The earlier *Godfather, Part II* (1974), for which he won an Academy Award, is arguably a performance of equal stature, and his work on that script is fascinating for a number of reasons explored in our earlier chapters; but by contrast with *Taxi Driver*, for *The Godfather* he is building a character within definite boundaries that have been set by Marlon Brando's prior performance as the older Vito, while De Niro is also eager to learn from the film's director and screenwriter, Francis Ford Coppola, who exerts considerable control over all aspects of the production. On *Taxi Driver* De Niro, taking all of the knowledge he has acquired by this point, is now able to be an active collaborator with screenwriter Paul Schrader and director Martin Scorsese in creating the character for himself.

In Chapter 5 we take a detailed look at *The Last Tycoon*, a much less well-regarded and rarely studied film, also released in 1976. The archive helps to explain why the extraordinarily detailed work De Niro put into preparing for this role did not ultimately result in a more compelling film. As always, however, with *The Last Tycoon* he learned from experience, including what kinds of project were best avoided, and he accordingly re-dedicated himself to the value of improvisation, which he approached in very different ways in each of *New York, New York* (1977), *Raging Bull* (1980) and *The King of Comedy* (1982), all of which we discuss in Chapter 6. In Chapter 7 we look at *The Untouchables* (1987) and *Goodfellas* (1990), two examples of films made after that point in the early 1980s when De Niro changed his working practices and started to take on more parts as a supporting or cameo actor, and fewer in which he was expected to carry the film as the lead. Instead he gave himself the freedom to select smaller roles that engaged his interest for specific reasons. In our Conclusion we note the various ways in which the kinds of material we have considered in the book continue to demonstrate their timeliness and relevance: a new approach to acting in *The Irishman*, an unusually voluble De Niro giving many interviews to promote the film (and to engage in a revealing and ongoing dispute with President Trump), and his discussion of his father's own newly published and starkly personal notebooks all occurred in late 2019 as we were preparing the final version of this book for publication.

Actors are often ridiculed for the seriousness with which they approach their roles, yet they work in an enormously expensive business where they are often the costliest item on the balance sheet. It is scarcely surprising that a serious actor—and De Niro is nothing if not serious—needs to prepare in order to perform when the camera is rolling. What the archive shows are the various strategies he has employed to play the character in the ways that he thinks will most benefit the film. Film studies has tended to regard the actor as text, or as star or celebrity, or as the object of the spectator's gaze. What these approaches often omit is the actor as collaborator, and co-author, ultimately responsible for carrying the story into the film's own world of light and shadow and convincing the audience to follow them. Actors work, both when they appear in front of the camera and when they prepare. What we have learned about Robert De Niro's preparations, from the marks and traces in his archive, is the subject of the following pages.

BIBLIOGRAPHY

Macdonald, Ian. *Screenwriting Poetics and the Screen Idea*, Basingstoke: Palgrave Macmillan, 2013.
McDonald, Paul. 'Supplementary Chapter: Reconceptualising Stardom', in Richard Dyer, *Stars*, 2nd ed. (London: BFI, 1998), pp. 177–200.
Naremore, James. *Acting in the Cinema*, Berkeley: University of California Press, 1988.

CHAPTER 2

The Robert De Niro Archive and the Screenplay as a Boundary Object

In 2006 Robert De Niro donated his entire archive to the Harry Ransom Center at the University of Texas at Austin, and after three years of cataloguing it was opened in 2009. De Niro's archive is remarkable in its completeness both chronologically going from his very first feature films to the present, and in its depth, with multiple versions of screenplays and other documents. This astonishing resource for researchers gives an unparalleled insight into how an actor engages with a screenplay. For the researcher, it is a reminder that the screenplay is a material text, a working document which accompanies the actor to the set, which is used to organise props and costumes and where the actor prepares their performance, both in discussion with other actors and directors in rehearsal and on their own. The annotations and associated materials reveal the analysis, research and reflection involved in preparing a performance.

What the archive tells us above all is the enormous amount of work De Niro commits to his job as an actor. A film actor has not just to perform the character—they must, to use Francis Ford Coppola's formulation, make themselves sufficiently welcoming that the character can temporarily make themselves at home. As Coppola states,

> the actors do not turn into the characters—in fact, the characters turn into the actors. This might be saying the same thing, but as the actor is flesh and blood, and the character is a spirit-like phenomenon, the process is more

© The Author(s) 2020
A. Ganz and S. Price, *Robert De Niro at Work*,
Palgrave Studies in Screenwriting,
https://doi.org/10.1007/978-3-030-47960-2_2

correctly understood as the effort that leads to the eventual inhabitation of the actor by the character.[1]

An actor must also curate the character across the times and spaces of the narrative and the production. The actor has, in consultation with the director, to find the patterns and rhythms of the drama, identify emotional highs and lows and the moments where the drama reaches its peak, and to find ways best to embody this. This therefore involves physical work: the actor has to be able to perform those tasks unexceptionally which are unexceptional for the character, whether driving a taxi, hosting a chat show, speaking a dialect, playing the saxophone, punching an opponent (or being punched by them), or killing someone and burying their body. The archive lays bare some of the work involved in being able to reproduce, many times if necessary, actions and gestures on screen that embody the screenplay and the character.

The actor's job is to be compelling: to be more present, or differently present. That has of course to do with an actor's natural gifts, their looks, their sense of rhythm, and their physical control, but it also depends on the quality of their research, their energy and physical control, the power of their imagination, and their ability to find striking physical equivalence for the dialogue and description in the screenplay. And this involves work. As De Niro said in 1989, in response to the question 'You once said that you wanted to feel that you've earned the right to play a character. What did you mean?':

> To have done enough research on the character to feel that you have the right to play that character the way you see it—bringing what you've experienced, what you've learned, making it your own. An actor hears these words all the time: 'Make it your own, make it your own.' Stella Adler would say, 'Your talent lies in your choice.' It's one thing to know that, it sounds great; it's another thing to really *feel* it. And then you have the right to do it.[2]

---

[1] Francis Ford Coppola, *Live Cinema and Its Techniques* (New York: Liveright, 2017), p. 39.

[2] Lawrence Grobel, '*Playboy* Interview: Robert De Niro', *Playboy*, Vol. 36, No. 1 (January 1989), p. 83; italics in the original.

The De Niro archive reveals the breadth and depth of the research that De Niro undertook to earn this right. As Steve Wilson, who was then the curator of the HRC's film collections, put it at the time of acquisition, '[t]his is what the Ransom Center is all about, the creative process […] I know of no other actor's archive that is as large and comprehensive as this one'.[3] Moreover, while many writers' archives have been sold to institutions for substantial sums, as for example when Harold Pinter's papers were acquired by the British Library in 2007 for a reported £1.1 million,[4] De Niro *donated* his collection, the value of which initial reports placed at over five million dollars.[5] It was, as a reporter at the time inevitably put it, 'an offer the University of Texas could not refuse'.[6]

For De Niro the archive has been an ongoing project, with the original donation being supplemented with further materials in 2012 and 2018. It comprises a vast range of textual materials pertaining to hundreds of movies, both completed films and projects that never came to fruition. Its physical expanse is enormous: at time of writing its meticulously catalogued holdings are arranged in over 500 boxes, in addition to hundreds of books and other bound volumes, as well as an extensive collection of costumes, props and other personal effects and artefacts. Such a vast deposition required years of processing, and it was not until April 2009 that the collection opened to researchers and the public.[7]

On first viewing it, the researcher may feel an almost otherworldly thrill in being confronted with the handwritten marginalia associated with near-legendary films and artists, and experiencing the erasure of time between that moment perhaps forty or fifty years ago when the actor's pen first

---

[3] Steve Wilson quoted in Jim Vertuno, 'De Niro Donates to Texas' Ransom Center', *AP News*, 7 June 2006, https://apnews.com/677908d9d6406ff5bfe41daef7a72bfb [Accessed 29 September 2019].

[4] Mark Brown, 'British Library's £1.1m Saves Pinter's Papers for Nation', *The Guardian*, 12 December 2007, https://www.theguardian.com/uk/2007/dec/12/books.theatrenews [Accessed 29 September 2019].

[5] Kimberley Jones, 'HRC Opens the Doors on De Niro: The Harry Ransom Center Bulks Up Its Movie Holdings', *The Austin Chronicle*, 28 April 2009, https://www.austinchronicle.com/daily/screens/2009-04-28/hrc-opens-the-doors-on-de-niro/ [Accessed 29 September 2019].

[6] Vertuno, 'De Niro Donates to Texas' Ransom Center.'

[7] 'De Niro's Film Materials Collection Opens at Ransom Center' (Press Release), *Harry Ransom Center*, 27 April 2009, https://www.hrc.utexas.edu/press/releases/2009/robert-de-niro-collection.html [Accessed 16 June 2019].

scrawled across the page and the tangible immediacy of the document's existence in the present. The HRC goes out of its way to preserve this effect as much as possible:

> Special Handling Instructions: Most of the scripts in this collection have been left in an unaltered or minimally processed state to provide the reader with the look and feel of the original as De Niro used it. When handling unbound scripts, or scripts with inserted materials, users are asked to be extremely careful in retaining the original order of the material. Script pages folded length-wise by De Niro are likewise to remain folded in keeping with original order.[8]

There is an uncanny immediacy in, for example, exploring the contents of De Niro's self-created folder for *The Godfather, Part II* and witnessing the disciplined methods by which the actor organised his approach to creating the role. There are annotated versions of the screenplay in both English and the Sicilian dialect which De Niro's character spoke for the majority of the film. We can read in capital letters in the script: '*CI FÁZZU N'OFFERTA KUN PO RIFIUTARI*' ('make an offer he can't refuse'); when we see De Niro providing a detailed note from his '*Last viewing of other me*',[9] in which he lists strategies to incorporate into his performance the gestures and actions he has absorbed from his latest viewing of Marlon Brando in the previous *Godfather* film, we come to understand the complexity of the process.

Bringing a Text to Life

The modern American screenplay form is characterised by scene headings, minimal scene and action descriptions, and dialogue running down the centre of a page that as a consequence typically has the appearance of containing a large quantity of 'white space'. This then becomes an invitation for different workers to supplement the writer's script with

---

[8] 'Robert De Niro: A Preliminary Inventory of His Papers at the Harry Ransom Center', https://norman.hrc.utexas.edu/fasearch/findingAid.cfm?kw=ronin&x=42&y=8&eadid=00481&showrequest=1 [Accessed 18 May 2020].

[9] *The Godfather, Part II* (1974), Shooting script, with RDN notes, lacks title page; contains 'old script' and 'new script' pages, with additional script pages and extensive RDN notes re character development, undated, Box 182 [RDN].

annotations appropriate to their task (a director can turn the master-scene script into a shooting script by adding appropriate directions, for instance), and this means that the 'same' script can have multiple uses for different kinds of worker. For De Niro, white space provides the arena in which he can work out his approach to embodying and performing the character in ways on which the writer's script itself may be silent.

While most of the typewritten screenplay texts De Niro annotates broadly follow the conventional template, there are significant variations. For *Once Upon a Time in America*, director Sergio Leone developed the story with two screenwriters, Leonardo Benvenuti and Stuart Kaminsky. The visual presentation of the screenplay may appear unusual to the Anglophone reader, since it follows the Italian convention that divides the material into two columns, with the scene text appearing on the left-hand side of the page and the dialogue on the right.[10] This format allows De Niro ample room to position his handwritten annotations directly alongside the material on which he is commenting, as is seen clearly in Fig. 2.1.[11]

Once Upon a Time in America offers an excellent introduction to the subtleties of De Niro's annotations. For example, at the beginning of the scene in which the elderly Noodles (De Niro) visits the cemetery where his friends were buried, on the same street where he grew up, Noodles sees (in the words of the screenplay) that '[t]he cemetery next to the synagogue is being torn up'. The writers' final paragraph describes his reaction: 'NOODLES' gaze softens with the nostalgia that even the most desolate places of our past produce in us when we go back to them again. He looks once more towards the cemetery, then goes to the synagogue and enters'. The first sentence contravenes the conventional wisdom that screenplays should avoid narratorial comment: the generalisation about 'the nostalgia that even the most desolate places of our past produce *in us*' cannot be filmed. But in this screenplay, overseen by the director, the affective reading of an image is an essential component of its creation. It is not just that the writer(s) introduce a narrative mode, but that the mode gives a fair indication of how the scene could be filmed, because it

---

[10] For a recent discussion of some Italian script conventions, see Claudia Romanelli, 'From Dialogue Writer to Screenwriter: Pier Paolo Pasolini at Work for Federico Fellini', *Journal of Screenwriting*, Vol. 10, No. 3 (2019), pp. 323–337.

[11] *Once Upon a Time in America* (1984), Script in 151 scenes (291 pages); extra scenes laid in, with RDN notes, undated, Box 120.4 [RDN], p. 200.

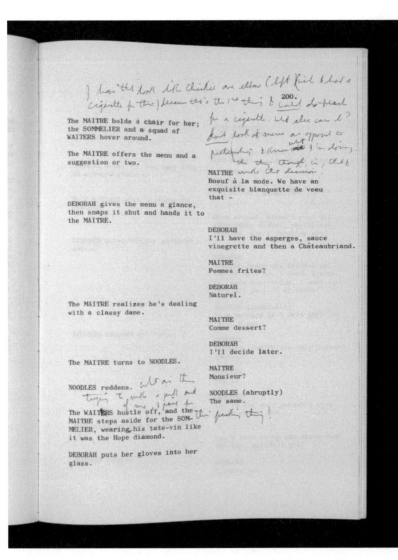

The MAITRE holds a chair for her;
the SOMMELIER and a squad of
WAITERS hover around.

The MAITRE offers the menu and a
suggestion or two.

MAITRE
Boeuf à la mode. We have an
exquisite blanquette de veau
that –

DEBORAH gives the menu a glance,
then snaps it shut and hands it to
the MAITRE.

DEBORAH
I'll have the asperges, sauce
vinegrette and then a Châteaubriand.

MAITRE
Pommes frites?

DEBORAH
Naturel.

The MAITRE realizes he's dealing
with a classy dame.

MAITRE
Comme dessert?

DEBORAH
I'll decide later.

The MAITRE turns to NOODLES.

MAITRE
Monsieur?

NOODLES reddens.

NOODLES (abruptly)
The same.

The WAITERS hustle off, and the
MAITRE steps aside for the SOM-
MELIER, wearing his tate-vin like
it was the Hope diamond.

DEBORAH puts her gloves into her
glass.

Fig. 2.1 *Once Upon a Time in America*, Box 120.4, RDN, p. 200

specifically invokes a nostalgic effect that could be evoked in any number of ways (music, soft focus, close-up on the character's face, to mention just some possibilities).

Following Sergei Eisenstein, we may suggest that the screenplay here outlines the 'emotional requirements' of a scene for which the director must find appropriate equivalences—a 'different language', as Eisenstein put in a 1929 article in which, discussing *The Battleship Potemkin* and citing the phrase 'A deathly silence hung in the air', Eisenstein suggests:

> Let the scriptwriter and the director expound this in their different languages. The scriptwriter puts: 'deathly silence'. The director uses: still close-ups; the dark and silent pitching of the battleship's bows; the unfurling of the St. Andrew's ensign; perhaps a dolphin's leap; and the low flight of seagulls.[12]

For Eisenstein it is quite appropriate for the writer to call for an emotional affect that does not have a precise visual equivalent, since finding these is the province of the director and not the writer. The *Once Upon a Time in America* screenplay is similarly written with affect in mind.

Yet it is surely significant that in a film with a justly celebrated musical score by Ennio Morricone, Leone does not use music, soft focus or even extended close-ups of the actor's face to create the nostalgic mood—the soundtrack at this point consists solely of diegetic street sounds, and De Niro is filmed mostly in medium shot from the back and from the side. The sentence 'NOODLES' gaze softens with the nostalgia that even the most desolate places of our past produce in us when we go back to them again is specifically asking for the *actor* to find an appropriate 'language' into which to translate the script, which at this point describes not just an image but an action: the gaze must 'soften'. The script places its faith in the actor to enact a complex evocation of nostalgic recollection that will prompt the appropriate affective response in the spectator.

It is the kind of challenge to which De Niro has responded again and again in his career, and we shall see throughout this book that his annotations typically tease out extraordinarily nuanced and ambiguous emotional responses that he then challenges himself to create on the screen. De Niro's marginal gloss to this paragraph in *Once Upon a Time in America*

---

[12] Sergei Eisenstein, 'The Form of the Script', in *Selected Works, Vol. 1: Writings, 1922–34*, trans. and ed. Richard Taylor (London: BFI, 1988), pp. 134–135.

is a fine example: '*Almost an* [illegible in the notation—probably 'emotional', possibly 'immaterial'] *reaction to cry. But to stop to hold in my reaction. Because of all those years away + to be happy to see it and also the sadness (yet happiness) to see how it's changed, how I've changed*'.[13]

It is typical of De Niro to write the note with this kind of halting, nuanced syntax, which here mirrors the complex movement of Noodles' response: (1) first to be moved almost to tears, but then (2) to try to arrest his response before the tears can come; and then (3) to be self-conscious enough to analyse the emotion—the 'nostalgia' called for in the script—and the self-restraining desire to hold it in; (4) to locate the cause of this complex, seemingly self-contradictory response—'sadness (yet happiness)'—in the recognition that the character has changed, but also that 'it' has changed, with the 'it' being seemingly the synagogue and cemetery, but also the street scene and everything the street represented in his boyhood; and finally (5) a qualification of the nostalgic response in the 'happiness' arising from the recognition that the changes are not purely of loss: clearly, something must have been gained too. De Niro's annotations show a perception of himself as simultaneously present in and absent from the scene, thereby using this moment as an opportunity to illustrate the structural effect of the film's complex time scheme and Noodles' position within it.

MONTAGE AND *MISE-EN-SCÈNE*

The *Once Upon a Time in America* screenplay is fairly unusual in the emphasis it places on emotional affect within the screenplay text. Many of the scripts on which De Niro worked are more conventional in presenting the action as a series of uninflected images; in such cases, as we shall see throughout this book, De Niro frequently conducts the same kind of work we have seen above in order to hypothesise ways of achieving the emotional affect—firstly in the annotations and then in the performance—that his reading of the script regards as being required, if not specified, in the writing.

This brings us to another, associated convention that has developed in connection with screenwriting. A consequence of avoiding the writing of affect is that the script will not usually linger on an image: the scene text

---

[13] *Once Upon a Time in America* (1984), Box 120.4 [RDN], p. 200.

will present an image in uninflected terms, and then move onto the next image. The rule of thumb whereby a page of screenplay text is presumed to approximate a minute of screen time also contributes to this minimalist mode of description (although as Kristin Thompson notes, this convention requires the cooperation of the director).[14]

Nevertheless, it is broadly true that most screenwriters will tend to write the action as an *implied* series of shots, to approximate the anticipated effect of seeing the film as a cinematically constructed narrative. It is in this sense that Claudia Sternberg can describe the screenwriter as a '*hidden director*', writing in such a way that the script suggests, without overtly specifying, a series of cuts and shot types.[15] In our present example, if we were to remove the narratorial comment about nostalgia we would be left with a description that clearly implies a particular sequence of shots: '1. NOODLES' gaze softens [...] 2. He looks once more towards the cemetery, 3. then goes to the synagogue and 4. enters'. We might think that even the shot type is specified (we may see the first shot as a close-up, for example), but in any case, stripped of the unusual narratorial comment it reveals the script as a montage of shots edited in a particular sequence to further the story, without at any point having overtly to specify either editing (cuts), or cinematography or direction (the type of shot) within the screenplay itself.

In these ways the conventional contemporary screenplay tends to prioritise montage (the idea that the meaning of a particular shot is generated by its position within a sequence of other shots, as in the Kuleshov effect) over mise-en-scène (the immanent meaning of the image captured within the frame of the shot). In short, it tends to prioritise editing over such matters as costume and set design—but also *performance*—which are the province of other specialists who may utilise the white spaces of the script, and supply paratextual illustrations, in working on the film. Unwittingly perhaps, screenwriting orthodoxy, like much of film theory, has thereby tended to construct the actor as something passive (Hitchcock's notorious 'cattle'): as something to be looked at, as the object of the gaze, as something manipulated by the plot, rather than as someone who is active, who has to make conscious decisions at every moment about

---

[14] Kristin Thompson, *Storytelling in the New Hollywood: Understanding Classical Narrative Technique* (Cambridge, MA: Harvard University Press, 1999), p. 367.

[15] Claudia Sternberg, *Written for the Screen: The American Motion-Picture Screenplay as Text* (Tübingen: Stauffenburg, 1997), p. 231; italics in the original.

how things will appear on the film. De Niro's annotations explore these conscious decisions, and in so doing reverse the priorities of the screenplay text: they demand that the actor take centre stage as a conscious, emotive agent whose decisions need to be made visible within the shot, and not just as an effect of the editorial juxtaposition of shots.

In working on the script, then, De Niro is consciously exploring some of the emotional affects of performance that cannot adequately be catered to in the writer's text. This is particularly the case with many of the wordless close-ups for which he has become celebrated. His partner at his film company Tribeca Productions, Jane Rosenthal, told an interviewer that '[t]he way his eyes make love to the camera—no one, not even the director, can see it at the time [...] No one sees it except the camera'.[16] As Shawn Levy writes of a different moment in *Once Upon a Time in America*, when the older Noodles visits Mo's restaurant, finds the peephole through which he used to peer voyeuristically at Deborah as she danced, and now peeks through it once again:

> [He] gazes through it as if at his own youth. Leone's camera stares into De Niro's eyes for a long, long while, and De Niro demonstrates his ability to become a transparent vessel for emotions. This is the sort of thing he loves best in film—acting without speaking, conveying an inner state through delicate physicality. His eyes—brown, moist, limpid, filled with pain and wistfulness—are the windows into the movie, and Leone holds focus on them for a daringly extended shot.[17]

The wordless close or medium shot on De Niro's face, as the spectator is asked to register the complexity of emotions that the character is experiencing, is very common in De Niro's films. Another striking example is the moment in *The Untouchables* when news is brought to De Niro/Al Capone, as he watches Caruso sing at the opera, that an enemy has been successfully assassinated. De Niro's face slowly forms into an expression that the spectator must recognise as of simultaneously sinister, oxymoronic laughter on hearing of a killing, and of the again oxymoronic tears shed at Caruso's singing, with Capone seemingly both sincerely moved by the emotional affect of the opera and yet at

---

[16] Jane Rosenthal quoted in Barry Paris, 'Maximum Expression', *American Film*, Vol. 36, No. 5 (October 1989), pp. 34–35.

[17] Shawn Levy, *De Niro: A Life* (New York: Three Rivers, 2014), p. 273.

the same time giving a response that looks melodramatically excessive, a vulgar masquerade of emotion.

A similar effect is achieved by slightly different means at the end of *Once Upon a Time in America*, as a minutes-long freeze frame audaciously holds on an even more intense and ambiguous smile on De Niro's face in the opium den in 1933. As the credits roll over it, the audience is invited to relive the meaning of the whole film as it is expressed in this frozen image of the younger Noodles' face. The immediate impression is that the smile registers the 'hit' just as the heroin kicks in, but as time passes and the spectator continues to stare, we are undoubtedly asked to think that the emotions passing through Noodles' mind will include contradictory feelings: of relief at having escaped from the violent thugs pursuing him, alongside a consciousness of having betrayed his friends who are now dead. We also see the image from the outside, as spectators who perhaps have developed an affection for the older Noodles that this man will become, but also disgust for the younger Noodles—and his own knowledge that he is a serial rapist who has destroyed his one true love, Deborah. We tell ourselves that this thought is surely also playing through his mind at this moment. All of these perceptions, meanwhile, are rendered more problematic by the complexity of the time scheme—at the end of the film both we and the older Noodles know much more about the ironies of this moment than the younger Noodles can be aware of—and by the cloudy effects of the narcotic daze that render moot all confident assertions about what is really passing through his mind.

These are the kinds of emotional impact that may or may not be adequately explored by a screenwriter on the page, but which only an actor can manifest on film, and which De Niro dedicates himself to examine via his preparatory analytical work that enables him to bring the text from screenplay to screen performance. The effect of the archive on one's understanding of screenplays is almost classically deconstructive, in the sense that deconstruction tends to propose that what is marginal, or 'supplementary', can in fact displace, undermine or otherwise challenge one's understanding of centrality and structure, and that origin, centre and structure are in fact dependent on whatever it is that they attempt to marginalise or efface.[18] In looking at the De Niro screenplays in this

---

[18] The foundational (if such a word can be used in this context) discussion of the 'supplement' is Jacques Derrida, 'Structure, Sign, and Play in the Discourse of the Human Sciences', in *Writing and Difference*, trans. Alan Bass (London: Routledge,

form we are constantly reminded of the role of the actor, whose body and agency are usually significantly absent within screenplays. The screenplay is the tool the actor uses to access the drama, and the portal through which they use their physical body to write the text as traces of light and shadow on a screen with accompanying sound.

The De Niro archive tends to overturn the investigator's prior understandings of what screenplays are, of how they are written, and of what is central to them. In the archive, the margin takes priority over the centre; the spaces of the script pages and the handwritten commentary that occupies them are often more revealing than the iterations of typescript; the modifications are more important than the prior, 'original' structure; and above all, the actor now takes centre stage, becoming as much, or more of, a creator of the final text than the screenwriter.

MARGINALIA AND COMMENTARY

The very existence of the archive invites us to think differently about screenplay texts—not just as the creation of a screenwriter or a stage in the pre-production of a film project, but as a piece of writing or artwork to which the actor has made material contributions that are visible on the page. The interest is immediately in what the existence of the script tells us about De Niro, what we can deduce about the script from the paratexts and other research materials that he has retained and archived along with the screenplay, and of course what his annotations tell us about his reading of the script and what he proposes to bring to his performance.

This will give a very different perspective on the screenplay than reading the unannotated script or the comments and revisions of the screenwriter or director. Consequently, copies of the 'same' screenplay in different archives immediately invite different readings of this 'same' text. An example is provided by the archival holdings for *Ronin* (1997), a project that began as an original screenplay by J. D. Zeik. De Niro's archive contains three lightly annotated or unannotated drafts by Zeik, culminating in draft 7, dated 30 September 1997 (RDN 131.4).[19] De Niro's marginal comments on the seventh draft of *Ronin* are brief—yet

---

1978), pp. 278–294. Jacques Derrida, *Margins of Philosophy*, trans. Alan Bass (Brighton: Harvester, 1982) collects a number of extended reflections on concepts of marginality.

[19] As the archive does not contain drafts 1–5 we can assume that the work had already proceeded through several iterations before De Niro committed to the film.

pithily telling. In several places he writes a comment, sometimes of a single word, that reveals his exasperation at an unmotivated or incredible action (*'possible?'*), unnecessary explanation (*'all this exposition'*), or on-the-nose dialogue (*'please!'*). Some pages have been folded carefully in half to indicate that it contains a comment by him of particular significance.

The eighth draft, dated 26 October 1997 (RDN 131.5), sees the material changed almost beyond recognition. Certain action scenes (especially the car chases, for which the completed film quickly became renowned) survive without modification, but much of the plot has been radically altered, with whole sequences jettisoned and others entirely new, while the dialogue has been entirely rewritten. The explanation for this can be found in the archive of screenwriter David Mamet, also held at the HRC, which retains correspondence to Mamet from Jane Rosenthal, producer at De Niro's production company Tribeca, alerting the writer to a request from De Niro and *Ronin* director John Frankenheimer for Mamet to polish the dialogue on the accompanying script.[20] The screenplay that Mamet delivered on 25 October[21] is verbally identical to the eighth, 26 October draft in De Niro's files.

The existence of these two archives allows us to see that Mamet jettisoned the preceding draft almost completely—as he had also done the previous year for *Wag the Dog* (1997), another film starring De Niro—and that the film as released was made from his new iteration, helping to confirm Mamet's status as one of the major American screenwriters of the 1990s. Simultaneously, however, the quantitively much smaller contribution of De Niro, amounting to a minimalist handwritten critique of the Zeik script and an invitation for Mamet to re-write, establishes him as instigator of the film that ultimately appeared on the screen.

The relatively spare annotations on the *Ronin* scripts are quite typical of the later screenplays in the De Niro archive. His marginal commentary tends to be much more extensive on the scripts with which he worked earlier in his career, up to and including *Goodfellas* (1990). On scripts until that date it is not unusual for his handwritten words greatly to exceed in quantity the printed words, especially on pages where the character to be played by De Niro appears. Individual script pages of *The*

---

[20] Correspondence from Jane Rosenthal to David Mamet, 25 October 1977, Container 176.2-4, David Mamet Papers, HRC.

[21] *Ronin*, Typescript draft by David Mamet, with typed and handwritten revisions, 25 October 1997, Container 176.1, David Mamet Papers, HRC.

Godfather, Part II, *The Last Tycoon*, and many others throughout the 1970s and 1980s are simply plastered with commentary.

Very frequently De Niro also uses his preferred ring-bound format to create marginalia to the marginalia: with the screenplay pages hole-punched and bound, the opened folder will present the printed text on the right-hand (recto) page, with De Niro's annotations upon it, while the left-hand page (the verso)—the blank reverse of the preceding page—allows him ample space for additional comments, frequently taking the form of a numbered list of further points pertaining to the recto text, sometimes using arrows to connect the observations on the verso page to the script on the recto. And for certain other scripts that we shall examine later in this book, especially *Raging Bull*, although De Niro's handwritten annotations can appear literally marginal he is in fact a central writer in originating and developing the script, and in writing the final draft. Although claiming formal credit for writing was never something in which De Niro appears to have taken any interest, the archive demonstrates that in some cases at least his contribution would have been sufficient to be awarded it. The process of annotation places the actor both literally and figuratively both at the margins and, simultaneously, at the centre of the writing process.

THE BOUNDARY OBJECT AND THE SCREENPLAY

If De Niro's annotations cause us radically to re-think what is a screenplay is, that does not of course mean the work of the writer is erased. On the contrary, writer and actor share the same text. Different uses are being made of the 'same' document by collaborators with different roles and emphases as the actor prepares both to inhabit and embody the words of the writer. and other collaborators make use of the text in different ways to enable that transformation to occur, in every possible way.

One approach to exploring these possibilities is to consider the screen-play as a 'boundary object'. Although screenplay studies has only picked up on this idea surprisingly recently, it has been a very well-established concept in the social sciences since 1989, when Susan Leigh Star and James R. Griesemer introduced the term as a means of exploring how groups of scientists of different specialisms work together towards a common goal[22]—'building a system to communicate across social worlds', as Star puts it in her later article 'This Is Not a Boundary Object: Reflections on the Origin of a Concept', where she also clarifies the meaning of the term itself. Instead of the common meaning of an 'edge or periphery', 'boundary' here 'is used to mean a shared space, where exactly that sense of here and there are confounded. These common objects form the boundaries between groups through flexibility and shared structure—they are the stuff of action'.[23] Meanwhile, '[a]n object is something people [...] act toward and with. Its materiality derives from action [...]. So, a theory may be a powerful object'.[24]

It is this idea of a 'shared space' that makes the idea of the boundary object so attractive to screenwriting studies, which for a long time has been hampered by the metaphor of the script as a 'blueprint': a fixed object that completed the 'conception' stage of pre-production, which was then realised in the 'execution' stage of filming.[25] As the De Niro archive overwhelmingly demonstrates, in most practical contexts in which De Niro works the screenplay is a multiply-authored and constantly changeable site of negotiation between different participants with different specialisms. Moreover, although De Niro himself has acquired sufficient status within the industry to ensure his own suggestions will be considered if not necessarily implemented, even in his earliest film performances the archive shows how his ideas about and commentaries upon the script comprise a material intervention between a screenplay as one iteration of the screen idea and what appears on the screen as another. Indeed, as we shall see in Chapter 5, the best example in his career of a screenplay that could be considered a 'blueprint', *The Last Tycoon*, is also for precisely that reason the best example of a film that

---

[22] Susan Leigh Star and James R. Griesemer, 'Institutional Ecology, "Translations" and Boundary Objects: Amateurs and Professionals in Berkeley's Museum of Vertebrate Zoology, 1907–39', *Social Studies of Science*, Vol. 19 (1989), pp. 387–420.

[23] Susan Leigh Star, 'This Is Not a Boundary Object: Reflections on the Origin of a Concept', *Science, Technology, & Human Values*, Vol. 35, No. 5 (2010), pp. 602–603.

[24] Star, 'This Is Not a Boundary Object', p. 603.

[25] For critiques of the 'blueprint' metaphor in screenwriting see Steven Maras, *Screenwriting: History, Theory and Practice* (London: Wallflower, 2009), pp. 11–16; and Steven Price, *The Screenplay: Authorship, Theory and Criticism* (Basingstoke: Palgrave, 2010), pp. 44–47.

failed to benefit fully from the work he put into annotating the screenplay text.

There is a suggestive overlap of terminology between Star and Griesemer's work and the discourses surrounding screenwriting. The boundary object is a pragmatic means of understanding how groups and workers with diverse interests and strategies may nevertheless collaborate productively around a particular structure—in our case, the screenplay. More fortuitously, perhaps, Star and Griesemer use the term 'actors' to describe the different groups that can cooperate via the boundary object:

> Because these new objects and methods mean different things in different worlds, actors are faced with the task of reconciling these meanings if they wish to cooperate. This reconciliation requires substantial labour on everyone's part. Scientists and other actors contributing to science translate, negotiate, debate, triangulate and simplify in order to work together.[26]

Star and Griesemer use the term 'actors' to mean 'participants'. They are studying what happens when people from different fields or with different expectations and needs are making use of the same documentation or system, a boundary object which is scrutinised by different participants from different positions. It is, though, eminently applicable to actors in a film and how they contribute alongside directors, writers, technicians and other crew to its development and realisation.

Pascale Trompette and Dominique Vinck, in an article reviewing the impact of Star and Griesemer's article twenty years after its initial publication, described the process as follows: 'Those involved succeeded in coming to an understanding by working around objects. The process allowed them to maintain a plurality of points of view. Each of the parties was able to keep its identity and its targets and was able to carry on its work whilst articulating with others'.[27] They cite Étienne Wenger's identification of four elements within the notion of the boundary object:

1. Abstraction: it facilitates dialogue between worlds
2. Multi-tasking: several activities or practices are possible

---

[26] Star and Griesemer, 'Institutional Ecology', pp. 388–389.

[27] Pascale Trompette and Dominique Vinck, 'Revisiting the Notion of Boundary Object', *Revue d'anthropologie des connaissances*, Vol. 3, No. 1 (2009), p. 3 (c).

3. Modularity: different parts of the object can serve as a basis for dialogue between actors
4. Standardisation of the information contained in the object: rendering the information interpretable.[28]

Trompette and Vinck show how this is applied to various concepts, including design management theory; others have applied it to communications and the various stakeholders in television programming.[29]

Given that the concept of the boundary object has been deployed in so many fields, it is curious that it has been used comparatively rarely in relation to screenwriting. The film is of course a well-established and highly visible industry that employs specialist workers from a range of disciplines who come together to work on particular projects, and screenplays very frequently function as the objects that many of these collaborators 'work around' (to borrow Trompette and Vinck's felicitous expression). Yet to the best of our knowledge it was not applied to screenplays prior to Rosamund Davies' account (in a paper co-written with Ryan Flynn) of how the screenplay became a contested site in a collaborative project writing videogame on which she worked, which explored public health issues on a project where

> the concept of the serious game, the scenario, the story outline, the script, the learning objectives and many other elements might all be considered boundary objects. Although they facilitated collaboration and discussion between writers, designers and health educators, each focussed on different priorities in their use and understanding of these objects. They therefore also became sites of communication breakdown and conflict, when these differences in interpretation were fully revealed.[30]

Jacob Ion Wille and Anne-Marie Waade also use the term in discussing the Danish television series *The Legacy*, applying it to all of the objects

---

[28] Trompette and Vinck, p. 5 (e).

[29] See for example Gail Davies, 'Science, Observation and Entertainment: Competing Visions of Post-war British Natural History television, 1946–1967', *Ecumene*, Vol. 7, No. 4 (2000), pp. 432–459.

[30] Rosamund Davies and Ryan Flynn, 'Explicit and Implicit Narratives in the Co-design of Videogames', in Anastastions Maragiannis (ed.), *Proceedings of the Digital Research in the Humanities and Arts Conference, DRHA2014* (London: University of Greenwich, 2015), pp. 73–80, p. 75.

(including the screenplay) that enable the development of 'a shared understanding within the creative team and to communicate ideas and knowledge to stakeholders'.[31]

The screenplay, then, is in many ways a perfect example of the boundary object, and the term has recently begun to build traction within this area of study. 2019 saw the publication in the *Journal of Screenwriting* of two quite separate articles that drew centrally on the concept in developing ideas about how the screenplay works within a community of practice. Noting that '[t]he strong element of shared practice in filmmaking reveals it to be a complex social process where boundary objects serve to align and coordinate action and meaning',[32] Vincent Giarrusso reflects on his own experience as a scriptwriter via the boundary object, drawing on Star and Griesemer's work but also, like Trompette and Vinck, on Étienne Wenger's 1998 study *Communities of Practice: Learning, Meaning and Identity*. Giarrusso's interest here is focused on three interrelated aspects of such relationships unpacked by Wenger: they are *'negotiable'*, because participants collaborate via 'Mutual Engagement'; they are *'relational'*, with practitioners negotiating a 'shared understanding of what keeps them together' in a 'Joint Enterprise'; and they develop a 'Shared Repertoire' of 'practices and resources' which 'can include both literal and *symbolic* meanings'.[33]

In a still more recent article, Rosamund Davies notes 'that the various sub-groups involved in a large-scale collaborative project will tend to generate tailored versions or off shoots of the original boundary object, for their own more specific use'.[34] This is exactly what happens to screenplays as De Niro works on them. As noted, he adds enormous quantities of information to the often minimalist form characteristic of screenplays, and even to the more inflected text of a Sergio Leone or a Paul Schrader, both in order to explore it critically and to realise it practically, just as

---

[31] Jacob Ion Wille and Anne Marit Waade, 'Production Design and Location in the Danish Television Drama Series *The Legacy*', *Kosmorama* #263, 16 May 2016, https://www.kosmorama.org/en/kosmorama/artikler/production-design-and-location-danish-television-drama-series-legacy [Accessed 20 May 2020].

[32] Vincent Giarrusso, 'An Insider Perspective on the Script in Practice', *Journal of Screenwriting*, Vol. 10, No. 1 (2019), p. 43.

[33] Giarrusso, p. 43; emphasis in the original.

[34] Rosamund Davies, 'The Screenplay as Boundary Object', *Journal of Screenwriting*, Vol. 10, No. 2 (2019), p. 151.

a director, for example, may transform a master-scene screenplay into a shooting script by adding shot numbers, shot specifications, and so on. We can also see how annotations touching on material aspects of the film that involve costume, hairstyle, props, or other actors can be picked up and explored as another boundary object; each text can generate another set of texts, to determine how to realise what will appear on screen. For example on *The Mission* (Roland Joffé, 1986), in which De Niro played a reformed slave trader, the actor suggested that he might shave his head—a possible authentic action from a Catholic sinner in search of redemption. The archive retains several documents exploring the logistics of this, in terms of the numbers of wigs necessary to enable this effect to appear on screen. Once the logistical complexity of realising gesture was explored by others, the idea was abandoned.

TEXTUAL ANALYSIS

If to interpret something is to criticise it then actors are critics, and De Niro's annotations offer many kinds of textual criticism, albeit usually of particular kinds that are primarily directed towards performance. Frequently this involves parsing a line to explore what the words mean to the character as De Niro conceives him, as we saw in the example from *Once Upon a Time in America*. Less pervasive but nonetheless frequent is actual rewriting: subtle, nuanced modifications to individual words and phrases. In one of the most famous speeches in *Taxi Driver* De Niro modifies the draft, in which Travis recites in voice-over his diary description of himself as a man who 'wouldn't take it any more'. De Niro changes this to 'would not', and contemplates changing 'any more' to 'no more'.[35] His marginal annotation indicates that the revisions are less to do with rhythm than with an understanding of how the character would use language in different contexts: '*Very formal when writing to self, but in conversation informal using improper Eng[lish]*'.[36]

In analysing the voice-over recitation of Travis's diary De Niro often conflates oral delivery and textual analysis, and adds to or alters Schrader's

---

[35] *Taxi Driver* (1976), Screenplay by Paul Schrader, 29 April 1975, Shooting script with revisions to 29 May 1975; shooting schedule and extensive RDN notes throughout; one page of RDN notes re wolves in back pocket, Box 221 [RDN].

[36] De Niro, ibid.

comments about Travis in the screenplay. For example, there is the potential for melodrama in the final diary entry ('My whole life has pointed in one direction. I see that now. There never has been any choice for me'), a danger accentuated by Schrader's suggestion that the 'normally monotone narration voice' should now contain '[a] note of despair and doom'. De Niro's analysis avoids this trap by observing that '*this could be done with little sense of the dramatic, a cadence, a sense that what I'm saying is developing into something imp[ortant]*'.[37]

On other occasions he devotes himself less to analysis of the words than to what the action expresses about the character and situation. An example is another scene in *Once Upon a Time in America* when Noodles, attempting to woo Deborah, pays for them to have a luxury restaurant exclusively to themselves for the evening. In the script, 'The Maitre realises he's dealing with a classy dame', and asks her in French what she would like for dessert, to which Deborah responds: 'I'll decide later'. 'The Maitre turns to Noodles' and 'Noodles reddens'. The annotation— De Niro's analysis of the subtext of the scene—perfectly captures the ambivalent power dynamics and the character's self-consciousness about social status: '*What are they trying to make a jerk out of me I paid for the fucking thing!*'[38] (see Fig. 2.1).

This exploration of meanings that underlie a conversation, often highlighted by a discrepancy between words and physical behaviour, is what is generally meant by 'subtext'. Austin E. Quigley has noted a logical fallacy in this commonly used word, because it implies that meaning is hidden behind or underneath the language, and 'critics, in general, have found it a great deal easier to perceive "hidden" meanings than to explain how the "hidden" is, or becomes, visible'.[39] As he proposes, a solution to this difficulty is provided by speech-act theory, a philosophy of language initially advanced by J. L. Austin. In his book *How to Do Things with Words*, Austin began by making a distinction between 'constative' (true or false) utterances, and 'performative' utterances, such as making a promise, in which 'the issuing of the utterance is the performing of an action'.[40]

---

[37] De Niro, ibid.

[38] *Once Upon a Time in America* (1984), Box. Folder 120.4, HRC, p. 200.

[39] Austin E. Quigley, *The Pinter Problem* (Princeton: Princeton University Press, 1975), p. 15; emphasis in the original.

[40] J. L. Austin, *How to Do Things with Words* (Oxford: Oxford University Press, 1962), p. 6.

Austin soon realised that the distinction breaks down, however, because utterances are always spoken within a situation; and '[o]nce we realise that what we have to study is *not* the sentence but the issuing of an utterance in a situation, there can hardly be any longer a possibility of not seeing that stating is performing an act'.[41]

Act, situation, performance, utterance: this is the language of the actor, and De Niro's screenplay annotations are often devoted to exploring the ways in which he as an actor can find the most powerful meanings of what is and what is not uttered in the situations in which he is performing. Sometimes, as in the examples above, this takes the form of textual commentary. De Niro parses the text, analysing its meanings and looking for inconsistencies within the screenplay, often cross-referencing to other parts of the script in a kind of concordance of the interconnections between character and drama which he will need to realise on screen. Much of this analytical work on a script can be described as *embodied criticism*, which comes from having to produce or reproduce a character in gesture, action and emotion.

At this level, the actor is going beyond the words themselves to find how the words and whatever might be admixed with them assume form and meaning through the body of the actor in space. Moreover, the space where that body is found in action is peculiar. The film actor usually moves in three dimensions in a set or a location dressed for the film. Most of the time they are subject to the physical rules that affect bodies: they have weight, and action and reaction. But the action is viewed in two dimensions on a screen, where they are traced in patterns of light and shade, and where their simulacrum has neither weight nor the other physical properties we expect. Successfully rendered in this new medium, the actor need no longer necessarily obey the rules of the physical world, as long as they are at home with the illusion of cinema, and aware how the camera sees the world, and how they are now suborned to the rules of narrative, whatever they might be.

In this screen world the characters De Niro plays love, and are hurt, kill and are killed, can grow older or younger. When his job is done well the viewer effortlessly enters the storyworld, heedless of how it is achieved by the actor, through interactions with the materialities and technologies which will achieve those effects. To take just one example, when David

[41] Austin, p. 139; emphasis in the original.

Mamet (a director as well as a writer, and originally an actor) analyses one of the cinematic deaths for which De Niro is responsible, he reveals the complexities involved in achieving just one illusion:

> Look at the shot in *The Godfather Part 2* where Robert De Niro shoots the vicious mafioso don somebody-or-other. De Niro puts a gun to his head, pulls the trigger and a vast wound opens up in the don's forehead.
>
> I ask how it was accomplished – did the gun spray the wound on? How could that be, as the wound appeared to have great depth? Here's how they did it. The makeup man built the wound into the actor's forehead, covered it with a layer of flesh, and ran an ultrathin monofilament from the flesh covering to the muzzle of De Niro's pistol. When De Niro shot he jerked his hand back, mimicking recoil; the line tore the covering free; and the wound appeared.[42]

But as he manages these material complexities De Niro still has to provide the sincerities we find in his close-ups, the precision in his gestures, and the delicacy of his inflexions and line readings, to enable the audience to commit to the story he is telling.

The Screenplay as a Material Object

Considering the screenplay as *boundary* object also requires us to consider the screenplay as *material* object. How precisely does an actor engage with a screenplay? The actor's relationship with the screenplay as both text and physical article is intimate. Until recently an actor's first engagement with a screenplay would be as a material object, for example as a package arriving via FedEx; and even in the era of email and digital dissemination, most actors will work with a hard-copy printout. Partly this is to facilitate written annotation, but a screenplay is read by actors when deciding whether or not to take a part, and pored over in the rehearsal room; it is an object that accompanies the actor to the set every day. Many of the uses De Niro makes of a screenplay involve modifying, exploiting and framing the text as a material object that can be used for multiple practical purposes.

---

[42] David Mamet, *Bambi vs Godzilla: On the Nature Purpose and Practice of the Movie Business* (New York: Simon and Schuster, 2007), pp. 94–95.

In their foundational article on the boundary object, Star and Griesemer propose that it is exemplified in the museum or archive itself: an arena in which the 'same' object becomes a medium for communicational exchange between multiple different users. The lens of microhistory is equally appropriate here. Every working screenplay is a historical document whose materiality reveals an enormous amount about the film the actor and the wider social relations and technology in the industry at the particular historical moment of its creation.[43] Like Star and Griesemer, John Brewer finds a potential for microhistory in re-thinking of the curation of archives:

> Over the last thirty years, historical archives have undergone a major transformation. What has been indexed, catalogued, made available, included in the archive (and therefore deemed a legitimate historical source) has changed profoundly. This has been accompanied — indeed was preceded by — a re-reading of the archive. Italian *microstoria*, in particular, repeatedly and brilliantly uses the nation's rich institutional records — of the church, state, and local authorities — not to write a history of the exercise of power but to reconstruct the vision and experiences of those who were its subjects.[44]

De Niro's decision to archive his process makes it possible to assemble a different kind of narrative to those with which we are more familiar in popular histories of famous performers. In the archive the actor is present not as star but as worker, whose labour is visible not just in its results but also through its previously invisible acts of preparation and analysis. It shows the conscious choices and decisions of an actor, and the restrictions under which they are made. Over De Niro's career the materiality changes from a plastic folder to leather-bound prestige object, and the technology of its reproduction changes, but in every case the screenplay expresses a set of material relationships and practices through which the actor is helping to define the story, the manner of its telling, and its perception by the audience.

---

[43] Carlo Ginzburg, 'Microhistory: Two or Three Things That I Know About It', trans. John Tedeschi and Anne C. Tedeschi, *Critical Inquiry*, Vol. 20, No. 1 (1993), pp. 10–35.

[44] John Brewer, 'Microhistory and the Histories of Everyday Life', *CAS-LMU eSeries*, No. 5 (2010), p. 11; emphasis in the original.

John Gielgud's copy of *Arthur* (Steve Gordon, 1981) in the British Library provides an illuminating example from another actor.[45] The script is held within a dark red plastic folder, with the title embossed on the front from Studio Duplicating Services. On the front page, Gielgud has written his name and the name of his hotel (the Lombardy on East 56th St.), a reminder that the screenplay is a working tool with many different copies are in circulation, labelled to ensure it is not picked up by mistake, and containing important intellectual property, industrial secrets that command a price from journalists or competitors. But Gielgud's screenplay shows a different approach to performance. All the pages in which he does not appear are torn out. His working method was to write the dialogue out by hand beside the printed text. His handwriting personalises it, and occasionally he also adds relevant stresses and pauses, but there are no annotations, no explorations of meaning or subtext, no suggestions for different line readings. The text is what it is, and it is his job to deliver it.

The actor's script is their portal into the fictional world, the means whereby their identity is extended into that of the character and the world of the script. The annotations and other material inscriptions are maps of how the actor has planned this journey. Today the archived screenplays allow the scholar to see the work of the actor, but also to reconstruct where and how they came together with others who made the same trip. De Niro's HRC archive copy of the script for a Brian De Palma then called *Son of Greetings* (it was a sequel to De Palma's 1968 film *Greetings* and was released as *Hi, Mom!* in 1970) is labelled with the actor's typewritten name and address, fixed with transparent tape onto the black plastic binder holding the screenplay. As De Niro's career progressed, and the films and roles on which he worked became more complex and expansive, he adapted the script and binder to meet his requirements, for example to allow him to carry his research together with the screenplay. The binder could thereby become a container for paratexts, the documents, commentaries and research materials with which he worked alongside the screenplay itself; the artefact becomes De Niro's para-screenplay. In his copy of *The Deer Hunter*, for instance, the paratexts are held in a pocket built into inside of the binder, thereby keeping

---

[45] *Arthur* (1981), by Steve Gordon, with John Gielgud notes, ADD MS 81370, John Gielgud Archive, British Library, London.

these materials separate from, yet alongside, his copy of the screenplay itself (Fig. 2.2).

Another striking example is his copy of the shooting script for *The Godfather, Part II*,[46] the film that would propel De Niro to international acclaim. His approach to organising the script and associated materials in a ring-binder would become something of a template in preparing written and print texts on many of his later projects. His *Godfather* ring-binder is used not just as a protective folder for the script but as a means for organising his work, with section dividers and coloured tabs creating separate repositories for different versions of the screenplay, and for different kinds of research material and commentary. The binder is divided into the 'new script' (revised pages), with one side of notes preceding the rewritten script pages for his character of Vito Corleone; and, prior to this and much more expansively, the 'old script'. This has excerpted from Coppola's enormous draft only those pages in which De Niro's character appears. Following this, De Niro has created a 'Notes' section containing 25 general notes on four sides of paper, and further notes specifically on make-up (four entries), props (another four) and costume (six).

Then comes a separate tab for 'Tapes'. This section brings together De Niro's observations that resulted from the unique performance context in which he reviewed videotapes made for him by Coppola from the first *Godfather* movie alongside recordings of De Niro's own scenes. De Niro had to study Marlon Brando's performance as the aged Don Corleone in order to prepare a performance that could credibly capture the gestures, movement and speech of the younger version of the character that De Niro would personify. This section of notes begins with three pages of 'impression[s] of older me', followed by sixteen 'Notes from watching self (1st set tape)'; then 'last viewing of tape sent 3/2/74 (all of older Vitri stuff)' (seven notes, with others on the verso), and finally ten notes made during his 'last viewing of older me 3/18/74'. Additional tabs separate out De Niro's notes on further 'Things to do' (five notes), and 'Character', which contains 23 notes and a further seven from 'Francis' (Coppola).

Within the same folder De Niro has bound additional paratexts: a two-page list of Sicilian expressions, and another two-page set of phonetic transcriptions of the Sicilian dialogue between Vito, Tessio and Clemenza.

---

[46] *The Godfather, Part II* (1974), Box 182, HRC.

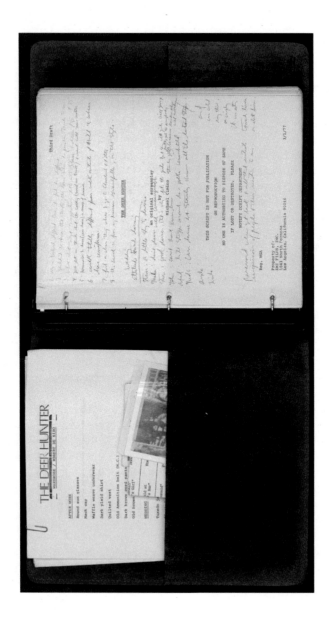

Fig. 2.2   Robert De Niro's copy of the shooting script for *The Deer Hunter*, Box 183, RDN

In this way the screenplay artefact is also transformed into a kind of dictionary, with the paratexts accompanying De Niro's translations of Sicialian dialogue on the screenplay pages themselves. This in turn is a subset of another kind of transformation of the screenplay, into a notepad on which the actor will record innumerable thoughts and observations as he works on the script. This kind of work is further encapsulated in his frequent selection of a particular design of binding that includes a pen-holder, with the artefact becoming an all-purpose container for script, notes, additional paratexts, and the actual writing materials with which De Niro would make his notes.

In summary, a text that could be described as a single object (Robert De Niro's copy of a screenplay) is always also at least some, and potentially all, of the following: (1) *an extension of his own identity*: as actor, character, and owner of the screenplay as a property; (2) a *container* for paratextual materials, including research documents and commentaries, as well as writing materials; (3) a *notebook* for recording research findings as well as conversations with directors, screenwriters, actors, etc.; (4) an *organiser*—a means of arranging primary and secondary materials into discrete sections; (5) a *dictionary* and pronunciation guide; (6) a *textual laboratory*: a place to explore, via textual commentary, the notation of affect, of different possible ways of realising and embodying the script in performance; and (7) a *critical analysis* of the screenplay from the perspective of the actor. If the screenplay is a tool, then the container and paratexts all form part of the tool kit.

All of these functions are necessary for De Niro when working on a film, and they can all offer the researcher insights into piecing together the narrative of the filmmaking process and the role of the actor within it. Looking at these tools and their use reveals a great deal about the work of the actor, and the social relations under which it takes place. De Niro used his toolkit in the course of his contribution to a work of storymaking, but analysis of the way he used screenplays in the course of his career allows another story to be told, just as John Brewer's essay connects the process of piecing evidence together to Italian neo-realism, which, he observes, is

best known outside Italy through the films of Rossellini, De Sica and Visconti – *Paisa*, *Roma*, *Citta Aperta*, *Ladri di Biciclette*, and *La Terra Trema*. (Indeed I would argue that Rossellini's *Paisa* was one of the first works of Italian microhistory) [...] as the critic Cesare Zavattini noted,

'What we are really attempting is not to invent a story that looks like reality, but to present reality as if it were a story'.[47]

Brewer looks at the routes that a historian takes to understand narrative and points to the importance of fiction in assembling historical narratives: 'The best (most plausible, most real) versions of this world in the nineteenth century were literary fictions (Dickens, Balzac, Flaubert, Tolstoy) [...] As Ginzburg puts it, "A writer is someone who is able to make us aware of certain dimensions of reality"'.[48] De Niro's position as a researcher incorporates practices of the historian, speaking to primary as well as relying on secondary sources to find out about boxers in the 1950s (*Raging Bull*), filmmaking in the 1930s (*The Last Tycoon*), firefighting in Chicago (*Backdraft*) or the methods of autograph collectors and the modalities of fan culture (*Taxi Driver*). These kinds of practices would be deemed completely normal in an academic sociologist or ethnographer, but are sometimes seen as eccentric in an actor, as we shall see in Chapter 6. The process of storymaking, which must be taken seriously whether by writer or actor, is dependent on kneading together the real and the invented until they become one and the same, in a new entity that combines both elements and yet is different from either. If the actor is a co-writer, both in the way they amend the text for performance and in how they embody it on screen, this includes many different kinds of writing: from the purely imaginative and associative, to the specific and grounded. And like a historian, De Niro uses narrative techniques to assemble them into a cohesive whole.

Seeing the actor as researcher allows proper consideration to the role of preparation in performance. As producer Art Linson, who worked with De Niro on *The Untouchables*, said when trying to persuade him to take the part of the convict in *Great Expectations*: 'I kept De Niro current with the progress of the script and meanwhile he did his homework. Bob always did his homework. He saw the David Lean movie. He read through the Dickens book'.[49] De Niro's research is thorough, but he is also able to build on that research through his fluency in a number of different fields of visual representation, which he is able to harness in the

---

[47] Brewer, 'Microhistory', pp. 11–12.

[48] Brewer, p. 12.

[49] Art Linson, *What Just Happened. Bitter Hollywood Tales from the Front Line* (New York: Bloomsbury, 2003), p. 107.

annotations and marks he makes on scripts. As the annotations make clear, he thinks about acting not in the abstract, but as a mediated performance. Perhaps because of the fine art background of both of his parents, he seems able simultaneously to inhabit his performance in three dimensions and to visualise it as the projected two-dimensional image the audience will see and hear on screen. In later chapters we look at what the annotations reveal about the way he conceives of his performance as image, and how he also finds ways of visual notation of affect and preparation for performance in both two and three dimensions; and we consider how he distils ideas of character for representation on screen, and how those ideas change from film to film.

PART AND WHOLE: THE NARRATIVE CONSTRUCTION OF REALITY

De Niro's annotations reveal the screenplay as a document that is always amendable, in the iterations of drafts and in the differently coloured pages circulated during production. In archives, these coloured pages are usually collected together in their 'final' iteration in a single text (commonly known as a 'rainbow' script) sequenced according to the narrative order of the completed film. During production, of course, script revisions are generated day by day, not in narrative sequence but in the order in which particular scenes are to be filmed, and/or in the order in which scenes have been rewritten. These pages, then, move between chronologies but also between understandings of what the film is projected to be at different moments in time. The rewriting and sequencing of these pages is therefore dependent on the relationship between part and whole. As we have seen, much of De Niro's focus is on concordance and exegesis, but this form of annotation takes its place alongside a concern with how the minutiae of a scene or even a line corresponds with his overall conception of the character, and of how that character functions within the narrative and structure of the film as a whole.

This relationship between part and whole is one of the key aspects of narrative considered by psychologist Jerome Bruner in considering how narrative operates 'as an instrument of mind in the construction of reality'.[50] Bruner lists ten features of narrative, each of which we briefly summarise below, followed by an explication of its relevance to the De Niro archive. Bruner is writing as a professor of psychology investigating arguments surrounding 'reality construction', and his article summarises and critiques narratological theories advanced by (primarily) literary critics, but it is remarkable how much of De Niro's detailed script annotation focuses on precisely the areas of narrative identified by Bruner. De Niro has a role here as a critic and textual analyst who is co-creating the film text, using a heuristic understanding of the narrative principles Bruner outlines. Once again, then, we find that the 'same' texts can be of value as boundary objects in many different kinds of investigation and practice.

1. *Narrative diachronicity*: the organisation of events in time as a meaningful temporal pattern. This of course is a central structuring principle in such key De Niro films as *The Godfather, Part II* and *Once Upon a Time in America*, but a striking example of De Niro's own concern to develop a character in relation to narrative diachronicity is found on the cover sheet of *Bloody Mama*, his first substantial professional role, where he makes a point of making notes about the chronology of the character (Fig. 2.2)[51]:

> Pages 1-4 1890's.
> 5-9 1912
> 10-19 1923
> 20-43 1927
> 44-80 1929
> 81-End 1933[52]

He inserts this kind of information about chronology on each scene within the screenplay. Elsewhere in the script he makes a point of marking in blue pencil the date and his age, for example reminding

[50] Jerome Bruner, 'The Narrative Construction of Reality', *Critical Inquiry*, Vol. 18, No. 1 (Autumn 1991), p 6.

[51] *Bloody Mama* (1970), Screenplay by Robert Thom, Shooting script; final draft with shooting schedules, photographs of RDN, research photographs, and song lyrics inserted; extensive RDN notes, Box 178 [RDN].

[52] *Bloody Mama* (1970), Box 178 [RDN], cover sheet.

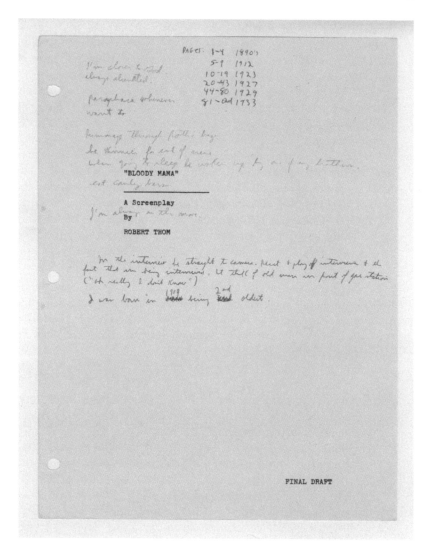

Fig. 2.3   *Bloody Mama*, Box 178, RDN, cover page

himself on page 11 that in 1923 his character would be 14 years old.

This reminds us that the actor has to engage with two types of narrative diachronicity: the events of the narrative, and the narrative of the film. Narratological literary and film theory commonly distinguishes between these two temporal dimensions as (i) story or 'fabula' (the chronological sequence of events as they actually happened), and (ii) discourse or 'sjužet' (the manner and sequence in which the events are narrated). Although the audience may receive the organisation of the events in non-chronological order, the performer needs to understand the narrative in both chronologies. This chronological curation, managed over the actual time the film takes to shoot, is a skill peculiar to filmmaking, the chronology and duration of which will probably have no relation to the time and space of the film narrative or the spectator's experience.

2. *Particularity*: the specific emblematic incarnation of a story that is nevertheless 'in some sense generic'. As Bruner says, 'a narrative cannot be realised save through particular embodiment',[53] and De Niro's is the particular body through which the film narratives he works on are realised; he becomes both the teller and a significant element of the tale.

3. *Intentional state entailment*: essentially, agency and choice. In his annotations De Niro focuses on the character's intentional state, perhaps consciously emulating his favourite dictum of Stella Adler: 'Your talent is in your choice'.[54]

4. *Hermeneutic composability*: the relationship between the meanings assigned to the whole of a text and its constituent parts, and the way in which we deduce the narrative from its constituent parts and then use the assembled narrative to decide which of those constituent parts don't belong—the 'hermeneutic circle'. Although De Niro will usually concentrate his annotations on those scenes in which his character appears, parsing the text to analyse character and motivation, he then uses that character analysis in deciding whether there are parts of the text that don't belong and should be

---

[53] Bruner, p. 7.
[54] Stella Adler quoted in Levy, p. 51.

excluded or changed. Almost all of the work we reference in this book involves De Niro's contribution to this iterative sorting of what belongs to the character and the film and what doesn't. A nice example is a note in De Niro's photostat of *The Hoods*,[55] the novel which was the inspiration for Sergio Leone's *Once Upon a Time in America*, where he notes a physical gesture: Noodles pulls the plait of Deborah, the girl he loves. De Niro marks with approval that the screenplay adaptation has retained the same gesture. What is notable is that this is not an action he will have to do as an actor: it is something his character will have done in the past, when he was Young Noodles (played in the film by Scott Schutzman Tiler). Yet because it is germane to De Niro's understanding of the character in the story it falls within the hermeneutic circle; it belongs to his fictional identity, and therefore when making the film at least in some senses to him. This is also an example of narrative diachronicity: for *The Godfather, Part II*, in constructing the younger Vito he worked backwards from the older Vito's embodiment in the person of Marlon Brando; in *Once Upon a Time in America* he has to move in the opposite direction, with part of his work in developing the older Noodles requiring him to formulate an understanding of the character as a boy, including the significance of physical gestures that can help him personify the character at two distinct stages of his later life, as a young hoodlum and as a wiser man approaching old age.

5. *Canonicity and breach*: 'what happened and why it is worth telling'; but more specifically, 'a tale must be about how an implicit canonical script has been breached, violated, or deviated from in a manner to do violence to what Hayden White calls the "legitimacy" of the canonical script'.[56] De Niro takes this beyond the realm of simple narrative to pinpoint what is unique or particular to his character's engagement with events; for example, as part of his preparation for *The Untouchables* he refers not just to films of Capone but his own performances of gangsters to discover both how and where this performance becomes exceptional.

---

[55] Photocopy of *The Hoods* novel by Harry Gray, with RDN notes, Box. Folder 120.1 [RDN].

[56] Bruner, pp. 11–12.

6. *Referentiality*: the reality effect constructed by the fiction so as to create a sense of verisimilitude. De Niro's preparation and research notes confirm his popular reputation as an actor willing to go to quite extraordinary lengths to gain this effect: not content with mere phonetic delivery of the Sicilian lines in *The Godfather, Part II*, he attended a language course and became sufficiently fluent to act as translator for the production, while even De Niro himself wondered if for *New York, New York* he spent too much time mastering the saxophone: 'I wonder if I should have saved a little more energy for other things and just worried about what was going to be seen'.[57]

7. *Genericness*: Bruner notes that genres comprise a means of organising both plot and the mode of telling (story and discourse, or fabula and sjužet, in the variant terminologies of narratological theory). It is striking that the films on which De Niro's early reputation was founded tend to be irreducible to genre, other than perhaps by content: we might think of *Bang the Drum Slowly* as a 'sports movie', *The Godfather* as a 'Mafia movie', *The Deer Hunter* as a 'Vietnam movie' and so on—though we might still find ourselves struggling to define *Mean Streets, Taxi Driver* or *The King of Comedy* other than as 'Scorsese' films (or more accurately, 'Scorsese and De Niro' films). Is *New York, New York* a musical, or 'a film *with* music', as Scorsese described it?[58] It perhaps makes better sense to define De Niro's films not by genre, content or narrative form than by mode of production. De Niro was drawn to directors and productions that enabled him to explore and shape not only his own character, but the 'hermeneutic composability' that defined the relationships between that character and other elements of the script. In such ways the most obvious way in which one can define De Niro's films is as precisely that: 'De Niro films'.

8. *Normativeness*: if narrative is in part defined by the transgression of a norm, 'narrative is necessarily normative. A breach presupposes a norm', and it can therefore be suggested that 'narrative is centrally concerned with cultural legitimacy'.[59] We must be clear what the

---

[57] De Niro quoted in Levy, p. 200.

[58] Martin Scorsese quoted in Levy, p. 199; emphasis in the original.

[59] Bruner, p. 15.

norm is in any given situation, so that we properly perceive the breach. De Niro conducts extensive research and exhibits boundless curiosity about almost every aspect of a character, from the right accent of Pennsylvanian steelworkers for *The Deer Hunter*, to the power of the Jesuit Church in Latin America for *The Mission*. There is a striking example in preparations for *Meet the Parents*, when De Niro proposed that the travel agent his character clandestinely meets should be called Thor Svenson and not Arnie Klein.[60] This is to make absolutely clear that the normative breach lies in introducing a potential Jewish son-in-law to the family, and therefore another Jewish character should not be visible; otherwise, the perception of the breach would be clouded. As these and innumerable other examples demonstrate, De Niro is both endlessly curious and pedantically yet creatively insistent that the decisions that are made should be legitimate and consistent.

9. *Context sensitivity and negotiability*: 'We seem to be able to take competing versions of a story with a perspectival grain of salt, much more so than in the case of arguments or proofs'.[61] De Niro is always concerned to establish the legitimacy of his character's perception of events, no matter how extraordinary or perverse it may appear to be. Whether he is speaking on behalf of studio head Monroe Stahr in *The Last Tycoon* or gangster Al Capone in *The Untouchables*, he takes pain to stress when he thinks the character believes themselves to be right in an assertion or a point of view, and his annotations reveal a scrupulous commitment to the integrity of the character in expressing why that character feels justified in taking the actions he does; and yet he is also able to separate out and negotiate between multiple perspectives, the 'I' of the character being distinguishable from the 'I' of the actor and the 'I' that is the object of the spectator's gaze.

10. *Narrative accrual*: the means by which individual instances of narrative become formulated into a tradition or a paradigm. In De Niro's case we should note that the cumulative work on preparation consolidates into something approaching a method, in the

---

[60] *Meet the Parents* (2000), Revised script, with RDN notes, bound script with inserted re-shoot pages, Box 101.5 [RDN].

[61] Bruner, p. 17.

sense that after a certain point in his career the proportional reduction in the amount of handwritten annotation is in part a consequence of the rehearsal of his approach to preparation via textual annotation on earlier scripts.

It is ultimately not surprising that what makes a great actor is a deep sensitivity to what makes a story and an understanding of how it manifests itself in action and affect, as De Niro's screenplay analyses show. As Bruner remarks, 'this is, perhaps, what makes the innovative storyteller such a powerful figure in a culture. He may go beyond the conventional scripts, leading people to see human happenings in a fresh way, indeed, in a way they had never before "noticed" or even dreamed'.[62]

Actors have to understand and interpret the screenplay, but they also have to become it in its new projected medium. That means equipping their body to determine the story and allowing the story to determine how their body moves, and what their body does. The body is the site of interaction between screenplay and film, and the actor's sensibility and understanding of what the story is, and how it is constituted and assembled by the audience, is crucial to its success. The actor has to see the story both far away and very close, aware of how it is manifested in details of costume and gesture and expression; and must also have a sense of its ebb and flow, its structure and rhythm and the dramatic transformations and revelations it contains. As Maurice Merleau-Ponty writes, 'To look at human beings from the outside is what makes the mind self-critical and keeps it sane'.[63] The ability to be simultaneously in the story and observing it, able to be absolutely in the moment of the action and able to bear in mind the way this is seen, is the essence of a film actor's art.

MATERIALITIES

The archives make visible the labour involved in realising a performance: not just the immense amount of work that the actor contributes in realising a role, but also how actors interact with others both formally and

---

[62] Bruner, p. 12.

[63] Maurice Merleau-Ponty, *The World of Perception*, trans. Oliver Davies (London and New York: Routledge, 2002), p. 68.

informally. The archives record all kinds of conversations and interactions in which De Niro engages: discussions with screenwriters, directors and producers, exchanges with other members of the crew, and with an extraordinarily wide range of people who can help with his research. These include steelworkers and Sicilian-language experts, autograph collectors and film producers, gangsters, historians and many others who can help him distil a role. The text is to a degree the result of those interactions, which the actor distils and embodies in performance. We have to remind ourselves, for example, that when De Niro created the role of the younger Don Corleone he was still a relatively inexperienced performer: he won an Oscar for the same performance for which he was also nominated for a BAFTA award for Most Promising Newcomer.

Moreover, the documents themselves can be quite ordinary. They have been catalogued and filed by film or project, and sometimes what finally ends up in the archive is as much a result of contingency as of planning. In the holdings for the Terry Gilliam-directed *Brazil* (1985),[64] for example, there is a note from Wardrobe Supervisor Joyce Stoneman about a pair of Fair Isle gloves:

ROBERT
FAIR ISLE GLOVES
AM BUYING WOOL THIS AFTERNOON FOR DARNING
PURPOSES. I WILL BE BACK AROUND LUNCH TIME
JOYCE STONEMAN
W/ROBE SUPERVISOR

This is about as mundane an exchange as one could imagine, yet it reveals the realisation of a screenplay as a film depends on an important nexus of materiality and relationships which are defined by and managed through the screenplay and enable it to be realised in a different medium.

De Niro's interest in costume is well known, and his costumes increasingly form part of the archive as his career proceeds. He is able to retain and donate a hat from *Hi, Mom!* (1970), another hat (*the* hat) from *Mean Streets* (1973), and his character's Italian passport from *The Godfather, Part II*. (Travis Bickle's jacket, shirt and boots from *Taxi Driver* are also in the archive, but only thanks to a donation by Paul Schrader

---

[64] *Brazil* (1985) screenplay by Terry Gilliam, Tom Stoppard, and Charles McKeown, undated, Box 20.2 [RDN].

in 2006.) Later he is able to archive his entire wardrobe: there are an astonishing 143 items from *The Untouchables*, from fat suits to cufflinks and underwear. Every single one of those costumes needed management. An actor is as dependent on the costumes as a racing driver is on the team that changes their tyres, to make sure the costumes are for the right scene, in the right state of wear, and in the right size. The wardrobe supervisor's attention to detail and to the materiality of the text needs to be at least as precise as De Niro's. The note from Stoneman to De Niro stands for thousands of communications between De Niro and the costume department, and how a relationship that is enabled and sustained through the screenplay manifests itself in a materiality which ranges from commissioning tailor-made suits to darning gloves.

De Niro shows a relentless commitment to the idea of the film, and the way it can be best realised. It involves all kinds of practices—writing, improvising, making casting suggestions—considering both the naturalistic aspects of the text and how to include the metaphorical resonances. De Niro can be seen at different points focussing on the overall narrative structure of the film, or considering a particular line reading in granular detail. Once he begins annotating a particular draft, we can see how the provisional text of the screenplay is in constant flux; it is not just a linear sequence of writerly iterations. The actor's role in realising the screenplay is of a different order to any other collaborator, and therefore their relationship to the screenplay text is different, because even if one imagines an actor's copy of the screenplay without annotations, their interpretation of the script will be written on film. Uniquely, the actor does not simply interpret the text: they embody it, they become it. In the mediated performance of the cinema the actor and the screenplay become literally inseparable. The evidence of the archive is of materialities, expressed in specific decisions that might be about props, costumes, line readings, gestures, or interactions with other performers; and speculation about the meaning of the script or motivations of the character will be addressed in *embodied* decisions about performance.

STORIES TOLD WITH PICTURES

Screenwriting guru Syd Field famously insisted that 'A screenplay is a STORY TOLD WITH PICTURES'.[65] Gary Davis's qualification—'a screenplay is a story told with word-pictures'[66]—helps to indicate the complexities surrounding the role of the screenplay as a written precursor text to a work created in a different medium. Our own formulation would read something like this: 'A screenplay is a story told in words that evoke pictures, and which is intended to be realised in an audio-visual medium'. A screenplay told with pictures, or with word-pictures, can be complete in itself in the sense that (for example) it tells a fully comprehensible story, but it is simultaneously incomplete in the sense that, in Pier Paolo Pasolini's famous formulation, it is a 'structure that wants to be another structure'—it wants to become a different kind of text.[67] It is written in words, but its intention is to be realised in an audio-visual medium. In other words, the screenplay is an *ekphrastic* text: it is a verbal representation, or in this case more properly *anticipation*, of a work of visual art.

The ekphrastic relationship of screenplays to films is peculiar. Generically, screenplays are examples of a kind of reverse or counter-ekphrasis whereby the written text invents the artwork it purports to describe; in such cases, 'ekphrasis creates the objects whose representations it purports to represent'.[68] Unlike most examples of ekphrasis, however, screenplays rarely describe these objects in any great detail. Indeed, novice screenwriters are routinely advised to avoid all but the most minimal scene description: partly because this would be to appropriate the work of the designer, partly because it would confuse the generic requirements of screenwriting with those of prose fiction, and partly because of the presumed 'rule' that one page of conventionally written screenplay text equates to one minute of screen time. Approaching the screenplay by way

---

[65] Syd Field, *Screenplay: The Foundations of Screenwriting* (New York: Dell, 1979), p. 7; emphasis added.

[66] Gary Davis, 'Rejected Offspring: The Screenplay as a Literary Genre', *New Orleans Review*, Vol. 11, No. 2 (1984), p. 92.

[67] Pier Paolo Pasolini, 'The Screenplay as a "Structure That Wants to Be Another Structure"', *American Journal of Semiotics*, Vol. 4, No. 1–2 (1986), pp. 53–72.

[68] Thomas Leitch, 'Adaptation and Intertextuality, or, What Isn't an Adaptation, and What Does It Matter?', in Deborah Cartmell (ed.), *A Companion to Literature, Film, and Adaptation* (West Sussex: Blackwell, 2012) p. 93.

of ekphrasis offers potentially productive answers to some of the practical and theoretical questions most commonly asked of the form, such as the importance or otherwise of description in screenwriting, and what is it that we see when we read a screenplay. What previous accounts of screenplay description have tended to overlook or underplay, however, is the role of the actor in anticipating the visual realisation of a character. Many of the scripts from which De Niro worked have the minimalistic scene description typical of the form, although others, such as *Taxi Driver*, are much more expansive. The kinds of texts he works with range from the philosophical to the heavily proscriptive or highly stylised. He does not necessarily object to being told what his character should be thinking, but he is constantly engaged in how and why they are thinking what they are. Sometimes working outwards from the script, but just as frequently researching the role before a screenplay had been fully developed, he painstakingly researches and explores the visual appearance of a character: everything from facial hair, weight, clothing and props. In this sense, the screenplay can act as a space for the actor (usually in dialogue with set designer, costume designer and so on) to perform the ekphrastic work to which screenplays ordinarily can only gesture.

BIBLIOGRAPHY

ABBREVIATION

RDN: Robert De Niro Papers, Harry Ransom Center, University of Texas at Austin.

PRIMARY

Arthur (1981), by Steve Gordon, with John Gielgud notes, ADD MS 81370, John Gielgud Archive, British Library, London.

Bloody Mama (1970), Screenplay by Robert Thom, Shooting script; final draft with shooting schedules, photographs of RDN, research photographs, and song lyrics inserted; extensive RDN notes, Box 178, RDN.

Brazil (1985), Screenplay by Terry Gilliam, Tom Stoppard, and Charles McKeown, undated, Box 20.2, RDN.

The Godfather, Part II (1974), Shooting script, with RDN notes, lacks title page; contains 'old script' and 'new script' pages, with additional script pages and extensive RDN notes re character development, undated, Box 182, RDN.

The Hoods. Novel by Harry Gray (photocopy), with RDN notes, Box 120.1, RDN.

Meet the Parents (2000), Revised script, with RDN notes, bound script with inserted re-shoot pages, Box 101.5, RDN.

Once Upon a Time in America (1984), Script in 151 scenes (291 pages); extra scenes laid in, with RDN notes, undated, Box 120.4, RDN.

Ronin, Typescript draft by David Mamet, with typed and handwritten revisions, 25 October 1997, Container 176.1, David Mamet Papers, Harry Ransom Center, Texas, Austin.

Rosenthal, Jane to David Mamet (correspondence), 25 October 1977, Container 176.2-4, David Mamet Papers, Harry Ransom Center, Texas, Austin.

Taxi Driver (1976), Screenplay by Paul Schrader, 29 April 1975, Shooting script with revisions to 29 May 1975; shooting schedule and extensive RDN notes throughout; one page of RDN notes re wolves in back pocket, Box 221, RDN.

SECONDARY

Austin, J. L. *How to Do Things with Words,* Oxford: Oxford University Press, 1962.

Brewer, John. 'Microhistory and the Histories of Everyday Life', *CAS-LMU eSeries,* No. 5 (2010), pp. 1–16.

Brown, Mark. 'British Library's £1.1m Saves Pinter's Papers for Nation', *The Guardian,* 12 December 2007, https://www.theguardian.com/uk/2007/dec/12/books.theatrenews [Accessed 29 September 2019].

Bruner, Jerome. 'The Narrative Construction of Reality', *Critical Inquiry,* Vol. 18, No. 1 (Autumn 1991), pp. 1–21.

Coppola, Francis Ford. *Live Cinema and Its Techniques,* New York: Liveright Publishing Corporation, 2017.

Davies, Gail. 'Science, Observation and Entertainment: Competing Visions of Post-war British Natural History Television, 1946–1967', *Ecumene,* Vol. 7, No. 4 (2000), pp. 432–460.

Davies, Rosamund. 'The Screenplay as Boundary Object', *Journal of Screenwriting,* Vol. 10, No. 2 (2019), pp. 149–164.

Davies, Rosamund and Ryan Flynn, 'Explicit and Implicit Narratives in the Co-design of Videogames,' in Anastastions Maragiannis (ed.), *Proceedings of the Digital Research in the Humanities and Arts Conference, DRHA2014* (London: University of Greenwich, 2015), pp. 73–80.

Davis, Gary. 'Rejected Offspring: The Screenplay as a Literary Genre', *New Orleans Review,* Vol. 11, No. 2 (1984), pp. 90–94.

'De Niro's Film Materials Collection Opens at Ransom Center' (Press Release), *Harry Ransom Center*, 27 April 2009, https://www.hrc.utexas.edu/press/rel eases/2009/robert-de-niro-collection.html [Accessed 16 June 2019].

Derrida, Jacques. 'Structure, Sign, and Play in the Discourse of the Human Sciences', in *Writing and Difference*, trans. Alan Bass (London: Routledge, 1978), pp. 278–294.

Derrida, Jacques. *Margins of Philosophy*, trans. Alan Bass, Brighton: Harvester, 1982.

Eisenstein, Sergei. 'The Form of the Script', in *Selected Works, Vol. 1: Writings, 1922–34*, trans. and ed. Richard Taylor (London: BFI, 1988).

Field, Syd. *Screenplay: The Foundations of Screenwriting*, New York: Dell, 1979.

Giarrusso, Vincent. 'An Insider Perspective on the Script in Practice', *Journal of Screenwriting*, Vol. 10, No. 1 (2019), pp. 41–61.

Ginzburg, Carlo. 'Microhistory: Two or Three Things That I Know About It', trans. John Tedeschi and Anne C. Tedeschi, *Critical Inquiry*, Vol. 20, No. 1 (1993), pp. 10–35.

Grobel, Lawrence. '*Playboy* Interview: Robert De Niro', *Playboy*, Vol. 36, No. 1 (1989), pp. 69–90, 326.

Jones, Kimberley. 'HRC Opens the Doors on De Niro: The Harry Ransom Center Bulks Up Its Movie Holdings', *The Austin Chronicle*, 28 April 2009, https://www.austinchronicle.com/daily/screens/2009-04-28/ hrc-opens-the-doors-on-de-niro/ [Accessed 29 September 2019].

Leitch, Thomas. 'Adaptation and Intertextuality, or, What Isn't an Adaptation, and What Does It Matter?', in Deborah Cartmell (ed.), *A Companion to Literature, Film, and Adaptation* (West Sussex: Blackwell, 2012), pp. 87–104.

Levy, Shawn. *De Niro: A Life*, New York: Three Rivers, 2014.

Linson, Art. *What Just Happened. Bitter Hollywood Tales from the Front Line*, New York: Bloomsbury, 2003.

Mamet, David. *Bambi vs Godzilla: On the Nature Purpose and Practice of the Movie Business*, New York: Simon and Schuster, 2007.

Maras, Steven. *Screenwriting: History, Theory and Practice*, London: Wallflower, 2009.

Merleau-Ponty, Maurice. *The World of Perception*, trans. Oliver Davies, London and New York: Routledge, 2002.

Paris, Barry. 'Maximum Expression', *American Film*, Vol. 36, No. 5 (October 1989), pp. 34–35.

Pasolini, Pier Paolo. 'The Screenplay as a "Structure That Wants to Be Another Structure"', *American Journal of Semiotics*, Vol. 4, No. 1–2 (1986), pp. 53–72.

Price, Steven. *The Screenplay: Authorship, Theory and Criticism*, Basingstoke: Palgrave, 2010.

Quigley, Austin E. *The Pinter Problem*, Princeton: Princeton University Press, 1975.

'Robert De Niro: A Preliminary Inventory of His Papers at the Harry Ransom Center', https://norman.hrc.utexas.edu/fasearch/findingAid.cfm?kw=ronin&x=42&y=8&eadid=00481&showrequest=1 [Accessed 18 May 2020].

Romanelli, Claudia. 'From Dialogue Writer to Screenwriter: Pier Paolo Pasolini at Work for Federico Fellini', *Journal of Screenwriting*, Vol. 10, No. 3 (2019), pp. 323–337.

Star, Susan Leigh. 'This Is Not a Boundary Object: Reflections on the Origin of a Concept', *Science, Technology, & Human Values*, Vol. 35, No. 5 (2010), pp. 601–617.

Star, Susan Leigh and James R. Griesemer. 'Institutional Ecology, "Translations" and Boundary Objects: Amateurs and Professionals in Berkeley's Museum of Vertebrate Zoology, 1907–39', *Social Studies of Science*, Vol. 19 (1989), pp. 387–420.

Sternberg, Claudia. *Written for the Screen: The American Motion-Picture Screenplay as Text*, Tübingen: Stauffenburg, 1997.

Thompson, Kristin. *Storytelling in the New Hollywood: Understanding Classical Narrative Technique*, Cambridge, MA: Harvard University Press, 1999.

Trompette, Pascale and Dominique Vinck, 'Revisiting the Notion of Boundary Object', *Revue d'anthropologie des connaissances*, Vol. 3, No. 1 (2009), pp. 3–25.

Vertuno, Jim. 'De Niro Donates to Texas' Ransom Center', *AP News*, 7 June 2006, https://apnews.com/677908d9d6406ff5bfe41daef7a72bfb [Accessed 29 September 2019].

Wille, Jacob Ion and Anne Marit Waade, 'Production Design and Location in the Danish Television Drama Series *The Legacy*', *Kosmorama #263*, 16 May 2016, https://www.kosmorama.org/en/kosmorama/artikler/production-design-and-location-danish-television-drama-series-legacy [Accessed 20 May 2020].

CHAPTER 3

Influences and Ideas of Performance

If anyone had come and told Napoleon that a man or a building is inces-
santly and continuously represented by a picture in the atmosphere, that
all existing objects project into it a kind of spectre which can be captured
and perceived, he would have consigned him to Charenton as a lunatic
[…] And yet that is what Daguerre's discovery proved!
—Balzac[1]

The main reason for examining De Niro's archive is to discover some of
the means by which he created the effects that are otherwise only percep-
tible to us as realised performances. It allows us to move from the study of
affect to the understanding of creative process and method. For example,
what kinds of work are involved in making something that has the appearance of naturalness and spontaneity? How does an actor create an illusion
of immediacy and presence while existing only as an effect of the play
of light and shade on a two-dimensional screen? These are some of the
questions that have been asked of the film actor since the medium came
into being, and in this chapter we indicate some of the ways in which
Robert De Niro went about answering them, and some of the formative
influences that contributed to his ability to do so.

---

[1] Honoré de Balzac, *Cousin Pons: Part Two of Poor Relations*, trans. Herbert J. Hunt
(Harmondsworth: Penguin, 1978), pp. 131–132.

© The Author(s) 2020
A. Ganz and S. Price, *Robert De Niro at Work*,
Palgrave Studies in Screenwriting,
https://doi.org/10.1007/978-3-030-47960-2_3

EARLY THEORIES OF FILM ACTING: WALTER
BENJAMIN AND SIEGRIED KRACAUER

Walter Benjamin devotes considerable space in his much-cited essay 'The Work of Art in the Age of Mechanical Reproduction' (1935) to the predicament of the film actor:

> The artistic performance of a stage actor is definitely presented to the public by the actor in person; that of the screen actor, however, is presented by a camera, with a twofold consequence. The camera that presents the performance of the film actor to the public need not respect the performance as an integral whole. Guided by the cameraman, the camera continually changes its position with respect to the performance. The sequence of positional views which the editor composes from the material supplied him constitutes the completed film. [...] Also, the film actor lacks the opportunity of the stage actor to adjust to the audience during his performance, since he does not present his performance to the audience in person.[2]

For the audience, then, the 'identification with the actor is really an identification with the camera', while for the actor 'the part is acted not for an audience but for a mechanical contrivance'.[3]

Consequently, filmed performance goes to the heart of perhaps Benjamin's most famous formulation, that the 'aura' of presence is disrupted by technological reproduction, because

> aura is tied to [the actor's] presence; there can be no replica of it. The aura which, on the stage, emanates from Macbeth, cannot be separated for the spectators from that of the actor. However, the singularity of the shot in the studio is that the camera is substituted for the public. Consequently, the aura that envelops the actor vanishes, and with it the aura of the figure he portrays.[4]

---

[2] Walter Benjamin, 'The Work of Art in the Age of Mechanical Reproduction', in *Illuminations*, ed. Hannah Arendt, trans. Harry Zohn (New York: Schocken, 1969), pp. 9–10.

[3] Benjamin, p. 10.

[4] Benjamin, p. 10.

It is perhaps the ability of De Niro to project something that seems to function like aura to the camera, despite everything, that makes him such an astonishing film actor; but he did not achieve this unaided, or without other histories of performance behind him. One story of post-war cinema is how a new generation learned to perform despite the problems Benjamin outlines; they drew on a new range of techniques and influences in response to the demands of the technology.

Susan Sontag similarly remarks that 'cinema is an object (a product, even) while theatre is a performance' and that 'making a film, like writing a book, means constructing an inanimate thing, every element of which is determinate'.[5] Everything may have been determined by the time the film is complete, but the specifics of what appears on screen are as dependent on specific choices and forms of authorship as are the words on a page. An actor has to imbue their gestures, sounds and movements with life, even if the film itself has none. The expressivity that we find in the best actors' work, the emotion we allow to be evoked in us, comes from their ability to make the medium communicate everything as if it were unfolding in front of us, just as when we hear the recording of a great musician, or engage with the work of an essayist, even after she is no longer alive.

Philip Auslander historicises the concept of 'live' and recorded performance in ways that go to the heart of Benjamin's concerns, and of how technology and acting have subsequently sought to address them. For Auslander,

> historically, the live is actually an effect of mediatization, not the other way around. It was the development of recording technologies that made it possible to perceive existing representations as 'live'. Prior to the advent of those technologies (e.g. sound recording and motion pictures), there was no such thing as 'live' performance, for that category has meaning only in relation to an opposing possibility.[6]

De Niro's great skill came in being able to reproduce the power of apparent liveness on film, and what the archives reveal is the sophistication of the techniques he developed to achieve this.

---

[5] Susan Sontag, 'Film and Theatre', *The Tulane Drama Review*, Vol. 11, No. 1 (1966), p. 31.

[6] Philip Auslander, *Liveness: Performance in a Mediatized Culture*, 2nd ed. (London: Routledge, 2008), p. 56.

Importantly, De Niro was able to bring to film performance methods he had learned from a technology whose full potential was only just becoming visible at the time Benjamin was writing his essay: television, which would in a sense become the medium through which live and recorded performance entered into dialogue with one another. Exploring the interplay between 'liveness' and mediatised performance, and the way that each form is influenced and informed by the other, Auslander notes that liveness was 'the one aspect of theatrical presentation that film could not replicate',[7] but that television in some ways could:

> As a camera-bound medium, television might well have striven to be cinematic; but instead it strove to be theatrical. The answer to this question lies in the way in which the essence of the televisual was understood, from television's earliest appearances, as an ontology of liveness more akin to the ontology of theatre than to that of film. Television's essence was seen in its ability to transmit events as they occur, not in a filmic capacity to record events for later viewing.[8]

De Niro was part of the first TV generation; he grew up in a mediated world. His understanding of performance was influenced by television, and this idea of liveness is a quality that he and his generation of performers brought to the screen. Very quickly, however, that line between liveness and recorded event was blurred, as Francis Ford Coppola recalls:

> I'll never forget one day in the mid-1950s when my mother came to my room to say that my father was on television. I ran down to the television in his studio two floors below and there he was—playing the flute on our TV. But I turned around, and there he also was, sitting at his piano watching the broadcast. It was astounding.[9]

Even in the 1950s the idea of liveness was already recorded. In jazz the work of engineers like Teo Macero was enabling Miles Davis to produce a kind of performance that had previously been impossible, something

---

[7] Auslander, p. 13.

[8] Auslander, p. 12.

[9] Francis Ford Coppola, *Live Cinema and Its Techniques* (New York: Liveright Publishing Corporation, 2017), p. 25.

improvised yet impeccably structured. The idea of performance began to change because television made a different kind of performance visible. The audience had seen itself on TV; for the first time there was a kind of mundane performance that was viewable as text, and with this came the idea of performed sincerity. Previously, TV performance didn't need to be 'sincere'; it just needed to be compelling. As John Ellis puts it:

> The new medium required new styles of performance right from the outset [...] In the initial phase of television, performance styles had to be developed, especially for non-professionals. In a second phase, the expression of emotions became more elaborated and confident, especially as TV fictions became more complex. Only then could the centrality of sincerely felt emotion begin to emerge, and at the same time the medium freed itself from the expectation that it should provide explanatory meta-discourses. Audiences were left to judge for themselves the degree of sincerity in the emotions displayed before them.[10]

De Niro's performance in *The King of Comedy* (1982) pushes these different levels of naturalism and self-referentiality in television acting to breaking point, with notorious cruxes surrounding the ontological matter of which parts of the film are to be understood as unfolding in the imagination of De Niro's character Rupert Pupkin, and whether or not we are to regard the stand-up monologue he finally gets to deliver on television as actually funny, moderately funny, or not funny at all.

In a post-Benjamin, media-saturated world of multiple interacting media platforms, 'aura' can never be wholly separated from 'image', although Benjamin was already alert to the issue: 'The film responds to the shrivelling of the aura with an artificial build-up of the '"personality' outside the studio. 'The cult of the movie star [...] preserves not the unique aura of the person but the "spell of the personality"'.[11] In his insistence on protecting his privacy as far as possible and resisting the cult of the movie star De Niro contests this 'cult', and manages to ensure that his aura remains within the boundaries of the film by making it inaccessible elsewhere. Conversely, however, this filmic aura became inextricable from his theatrical persona on a rare occasion when he returned

---

[10] John Ellis, 'The Performance on Television of Sincerely Felt Emotion', *The Annals of the American Academy of Political and Social Science*, 625 (2009), p. 104.

[11] Benjamin, p. 11.

to the stage. While the young De Niro's first public performances were as a stage actor, by the time New York's resident impresario Joe Papp persuaded him to appear in *Cuba and His Teddy Bear* in 1986 he was a film star; his 'authentic' presence in stage was therefore a box office draw. The *New York Times* critic Mel Gussow marvelled at his 'earthy naturalness and an ability to extinguish his own star charisma', and the *Village Voice*'s Michael Feingold celebrated his 'lead actor's authority, which in the theatre is a better asset than a star's mythical image'.[12] Nevertheless, in revelling in De Niro's 'naturalness' and 'authority' (as a stage actor) in contrast to his 'charisma' and 'mythical image' (as a film star), they unavoidably read his on-stage theatrical performance in relation to his off-stage screen persona.

The tension between performance and 'real life' that perhaps lies at the heart of Benjamin's foundational distinction was also explored by the Modernist film critic Siegfried Kracauer, who identifies the paradox of the film actor: 'The film actor must act as if he did not act at all but were a real-life person caught in the act by the camera. He must seem to *be* his character'.[13] Directors as different as Vsevolod Pudovkin and René Clair, asserts Kracauer, value 'projections of the unconscious', and 'the film actor [has] to advance the narrative by embodying "such psychic events as are before or beyond speech"'[14]:

> The film actor's performance, then, is true to the medium only if it does not assume the airs of a self-sufficient achievement but impresses us as an incident—one of many possible incidents—of his character's unstaged material existence. Only then is the life he renders truly cinematic. When movie critics sometimes blame an actor for overacting his part, they do not necessarily mean that he acts theatrically; rather they wish to express the feeling that his acting is sometimes too purposeful, that it lacks that fringe of indeterminacy or indefiniteness which is characteristic of photography.[15]

---

[12] Quoted in Shawn Levy, *Robert De Niro: A Life* (New York: Three Rivers Press, 2014), p. 314.

[13] Siegfried Kracauer, 'Remarks on the Actor' quoted in R. Knopf (ed.), *Theater and Film: A Comparative Anthology* (New York: Yale University Press, 2005), p. 325.

[14] Kracauer, p. 325.

[15] Kracauer, pp. 325–326.

Kracauer's insight into the need for actors to appear not 'too purposeful' alerts us to the danger of overlooking how much work can be involved in something which can appear so effortless. De Niro's archive is now perhaps the world's most important primary resource in providing the evidence of this work. He is of course, however, far from being the first actor to address the question of how to respond to the challenge of Benjamin's aura, and how to exploit the paradox of Kracauer's film actor.

THE ACTOR'S RESPONSE TO FILM TECHNOLOGY

Even at the time, perhaps, there was something a little naïve in Benjamin's assertion that '[t]he stage actor identifies himself with the character of his role. The film actor very often is denied this opportunity. His creation is by no means all of a piece; it is composed of many separate performances'.[16] Similarly, Kracauer's assumption that '[a]ny genuinely photographic portrait tends to sustain the impression of unstaged reality' today looks unsustainable. We can see now that actors adapted to the technology, just as painters adapted to having to paint on canvas or lying on their back, or en plain air. De Niro has specifically talked about the way in which he deals with being edited: 'I know [...] that if [the director]'s got any sense he'll cut away from the stuff that's not quite right. Or maybe he will feel it's OK and it's me being self-conscious'.[17] He differs from the actors Benjamin describes both in relation to the technology and in the nature of his collaborations with directors, screenwriters and other actors. In 1960 Jerry Lewis, with whom De Niro was to work on *The King of Comedy*, took out the patent on the video assist, and from then on it was possible for performers to see themselves in action. From as early as *The Godfather, Part II* De Niro was watching images of performances: first of Marlon Brando in the original *Godfather* and later of rushes, videotaped rehearsals, and his own performances. All of these techniques show De Niro working directly with film technology to produce, if not the technical impossibility of actual presence, an illusion of spontaneity and natural performance.

[16] Benjamin, p. 11.

[17] Quoted in Bert Cardullo et al. (ed.), *Playing to the Camera: Film Actors Discuss Their Craft* (New Haven: Yale University Press, 1998), pp. 281–282.

Very early on actors realised they needed to find ways to deal with the specific requirements of tracking their emotional rise and fall during the real time of a production. Just two years after Benjamin's essay, Robert Donat was exploring solutions to the problems Benjamin identified. Vicky Lowe has analyzed this actor's methodologies, drawing on 'Film Acting', an article Donat contributed in 1938 to the film production manual *Footnotes to the Film*, and on the 'emotion chart' he produced in preparing that same year to play the role of Manson in *The Citadel* (the chart is now in the John Rylands Library at the University of Manchester). In Lowe's account,

> The 'Emotion Chart' provided a visual representation of the levels of emotion required on a scene by scene basis throughout the film. This would then enable Donat to construct an emotionally coherent performance on screen, despite the restrictions of di continuous performance conditions. In Donat's description of its importance to him, the concept of control is highly evident as he said it enabled him to tell 'at a glance (…) at what tempo I had to control my emotions for the day'.[18]

As Donat describes it,

> In the end I worked out a scheme by which all the major points in Manson's life, its ups and downs, its triumphs and failures could be spread out in front of me like a map. This was drawn out on squared paper like a huge graph and pinned to my dressing room wall. Every incident was carefully noted by means of a line, which ran up and down, very much like a temperature chart. In this way, I was able to keep my finger on the pulse of Manson's emotional life, giving to each event just what the moment demanded and no more.[19]

Lowe compares the performance chart to the finished film, and examines the extent to which Donat's evaluation of the emotional pitch of the scene matches her analysis of the scene as acted in the film. She observes that the creation of the chart 'suggests that for Donat good acting implied a

---

[18] Vicky Lowe, 'Acting with Feeling: Robert Donat, the "Emotion Chart" and *The Citadel* (1938)', *Film History: An International Journal*, Vol. 19, No. 1 (2007), p. 75.

[19] Lowe, p. 75.

degree of authorship. With the "Emotion Chart", Donat wrote himself into the film, as conscious creator of his performance'.[20]

It is striking that what Lowe terms Donat's 'conscious awareness of the technical needs of the medium' seems almost a novel idea. Although there are many ways in which a film actor needed to understand technology and, if they came from the stage, relearn the nature of performance, the idea that actors are without agency or authorship in this new medium seems astonishing—especially an actor like Donat, who was already an international success after his starring role in Hitchcock's *The 39 Steps* (1935) was described by *Observer* critic C. A. Lejeune as 'the British equivalent of a Clark Gable or a Ronald Colman'.[21]

Donat's chart used the organisational principles of the screenplay—the breakdown into scenes—to work on what one might call the longitudinal performance: the process of sustaining a performance throughout the actual time of the filming process, which is one of the chronologies of the actor. All film actors from whatever formation who appear in a film for any length of time have needed to find a way to produce the appropriate intensity on the right day, curating the performance through the three chronologies the actor experiences: the timescale of the story (which may be in hours or decades), the real time of the shooting process (usually weeks or months), and the duration of the film as experienced by the audience (usually between 80 minutes and three hours).

Although Donat describes how (and where) he used his emotion chart, he does not reveal where he discovered this process from. We do know, however, that Donat, like De Niro, considered watching rushes to be a key part of an actor's process:

> [I]t is when one sits in the projection theatre at the studio the following day and sees one's previous day's efforts come to life, that the real strength of a mere moment becomes properly significant. Then, when one senses the value of detail and the unique opportunities afforded for perfection, the ultimate possibilities of film-making seem to gain a sort of sanctity.[22]

---

[20] Lowe, p. 80.

[21] Quoted in Jeffrey Richards, *The Age of the Dream Palace: Cinema and Society in 1930s Britain* (London; New York: I.B. Tauris, 2010), p. 229.

[22] Donat, quoted in Cardullo, p. 92.

Watching rushes is one means by which the screen actor addressed what Benjamin saw as a 'feeling of strangeness that overcomes the actor before the camera'.[23] Benjamin thought that this 'is basically of the same kind as the estrangement felt before one's own image in the mirror. But now the reflected image has become separable, transportable. And where is it transported? Before the public'.[24]

However, this is not quite right. The *camera* is not a mirror; the *screen* is more like one, but the actor can decide not to look at the same screen as the public, because that image is projected after the film is made. Rushes, however, allow the actor the use of a more private 'mirror' *during* production, facilitating changes to the performance to create a better one for the public. This does not mean, however, that the act of looking at rushes lacks a comparable sense of estrangement. For Donat, the actor

> must gauge his movements so that at the moment of the close-up, his head will be momentarily still and his eyes— almost imperceptibly— will flash their story; not into the lens itself [...] but at a spot dangerously close. And an exact spot [...] so insidiously faithful is the lens that it will blurt out the whole story if given half a chance.[25]

Rushes, then, can be both alienating and yet a factor in sustaining the illusion of naturalness, by making the actor aware of how they appear on screen. In an interview with Leigh Woods, Jeff Daniels said he no longer wanted to watch rushes, but he stressed: 'By now I know what my face looks like on film. It's very important to know what the muscles in your face are doing'.[26]

The invaluable anthology *Playing to the Camera: Film Actors Discuss Their Craft* reveals other methods that performers have adopted in addressing this strange paradox of trying to reconcile performance with naturalness while having to learn a new technology. Another British actor and Donat's contemporary, Michael Redgrave, says that 'in good acting there is a continual flow of improvisation',[27] and discusses how much he learned from directors, referencing Hitchcock, Czinner, Carol Reed and

---

[23] Benjamin, 'The Work of Art', p. 11.

[24] Benjamin, p. 11.

[25] Donat quoted in Lowe, p. 73.

[26] Jeff Daniels quoted in Cardullo, p. 257.

[27] Michael Redgrave, quoted in Cardullo, 100.

Fritz Lang. Working with Alberto Cavalcanti, Redgrave recalls that 'In the "Ventriloquist" section of *Dead of Night* we both felt it was impossible to tell where direction or acting ended or began'.[28] Albert Finney, too, saw improvisation, or the illusion of improvisation, as the key to successful film acting:

> I think my job as an actor is to produce the effect, if you like, of impro-
> visation in the final result. If improvisation seems more real than acting
> that may be because people have seen a lot of bad acting [...] Acting
> is the craft of knowing exactly what you want to communicate and then
> making it spontaneous, making it seem just to happen. And you have to
> know exactly what second I feel is the best moment in a scene to put that
> cigarette out. But don't do it as though you were beating time.[29]

Finney saw the actor's job as 'to be able in some way on the fourth take or for that matter the eleventh take to keep the life in it',[30] echoing Kracauer's paradox that the film actor must act as if he did not act. A film actor, then, needs to understand their medium, which is both film and themselves. They need to control how they appear on film and be able to modify their movements and expressions in two ways: how they control their own body and how to be aware of it in mediation, when it appears projected on a screen with all the distortions of a lens and reduced from three dimensions to two.

By the time Robert De Niro entered the profession, then, all kinds of techniques were available to encourage the development of a rehearsed spontaneity. Just as theatre design changed to accommodate electric lighting or film projection, film performance was changing to accommodate not only the technologies with which film was made, but the way the audience perceives the image. De Niro is developing his techniques as the relationship between subject and audience is changing; the audience knows what actors look like on screen, and the actor's understanding of truthful performance is different once they have encountered their sense of their own self. Over time, De Niro would synthesise the different approaches to performance he has encountered into something which is distinctly his own, which combines aspects of the naturalistic

---

[28] Ibid., p. 104.

[29] Albert Finney, quoted in Cardullo, p. 112.

[30] Finney, quoted in Cardullo, p. 112.

with the extensively stylised, which shifts the focus from representation to creation. These techniques come directly out of his developing practice, in which he brings together an understanding of performance, character and narrative within the medium of film.

FINE ART PRACTICE AND PERFORMANCE

Some of that sophisticated understanding also came not from film but from the world of fine art into which De Niro was born. Daniel Belgrad writes that 'Historically the development of spontaneous art was linked to the social issue of ethnic identity'.[31] De Niro's ethnic identity was complex, but his name and appearance led people to assume he was Italian; he spent time with his grandparents in Syracuse, and on trips to Europe he explored his Italian roots. But he was also visiting Peggy Guggenheim's gallery in Venice and his father's studio in France, as well as Erwin Piscator's in Berlin. He moved between worlds, and that fluidity matched a growing fluidity between disciplines.

He was born in New York in 1943. His father, also named Robert De Niro, was a painter who had studied with perhaps the two most influential American-based art teachers of the twentieth century: first with Hans Hofmann and then with Josef Albers at Black Mountain College, where he had a full scholarship for two years. De Niro's mother, Virginia Admiral, was also a student of Hofmann; indeed, she and Robert De Niro met at Hofmann's courses in Provincetown, and the courses attracted other painters including William De Kooning, Lee Krasner, Jackson Pollock, Larry Rivers and Mark Rothko. Growing up in this environment, Robert De Niro Jr quickly absorbed a remarkable range of different approaches to improvisation, process and representation.

Both Hofmann and Albers in their different ways taught the relationship between practice and theory, and the idea that practice was the only way to express and explore ideas. Hofmann had been in the US since the late twenties; Albers fled the Bauhaus when the Nazis came to power, and 'Much of what Albers brought from the Bauhaus was congenial to Black Mountain College: The principles of "practice before theory," "learning by doing," and "study, not art"; the dissolution of the hierarchy that elevated fine arts above everything else; recognising that art

---

[31] Daniel Belgrad, *The Culture of Spontaneity: Improvisation and the Arts in Postwar America* (Chicago and London: The University of Chicago Press, 1998), p. 40.

is an experience rather than a commodity'.[32] Albers used metaphors of drama and performance in teaching fine art. He encouraged students to think of objects and colours as having personality, and that the artist needed to look at them and consider their properties: '"What do you see in the chairs?" he'd ask [...] "Are they dancing teenagers? Sedate oldsters? Flying horses? These chairs aren't just sitting there. Look at them. They are dancing"'.[33] Albers also used to concoct little melodramas to help his students see the colour performances, one student recalling a conversation between yellow and orange: 'Look! the color orange is at the door and says to the yellow, "You go first." But the yellow is also polite and says, "No, you go first."'[34]

The Bauhaus had always put performance at the heart of its understanding of fine art practice. Oscar Schlemmer, who taught theatre at the Bauhaus, stressed the centrality of performance and theatre in the understanding of art practice. Noting that the Bauhaus's aims 'have valid application to the field of the theater', Schlemmer proposed that

> the stage is an orchestral complex which comes about only through the cooperation of many different forces. [...] It is the union of the most heterogeneous assortment of creative elements. Not the least of its functions is to serve the metaphysical needs of man by constructing a world of illusion and by creating the transcendental on the basis of the rational. From the first day of its existence, the Bauhaus sensed the impulse for creative theatre; [...] the un-self-conscious and naive pleasure in shaping and producing, without asking questions about use or uselessness, sense or nonsense, good or bad. [...] [This] was expressed in our exuberant parties, in improvisations, and in the imaginative masks and costumes which we made.[35]

---

[32] Frederick A. Horowitz, 'What Josef Albers Taught at Black Mountain College, and What Black Mountain College Taught Albers', *Journal of Black Mountain College Studies*, Vol. 11 (2011), http://www.blackmountainstudiesjournal.org/volume1/1-9-frederick-a-horowitz/ [Accessed: 15 May 2020].

[33] Josef Albers quoted in Frederick A. Horowitz and Brenda Danilowitz, *Josef Albers: To Open Eyes* (London: Phaidon Press, 2006), p. 178.

[34] Quoted in Horowitz and Danilowitz, p. 199.

[35] Walter Gropius and Arthur S. Wensinger (ed.), *The Theater of the Bauhaus: Oskar Schlemmer, Laszlo Moholy-Nagy, Farkas Molnár* (Middleton, CT: Wesleyan University Press, 1971), pp. 81–82.

Bauhaus Director Walter Gropius designed a 'Total Theatre' for Erwin Piscator,[36] who taught at the New School in New York; his wife Maria Ley-Piscator was De Niro's first acting teacher, and De Niro was later to visit him in Berlin on a tour of Europe.[37] Gropius' ambition for his theatre showed a relationship between externality and internality, the three-dimensional body and the mind of the audience: 'the playhouse itself, made to dissolve into the shifting, illusionary space of the imagination, would become the scene of action itself [...] if it is true that the mind can transform the body, it is equally true that structure can transform the mind'.[38]

The Bauhaus principles of learning through doing and an iterative methodology of practice, play and reflection used by artists can be seen in the Ransom Center archive in De Niro's improvisations and explorations, and his repeated close readings of the text. De Niro, then, grew up in an environment where debates about expression and authenticity and their relationship to performance were at the heart of the practices of both his parents: they learned to work. Moreover, the modes of expression they developed took the form of gestures, energies and emotions, all of which manifested themselves both visually and verbally, and connected to the new improvisational and embodied practices of the Abstract Expressionists.

As J. J. Murphy's recent study *Rewriting Indie Cinema: Improvisation, Psychodrama and the Screenplay* makes clear, improvisation reached the cinema via a number of different routes, and via an inter-medial approach to filmmaking in which '[w]ith the exception of Cassavetes, the early filmmakers were neither screenwriters nor actors [...] Robert Frank and Albert Leslie used other artists, such as poets, painters, and musicians'.[39] In Murphy's view,

[t]he shift from the emphasis on the written page to the performer has other implications. The movement [...] placed greater emphasis on the

---

[36] Gropius and Wensinger, p. 10.

[37] Andreas Conrad, 'Wie Robert De Niro per Anhalter durch die DDR reiste', *Die Tagesspiegel*, 11 February 2007, https://www.tagesspiegel.de/kultur/wie-robert-de-niro-per-anhalter-durch-die-ddr-reiste/809516.html [Accessed: 15 May 2020].

[38] Gropius and Wensinger, p. 14.

[39] J. J. Murphy, *Rewriting Indie Cinema: Improvisation, Psychodrama, and the Screenplay* (New York: Columbia University Press, 2019), p. 12.

human body. What was occurring in film was not an isolated gesture but an expression of a larger movement that occurred within all the arts in America. In poetry, for instance, Allen Ginsberg used his own breath to determine the rhythmic lines of his poems. In painting, Jackson Pollock used his own body to express his feelings on the canvas.[40]

Murphy cites Daniel Belgrad's *The Culture of Spontaneity: Improvisation and the Arts in Postwar America*: 'an accurate understanding of American Intellectual and cultural life in the post-war decades depends on recognising the existence of a coherent aesthetic of spontaneity and its social significance'.[41]

Robert De Niro had deep connections to these cultures of spontaneity, as he grew up at the heart of the New York avant-garde where all these worlds connected. Pollock and his wife Lee Krasner studied with his parents in Provincetown. Larry Rivers, a friend of Robert De Niro Senior who also studied with him at the Hans Hofmann School, was one of the actors in the 1959 short film *Pull My Daisy*, scripted by Jack Kerouac and directed by Robert Frank and Alfred Leslie. Both of De Niro's parents were connected with poetry, criticism and theatre, as well as film. Poet, playwright and MoMA curator Frank O'Hara (a supporter of Robert De Niro Senior's work), playwrights like Tennessee Williams, painters like Elaine de Kooning, and critics like Clement Greenberg, Pauline Kael and Manny Farber were all part of the Admiral/De Niro circle. (*Negative Space*, Manny Farber's collection of film writing is dedicated to Admiral.) Robert De Niro Senior worked alongside Jackson Pollock at the Museum of Modern Art, where his mother had a painting hanging, and both Virginia Admiral and Robert De Niro Senior had a stipend from the Guggenheim fund administered by Hilla Rebay. Admiral's work was purchased by the Museum of Modern Art in 1946 when she was still a student[42]; her work was included in the Peggy Guggenheim Collection and shown in the Venice Biennale in 1941, and in the film *Peggy Guggenheim: Art Addict* (2015) her son describes his pride as a young man at seeing her work in Venice.

---

[40] Murphy, p. 12.

[41] Murphy, p. 12.

[42] MoMA documentation for 'An Exhibition of Recent Acquisitions,' Held February 14 through March 18, 1945, *MoMA*, https://www.moma.org/documents/moma_master-checklist_325455.pdf [Accessed: 15 May 2020].

De Niro, then, was exposed to approaches to performance in theatre in art and in everyday life from an extraordinary wide range of people, from New York collectors to penniless European émigrés, from intellectuals poets and critics who expressed themselves in words to the painters and actors whose work was written with the body, to the street kids he hung out with on the Lower East side and who gave the pale-faced teenager the nickname 'Bobby Milk'.[43]

INTERMEDIALITY AND PERFORMANCE

Although it is easy to think of De Niro's parents as belonging to a world of 'high' art, and that they fell on one side of a distinction in the 1950s between highbrow and lowbrow cultures that would soon become unfashionable, it is important to emphasise that through them he was equally exposed to more 'popular' kinds of entertainment: an admixture perhaps epitomised in the fact that his mother was at one point writing erotica for Anaïs Nin and crime stories for *True Crime* magazine while his father was writing poetry in both English and French. Although both of his parents were highly regarded as visual artists they were also writers, and this facility in multiple kinds of artistic expression is equally evident in the work of their son, who is a writer as well as actor.

This conception of the actor resonates with James Naremore's previously cited categorisation of De Niro as 'a sophisticated theorist'.[44] British Actor Simon Russell Beale has described acting as 'three-dimensional literary criticism', and although he is speaking largely of performing Shakespeare on stage there is much in common between his practice and De Niro's:

> It is an important part of our job [...] to lead the audience through a detailed, thought-through argument or series of arguments. As a component of this, it is essential, it seems to me, to clarify and distil the line of thought in an individual character's head, before one begins to explore other, emotional areas. A large part of our time is taken up with this process and the benefits, if it is pursued rigorously, are three-fold. The first is obvious: an actor cannot safely open his or her mouth unless he or

---

[43] Levy, p. 41.

[44] James Naremore, *Acting in the Cinema* (Berkeley: University of California Press, 1988), p. 267.

she knows precisely the meaning of the words at their simplest level. The second is that it clarifies a character's function within the larger picture of the play; and the third benefit is that a careful analysis of a series of thoughts may lead the actor into unexpected emotional territory. If that happens, it can, in an ideal world, lead to discoveries beyond or without memory or desire.[45]

As noted earlier, De Niro's first acting experiences were not for film but for the stage. One of his first roles was in *Glamour, Glory and Gold: The Life and Legend of Nola Noon, Goddess and Star*, which was written by Jackie Curtis, 'a rising star in the firmament of Andy Warhol's Factory scene',[46] and which opened at Bastiano's Cellar Studio in August 1968. De Niro played no fewer than ten different parts, and received very positive reviews:

'Robert DeNiro [*sic*] appears in no less than ten cameo characterizations and is a standout comic actor,' said *Show Business*. 'He's a master of the art of underplaying'. The *Village Voice* concurred: 'DeNiro [*sic*] made clean, distinct character statements in a series of parts which many actors would have fused into a general mush. DeNiro is new on the scene and deserves to be welcomed.[47]

De Niro also performed at the experimental theatre La Mama. The connections between film acting and more mainstream Broadway theatre informed by the techniques of the Method have been more fully explored, for example regarding the careers of James Dean and Marlon Brando, but there are nevertheless significant 'parallel[s] between avant-garde performing and film acting', as the actor Willem Dafoe suggested to Auslander in 1985:

[Dafoe] told me that, from his point of view as a performer, what he does when performing in a Wooster Group piece is virtually identical to his acting in films [...] Dafoe is one of a growing group of American performance artists whose experiences in the avant-garde enabled them to make

---

[45] Simon Russell Beale, 'Without Memory or Desire: Acting Shakespeare', Ernest Jones Lecture organised by the Scientific Committee of the British Psychoanalytical Society, 21 June 2009. The British Psychoanalytical Society Archives, London, UK.

[46] Levy, p. 75.

[47] Levy, p. 76.

a smooth transition into acting on film or television; the careers of Laurie Anderson, Spalding Gray, Ron Vawter, Ann Magnuson, Eric Bogosian, Steve Buscemi, and many others are noteworthy in this regard. More important, their more experimental work itself has found its way into mass-cultural contexts in many cases: Anderson's performances as rock concerts, films, and videos; Gray's and Bogosian's monologues as movies.[48]

Although he comes from a slightly older generation, De Niro can be added to this list. One of the reasons why he is often overlooked in such contexts is that he transitioned to film acting very quickly and his success came so rapidly, but he grew up with improvisation and experimentation, the notion of liveness and the power of the traced gesture, whether expressed in marks on paper, in theatre or on film.

ADLER, STRASBERG, PISCATOR AND THE 'METHOD'

It is widely assumed that De Niro's achievements in creating effects of spontaneity and naturalness must be due to 'the discourse most closely associated with DeNiro as an actor: that of so-called Method acting with its attendant psychological concepts of acting out and working through'.[49] However, while the Method may be a way of reaching a level of emotional intensity, it is not a way of managing the filming process from the actor's perspective. How actors manage that process, and how they learn from other actors, directors and others working on the film with whom they come into contact, has been much less fully studied. Learning to perform a role of any duration successfully in a feature film is something that can be achieved only through doing, which is why the Bauhaus approach of iteration, of play followed by analysis and practice, is so important. Actors learn from scripts; they learn from other actors, as De Niro learned from Shelley Winters and Marlon Brando; they learn from directors, as Donat indicates (and in his early films De Niro worked with several outstanding directors—and some bad ones); and they learn from their practice. Ultimately, as Hans Hofmann wrote, 'the artist [...]

---

[48] Auslander, p. 33.

[49] Marco Abel, 'Becoming-Violent, Becoming-DeNiro', in *Violent Affect: Literature, Cinema, and Critique After Representation* (Lincoln: University of Nebraska Press, 2007), p. 137.

must then detach himself entirely from schools and directions and evolve a personality of his own'.[50] This is exactly what De Niro did.

The 'Method' ultimately derived from the ideas and 'system' of Konstantin Stanislavsky (via, in the United States, Richard Boleslavsky), and was concentrated in the 1930s at the Group Theatre, which counted Lee Strasberg and Stella Adler among its founders. Over time Strasberg and Adler would go in radically different directions, with their theoretical split being concentrated on the matter of 'affective memory'. Both of these figures would exert some influence over De Niro, although Adler was to have by far the greater impact on his work, and this influence has been expounded many times before.[51] Our aim here is to situate them in the broader context of De Niro's overall formation. Essentially, at the Actors Studio Strasberg, following a method strongly related to Stanislavsky's early emphasis on 'emotion memory', 'relentlessly promoted "affective memory" as the Holy Grail of realist acting'.[52] In this approach the actor was to find an emotional correlative for the character's emotions in her own experience, which could then be recalled in the performance of a scene via the actor's 'sense memory' that would correspond to the emotion required on stage at that moment.

De Niro's early training with Strasberg's bitter rival Adler reportedly persuaded the youthful actor against attempting to gain admission to the Actors Studio,[53] although as we shall see De Niro's recollection is slightly different; in any case, Strasberg was undoubtedly an influence. Some traces of his approach can be found in De Niro's annotations, at comparatively rare moments when in seeking to find the emotional core of a scene he will remind himself of an episode from his life—although it must be emphasised that, in the scripts we have examined, it is more common for him to recall instead a corresponding event in *someone else's* experience. Some of the best examples of this particular variation are found in his annotations for *The Last Tycoon* (1976), which was directed by another Group Theatre veteran, Elia Kazan, and made just a couple

---

[50] Hans Hofmann in Tina Dickey and Helmut Friedel, *Hans Hofmann: Wunder Des Rhythmus und Schönheit Des Raumes* (New York: Hudson Hills Press, 1998), p. 9.

[51] See for example Levy, *Robert De Niro*, pp. 48–54; R. Colin Tait, 'Robert De Niro's *Raging Bull*: The History of a Performance and a Performance of History', *Canadian Journal of Film Studies*, Vol. 20, No. 1 (2011), p. 28.

[52] Abel, p. 148.

[53] Levy, p. 77.

of years after De Niro acted alongside Strasberg in *The Godfather, Part II* in 1974. At moments in *The Last Tycoon* De Niro uses the technique he rarely deploys elsewhere of recalling an experience of a similar kind of emotion: '*Just think of the sadness of [X & Y] splitting*'. And in perhaps another reference to emotional memory he can draw on, '*What loss. Like [X] that first time*'.[54] (Our parenthetical letters indicate where De Niro names individuals he knew personally.)

Although Strasberg held continuously to affective memory, Stanislavsky himself was more flexible, and over time came to favour instead 'the method of physical actions'.[55] This differed from affective memory in emphasising that the actor should analyse 'the behaviour and motivations of the character rather than the actual experiences of the actor',[56] including via imaginative engagement with the text. This was the approach favoured by Adler, whose classes De Niro attended at the age of sixteen. By contrast to the occasional touches of affective memory in De Niro's annotations, the evidence of the archive is that physical action techniques are overwhelmingly more important to him, and that the foundation of his approach lies in the combination of methods advanced by Adler: the actor's preparatory work combined with rehearsal, in a 'laboratory setup'.[57] In De Niro's particular formation this involves detailed preparation via the script, a frequently improvisatory approach to rehearsal, and an attention to physical detail, including costume and props as well as the body. All of these aspects of his research permeate the archive in every detail.

The performed spontaneity which became the distinguishing feature of post-war film performance, then, did not itself arise spontaneously. Film performance was transformed after 'the Method' and Adler's studio-developed techniques to incorporate ways of learning how to act in the new medium. Adler drew on Stanislavsky, but she had also worked with Piscator's Dramatic Studio and the Yiddish Theatre in New York, as well as performing both on stage and in the cinema. The Dramatic Studio, which was sited within the progressive New School, was teaching radio

[54] *The Last Tycoon* (1976), 11 August 1975, Script Copy 20, with extensive RDN notes, additional mimeo and RDN notes in pocket at front, Box 191 [RDN].

[55] Foster Hirsch, *A Method to Their Madness: A History of the Actors Studio* (New York: Norton, 1984), p. 39.

[56] Abel, p. 149.

[57] Hirsch, p. 206.

television and film, and De Niro entered these classes very early on. As he recalled in 1993:

> My mother worked for a woman, Maria Ley-Piscator, who with her husband founded the Dramatic Workshop, which was connected to the New School. My mother did proofreading and typing and stuff or her, and as part of her payment, I was able to take acting classes there on Saturdays when I was 10.[58]

Significantly—and like his father at Black Mountain College in his own medium—he was exposed very early to new European ideas about the theorisation and exploration of artistic practice and performance, in both fine art and drama. Piscator, like Albers, had connections to the Bauhaus, and Piscator developed theories of political theatre based on his own practice. As De Niro goes on to point out, in a neat summary of his early progression, 'It was a big school with a lot of actors, some of whom were able to study acting on the G.I. Bill. Brando and [Rod] Steiger went there, the generation before me. When I was 15, 16, I studied with Stella Adler at the Conservatory of Acting, then I stopped again and went to the Actors Studio when I was 18'.[59] By that age, then, De Niro he had studied with three of the most influential teachers of acting in the twentieth century; and he had also, at the New School, been open to a European influence, which synthesised techniques from both the Russian and the German theatres, challenged an easy and unproblematic naturalism, and encouraged an intersectional environment in which writers and actors studied together.

Not surprisingly, then, De Niro's approach to acting exhibits a more diverse range of influence than that exerted by any particular school or teacher. He was single-minded in his pursuit of excellence, but he was never ideologically committed to a single means of achieving it in the way that Strasberg arguably was. An article posted on the web page of De Niro's Tribeca Film Institute quotes the actor at a 2014 question-and-answer session:

---

[58] Peter Brant and Ingrid Sischy, 'A Walk and a Talk with Robert De Niro', *Interview*, Vol. 23, No. 11 (1993), p. 92.

[59] Brant and Sischy, p. 92.

the best thing you can do, I always feel, is at the end of the day whether it's Stella Adler or Lee Strasberg, either technique—and they overlap a lot—at the end of the day actors use whatever can work for them. When you are in the moment you have to use what's good for you. You can think about your mother that died last week, you can think about this you can think about that, my two things are you don't hurt yourself, you don't hurt others and everything else is okay. Whatever your wildest imagination can make you arrive at that point at that scene, that's fine.[60]

This is a long way from what is generally meant by the 'Method', and critics eager to describe De Niro as a 'Method actor' have nevertheless routinely encountered something in him that resists this easy classification. As Lesley Stern remarks in summarising this problem, De Niro 'adopts some of the laconic, sardonic tropes of an earlier Hollywood masculinity, and yet has learnt from the Method boys a rhetoric of the body. Perhaps it is his more catholic and inventive rhetorical ploys that incite an uneasiness, and sometimes hostility, in critics who try to situate him squarely within a Method tradition'.[61]

By the time De Niro began preparing for *Taxi Driver* he had found a way to use whatever worked for him, a heuristics of performance that allowed him to use a range of techniques, textual analysis from Adler, aspects of the Method to reach emotional intensity, the chronological breakdowns visible in the Corman screenplay, and a flair for improvisation that comes from his sensibilities and his previous experience in working with Scorsese on *Mean Streets*. He has incorporated what he learned from his role in *The Godfather Part II*, where he breaks down Brando's performance and works out how to make himself embody his character as a young man.

De Niro's decision to archive his screenplays, working notes and costumes makes it possible to see the amount of thought and effort that has gone into the simulation of indeterminacy he achieves so well: the sense that this is happening for the first time in front of the camera. His style is both physical and verbal, articulate and embodied. As Stern describes it in her essay on *Taxi Driver*, 'De Niro uses his body not only

[60] Jason Guerrasio, 'What it means to be "Method"', *Tribeca Film Institute*, 19 December 2014, https://www.tfiny.org/blog/detail/what_it_means_to_be_method [Accessed: 20 May 2020].

[61] Lesley Stern, *The Scorsese Connection* (Indianapolis: Indiana University Press, 1995), p. 210.

to signify character but as a site of performative action; he conveys, across characters, a sense of acting through the body'.[62] His work is embodied with the physical precision and affective power of a virtuoso musician or a dancer. Perhaps an audience can more easily accept that musicians practice than that actors also rehearse to produce something as insubstantial as a mere projection, which moreover, unlike a musical recital, when it is most successful seems—in the dominant Western traditions of film and television acting, at any rate—deceptively indistinguishable from normal behaviour: 'one of many possible incidents',[63] as Kracauer puts it. Perhaps we are made uncomfortable by the sense that there is anything rehearsed about that spontaneity, because if there is, we can feel we have been fooled—though that should be a pleasure in itself, as in delighting in the seeming miracles of a stage magician. De Niro's performances result from prodigious effort, however lightly carried, and his annotations allow us to trace how much research, analysis and thought has gone into his constructing them. What we see on screen appears natural or effortless precisely because so much art has gone into its realisation.

By contrast with Marlon Brando, with whom De Niro is often compared but who is, significantly, nearly twenty years his senior, the younger man grew up in a United States in which it is television and not cinema or theatre that occupied the dominant position in popular conceptions of public performance; and also unlike Brando De Niro is in important senses an avant-garde artist, who quickly finds himself working in cinema, finds that he is good at it, and then works very hard to succeed at it. These three strands—the understanding of artistic expression as a serious, lifelong pursuit; an extremely diverse range of cultural and intellectual influences; and the rapid transition and transformation of the self between media forms and from one stage of his career to the next—help to define De Niro's particular formation as an actor.

By the early 1960s De Niro was able to draw on many different influences and notions of performance. Although it is important to note how his practice connects with previous approaches to acting, the then-dominant notions about stage and film performance that he learned while studying under Stella Adler and Lee Strasberg were admixed with ideas and influences drawn from painting, writing and avant-garde theatre.

[62] Stern, p. 52.
[63] Kracauer, p. 325.

These include the idea of improvisation as being at the heart of every art form; the environment in which he grew up, invested with the aesthetics and practices of the fine art movement and abstract expressionism; the many different kinds of writing and writer that surround him; the normative use of chance and contingency in the making of an artwork; and the use of the body in the making of such a work.

EARLY FILMS

De Niro's first screen role was in a short film called *Encounter* (1965), which deals with an accidental encounter in Times Square between a long-separated mother (Dyanne Thorne) and son (De Niro). It was directed by Norman C. Chitin, who had studied with Stella Adler and had advertised the roles through her school; but the film was never released. De Niro also appears as a background extra in *Three Rooms in Manhattan*, directed by the famed French director Marcel Carné. This is probably the film that De Niro is thinking of in 1989 when he recalled

> some walk-on for an independent film: I walked in and ordered a drink at a bar. I remember a bunch of other young actors hanging around, moaning and bitching, all made up, with pieces of tissue in their collars; it was the kind of thing you always hear about actors—where they're just silly or vain, complaining back and forth, walking around primping, not wanting to get the make-up on their shirts.[64]

During this period he is taking acting classes with Stella Adler while also working in Experimental theatre at La MaMa and a number of other experimental venues in New York, as well as acting in dinner theatre in North Carolina.

Before *Encounter* came out, however, De Niro had a more fully developed role in *The Wedding Party* (filmed in 1963, although it would not be released for another six years), directed by Brian De Palma, who was then a young and ambitious avant-garde director running a workshop at Sarah Lawrence College where he had studied. De Palma recalled that

---

[64] Lawrence Grobel, '*Playboy* Interview: Robert De Niro', *Playboy*, Vol. 36, No. 1 (January 1989), p. 86.

Bobby came into a casting session [...] And he's very quiet. Shy. And then he said he had something he prepared in class. Then he went out. [...] And then he burst through the door and does a scene from Clifford Odets's play *Strike*. I think about the cab strike. And it was like [...] you were like watching Lee J. Cobb. It was like: 'holy mackerel'.[65]

De Palma quickly realised that De Niro was 'the most captivating character', and that 'we've got to make him like the main character. This guy is fantastic'. The evidence suggests that De Niro was using Adlerian methods and thinking about character and costume, but was not yet exploring the character in great depth.

De Niro made another early film with Brian De Palma, *Hi, Mom!* (1970). This features a lengthy sequence on a piece of radical theatre called 'Be Black Baby', in which a black theatre group confronts participants with their prejudices. It is a happening, which as Michael Joshua Rowin writes in his essay on the film, 'intends for its white, liberal audience to not just 'intellectualize' being black, but to really 'feel what it's like'.[66] The satire shows a familiarity with the New York avant-garde art scene—perhaps not surprisingly, as De Palma had made *The Responsive Eye*, a short film documenting the opening night of the eponymous exhibition at the Museum of Modern Art in New York 1966. This combines interviews with artists, including Joseph Albers and Larry Rivers along with critic Rudolph Arnheim, and vox pops with visitors, foreshadowing the satirical approach to the art public of *Hi Mom!* De Niro's own connections with the New York art world, meanwhile, can be seen in his association with the 'Ginger Island Project'. In 1969, he accompanied George Maciunas and other members of the artistic community Fluxus to this uninhabited island in the Caribbean, which Maciunas intended to purchase with the aim of establishing an artistic colony there. The artist John Held reported that De Niro's mother 'was thinking about buying

---

[65] Brian De Palma, interviewed in *De Palma*, Color Digital (HD), Directed by Noah Baumbach and Jake Paltrow (USA, Empire Ward Pictures, 2016).

[66] Michael Joshua Rowin, 'Free Radical', *Reverse Shot*, 3 November 2006, http://reverseshot.org/archive/entry/906/hi_mom_depalma [Accessed: 31 May 2020].

a plot, so they sent Bobby to help Maciunas survey the island',[67] but ultimately nothing of this plan came to fruition.

Shortly before *Hi, Mom!* De Niro acted in Roger Corman's *Bloody Mama*, which he was reportedly brought to by Shelley Winters, who knew of his work from the New York stage. The film was shot on location in the Ozarks in Arkansas during 1969 and released in 1970. It was written by Robert Thom, a Yale graduate of whom Louis Black wrote: 'he is the original author or scriptwriter of several of the weirdest American films ever made', predominantly exploitation films of the kind that in the late 1960s and early 1970s represented, in Black's view, 'America's true renegade cinema [...] and yield[ed], both in front of and behind the camera, at least two generations of filmmakers who would mature into some of the medium's greatest talents. Thom wrote the scripts for four of the most significant and best of these movies', of which *Bloody Mama* was one.[68] On this film, De Niro begins to develop techniques for acting across a chronological timescale he has not encountered before, working with an extremely experienced director and practised actors. In the four weeks of shooting he has to cover almost forty years of his character's life, and as noted in the previous chapter, he develops a form of notation that allows him easily to access the key information he needs for each scene, and what he wants to bring to it in terms of thought, action and gesture.

His next film saw him take on his first Mafia-related role. Al Pacino was originally attached to *The Gang That Couldn't Shoot Straight* (1971), written by Waldo Salt, who had just won an Academy Award for *Midnight Cowboy*, and adapted from the book by New York journalist Jimmy Breslin. Pacino left to take the role of Michael Corleone in *The Godfather*, and De Niro was released from a much smaller role on the same film to replace him. De Niro got good reviews, even if the film did not. His next role was as an undercover cop on *Born to Win* (1971) for the Czech New Wave director Ivan Passer, who cast him after having seen him on stage in New York. Already, then, De Niro had worked with directors

[67] Oral history interview with John Held, Jr., 2017 September 28–October 3. Archives of American Art, Smithsonian Institution, https://www.aaa.si.edu/collections/interviews/oral-history-interview-john-held-jr-17514 [Accessed: 15 May 2020].

[68] Louis Black, 'Down We Go: Revisiting Renaissance man Robert Thom's prolific and hellish Hollywood visions', *The Austin Chronicle*, 10 August 2007, https://www.austinchronicle.com/screens/2007-08-10/517929/ [Accessed: 15 May 2020].

from a very broad range of backgrounds, though he still had no contact with Hollywood.

Bang the Drum Slowly (1973) was De Niro's breakout film. Directed by John D. Hancock, a Harvard-educated theatre director who had worked with Tennessee Williams, he plays Bruce Pearson, a dying baseball player befriended by a more successful teammate. It was a tearjerker buddy movie which had previously been made as a teleplay with Paul Newman in the role of the successful teammate. Roger Ebert singled out the 'very good acting' by De Niro in what he described as 'the ultimate baseball movie'.[69] The review from David Denby in *Film Quarterly* was less kind, but in some ways is a greater testament to the power of De Niro's performance, which seems to have touched the critic profoundly:

Perhaps audiences are moved, in part, because the film touches buried levels of wonder and sentiment: the relationship between the men evokes the awesome mysteries of school or summer camp friendships in which an older, popular boy would inexplicably make a young outsider, a loser, his personal favourite, protecting him against bullies. As kids we never questioned such attachments. As adults, looking at other adults, we might wonder about the motives of the stronger man. Vanity? Love of power? Repressed homosexuality? These are some of the nasty but hardly unusual realities of the moral life that an artist of normal curiosity might consider, even if he intended to dismiss them or mix them with predominantly 'good' motives.[70]

That De Niro, who had at that stage only played supporting roles, has provoked such an extraordinary stream of consciousness from the critic is in itself worthy of comment. De Niro's performances are often seen as being naturalistic, but in fact they combine energy, intense stylisation and rhythmic grace. They are like a sketch by a great painter: they refine and simplify.

[69] Roger Ebert, 'Reviews: *Bang the Drum Slowly*', *Roger Ebert*, 26 August 1973, https://www.rogerebert.com/reviews/bang-the-drum-slowly-1973 [Accessed: 15 May 2020].

[70] David Denby, 'Review: *Bang the Drum Slowly* by John Hancock', *Film Quarterly*, Vol. 27, No. 2 (1973), p. 50.

Mean Streets

Mean Streets, the first film De Niro would make with MartinScorsese, was a career-changing role, and the beginning of an enduring collaboration that changed cinema. De Niro describes how he came to get the part:

> I ran into Harvey [Keitel] in the street, and he told me. I said, 'Frankly, you know, I'm at a certain stage as an actor, so I have to ask for the lead. I'll be honest with you.' But another part of me said that it really doesn't matter— you want to do it, or you want to work with the director. That's the way it should be. Then I spent a period of time kicking around the four parts. [...] But I wanted to work with Marty. Finally, I just said, 'Okay, I'll do that'.[71]

Scorsese said of their early relationship: 'We feel many things the same way. We understand each other perfectly. We don't need words to work together. The communication between us is like a form of sign language'.[72]

The collaboration between De Niro and Scorsese has been thoroughly documented by Colin Tait in his research at the HRC. Tait shows how De Niro had established techniques of script analysis from his work with Adler, and explored improvisation with De Palma on *Hi Mom*, *Son of Sam* and *Greetings*, 'leaving him free to engage in a synthesis of flexible, on-screen, and in-character exploration, as well as teaching him how his characters dictate action in a film'.[73] Tait explores *Mean Streets* in great detail, identifies De Niro as author of the character of Johnny Boy, and uncovers the research he did, including attention to costumes (it was De Niro's hat—now in the HRC—that was the clincher in De Niro getting the part) and the specifics of the character's situation, including De Niro's detailed calculations about the total amount of money his character owes, and to whom. The focus on specific financial issues, and how money can

---

[71] Quoted in Fred Schruers, 'De Niro' (interview), *Rolling Stone*, 25 August 1988, https://www.rollingstone.com/movies/movie-news/a-rare-talk-with-robert-de-niro-242 940/ [Accessed: 15 May 2020].

[72] Quoted in Michael Henry Wilson, *Scorsese on Scorsese* (Cahiers Du Cinema) (Paris: Phaidon Press, 2011), p. 51.

[73] R. Colin Tait, 'De Niro and Scorsese: Director-Actor Collaboration in *Mean Streets* (1973) and the Hollywood Renaissance', in Yannis Tzioumakis and Peter Krämer (ed.), *The Hollywood Renaissance: Revisiting American Cinema's Most Celebrated Era* (London: Bloomsbury, 2018), p. 205.

work as pressure and motivation, is something we shall notice throughout De Niro's work.

In the *Mean Streets* annotations, as De Niro begins working with his most significant directoral collaborator, we can already see many of the methods of working with a script that he will retain and develop throughout his career:

1. Improvisation. A particularly interesting discovery is De Niro's authorial contribution to the Johnny Clams scene, where De Niro has written down dialogue or action which later make their way into the finished film. Tait also has found a written request from De Niro to Scorsese to improvise and shoot a (missing) scene, because 'People will want to know why I'm crying'.[74]

2. Writing monologues that will not appear in the film but that help him to explore a situation from the character's point of view:

> *mingea Madonna mi. (yet don't overdo cause hey don't unless character trait) to justify heaviness say in poolroom: I'm loving? with my friends of course but that don't have nothing to do with enemies and people I'm gonna fight with Having my friends and loving them has nothing to do with how I'd act especially for show (in reality crew etc. [Imp])with guys I don't like and am trying to fuck with us this would justify arrogance and certain toughness such as in pool hall ('don't fucking touch me- scumbag') and give color Or find out about from real guys what makes him a J.O.*[75]

What is most interesting here is that there is already a notion of performing performance (a theme throughout De Niro's work); he talks about what he does 'for show'.

3. Enumeration: De Niro's numbered lists of questions and observations, which feature throughout his screenplay analyses:

---

[74] Ibid., p. 218; emphasis in the original.

[75] *Mean Streets* (1973), Screenplay by Martin Scorsese, with RDN notes, Folder 93.10 [RDN].

> *1 Find out How I'm different from them*
> *2 I owe 9 thousand about 3 to Michael a lot of times I'm ducking*
> *guys in the neighborhood.*[76]

4. The concordance, in which De Niro tries to find the interrelationships and connections between the evidence presented in various scenes and, where there is contradiction, use techniques similar to those identified by Jerome Bruner (considered in Chapter 3) to decide which of the elements are at the heart of the story and which should be rejected as peripheral or irrelevant.

5. Questions. De Niro's constant questioning of directors, writers, figures on whom he can base a character, and others has been known to drive the addressee to distraction. On *Mean Streets* he has a number of 'questions for Marty' in which we can see his interest in the specifics of the shooting. Will they be shooting as specified in the shooting schedule? '*Can I be arrogant?*'

While breaking down the annotations into different categories can be helpful in understanding how De Niro works with a text, the overall impression is of a restless, ceaseless intelligence, alighting on detail after detail and posing himself questions to which he must attempt to find an answer. Sometimes he is thinking about his character's relationships with others: '*what's my feeling and attitude to Charlie Jimmy Michael Tony and everyone. Have it when enter each scene*'. Sometimes he is focusing on how he walks ('*hands in both pockets*') or how he should wear his hat ('*tilted to side*'). He is alert to particularities of dialogue ('*I say "You know but" "yea but" a lot*'); at other times he is thinking about larger ambition ('*I aspire to being a big shot but am slipping from that mold. That's why becoming a lot more sloppy*').

There are many script annotations, largely in pencil, in which he clarifies performance, speculates about line readings, or add actions where the script suggests ad lib improvisation. For example, when the police question everyone after a fight at the bar and ask who started it, the screenplay notes that 'everybody [...] covers for everyone else'.

De Niro suggests specific lines ('*can I call my mother my father my uncle my attorney*'), but also a reading: '*be serious...*' There is also a piece

---

[76] De Niro, ibid.

of advice that holds true for most of his work with Scorsese: '*Marty:* "*better that it goes than worry about the order of dialogue and how it goes*"'. This improvisatory approach to directing and acting would be one of the things that cemented the relationship between Scorsese and De Niro and proved one of the strongest influences on the actor. Scorsese drew inspiration for this approach from John Cassavetes, telling *The New York Times* that 'It was *Citizen Kane* that made me aware of what a director actually did [...] but it was *Shadows* that gave me the urgency and the courage to actually try to make films'.[77]

The near-ecstatic comments on De Niro's performance from prominent critics help to explain the rapidity with which *Mean Streets* propelled him into the limelight. Roger Ebert called it 'marvellous [...] filled with urgency and restless desperation',[78] and hailed De Niro as 'a bravura actor', who 'does something like what Dustin Hoffman was doing in *Midnight Cowboy*, but wilder; this kid doesn't just act—he takes off into the vapors',[79] while Pauline Kael in the *New Yorker* wrote that *Mean Streets* went 'beyond perfect ensemble acting into exhilaration'.[80]

The Godfather, Part II

His next role was as the young Vito Corleone in *The Godfather, Part II*, working with Francis Coppola who had, like both De Niro and Scorsese, worked with Roger Corman, but unlike Scorsese had studied at UCLA and not in New York. For this film De Niro won his first Oscar at the age of 31, for Best Supporting Actor, after which, as we shall see, he had more power to help get a film made.

In the *Godfather, Part II* the relationship between acting and character for De Niro was complex. He has to embody a character who has already

---

[77] Stephen Holden, 'The Movies That Inspired Martin Scorsese', *The New York Times*, 21 May 1993, https://www.nytimes.com/1993/05/21/movies/the-movies-that-inspired-martin-scorsese.html [Accessed: 20 May 2020].

[78] Roger Ebert, 'Reviews: *Mean Streets*', 2 October 1973, https://www.rogerebert.com/reviews/mean-streets-1973 [Accessed: 20 May 2020].

[79] Pauline Kael, '*Mean Streets*: Everyday Inferno', *Scraps From The Loft*, 11 January 2018, https://scrapsfromtheloft.com/2018/01/11/mean-streets-pauline-kael/ [Accessed: 20 May 2020].

[80] Kael, 'Everyday Inferno', *The New Yorker*, October 1973, https://www.newyorker.com/magazine/1973/10/08/everyday-inferno [Accessed: 20 May 2020].

been performed previously—and not by just any actor but by Marlon
Brando, considered probably the greatest actor of his generation, who had
won his second Academy Award for his performance as Vito Corleone in
the first *Godfather* film (1972). To use Coppola's formulation, the character who must inhabit De Niro lived with Brando a few years earlier,
though thirty years later in the life of the character. De Niro plays Vito
not only in a different decade but in a different language, the majority of
his lines being in Sicilian dialect. But De Niro says he

> wasn't intimidated. I just looked at it like a mathematical problem: Brando
> had already established the character, so I just figured out how to connect
> to what he had done. We videoed scenes from the movie with a little
> camera, and I'd play those back, look at them and see what I could do to
> connect it all.[81]

Asked what he had learned from Coppola, De Niro replied:

> He leaves you alone. He helps you in certain areas where you're having
> trouble. Makes it comfortable for you. [...] You've also got to develop a
> relationship with a director, so you can trust each other, so you can talk
> about the problems. Directors can't be condescending or patronizing to
> actors. Actors want to be helped, guided, given a lot of support.[82]

With the screenplay for *The Godfather, Part II*[83] De Niro also established
many of the methods he would come to use habitually in working with
the screenplay as a material text. He kept it in an Executive Folder from
Kroll Stationers of New York City. There are two versions of the script,
one in English and the other is Sicilian, interleaved; both are annotated.
As noted in our previous chapter, the screenplay also has colour-coded
tabs for Notes, Things to Do, Character Bio, and Events. In the front
pocket there are many dialogue notes and material for learning Sicilian,
and in the back pocket the brochure for the first *Godfather* film. The
material is beautifully organised, and to take it out of its archival box is to
be reminded of the materiality of the object. This is above all a working

---

[81] Grobel, pp. 81–82.

[82] Grobel, p. 82.

[83] *The Godfather, Part II* (1974), Shooting script, with RDN notes, lacks title page;
contains 'old script' and 'new script' pages, with additional script pages and extensive
RDN notes re character development, undated, Box 182 [RDN].

tool which accompanied the actor over the nine months of shooting; it would be in his dressing room, in his hotel room, on his knees between takes. It contained everything he needed.

De Niro focuses on the 'mathematical' problem he has described above: how will he become the character already established by Brando? He watches and rewatches the videotapes of Brando, and uses them to establish both specific gestures and the general demeanour that must be carried over from the older Vito to the younger. He kept these notes in his *Godfather* binder so they were available to him at all times on the shoot.

> *Note from watching self*
>
> *Be more still and listen. I'm a listener I don't move and do a lot, especially after kill Fanucci. Hand to chin (and face)*
>
> *Hands heavier I think.*
> *Lose weight I think*

He has also copied a list from Mario Puzo's novel of sentences he thinks are relevant. Underlined in red, for instance: '*His eyes did not smile*'.

There is a later, numbered list of eleven points from a '*Last viewing of older me*' where he notes gestures that Brando has established and where they could be used. Some of these are brief ('*Wedding ring*'); others are specific observations of Brando's performance:

> *Mouth little to side left as with baker Manzini. Will be helped by the brace*
> *Good thinking hands fingertips to face when thinking about Salozzo*
> *Touching tie as with Salozzo could be good in Sicily especially when older me sits and then straightens tie.*
> *Touching lips and thinking in this is too, good just for what it is*

Still others emphasise an attitude, sometimes very specifically gleaned from the earlier film:

> *remember that paesan[t] shrewdness mixed with older me (Vito)*
> *Remember you're a young Vito Corleone though there are other things I might see to do here. A workman's kind of thing for example.*

*Somewhere during our encounter might give Roberto an unexpected hostile
look (as older me did at wedding)*

In these annotations we can see De Niro's character becoming the Vito
Corleone we know, and he as a performer becoming Brando. The screenplay is fizzing with thought and suggestions and questions: about the
time span, about gestures and costumes, about whether he should smoke
or not. He thinks about the jobs that he does, cutting paper-thin prosci-
utto at the store. He wonders what kind of tasks he can do behind the
counter and '*still maintain that dignity, and still be seen as a big shot*'
even though he is not a big shot yet. He is calculating precisely how he
can establish the aura of Brando's Don Corleone when he is neither a
Don nor Brando.

When the script has Fanucci, the mafioso he will ultimately kill, saying
to him 'you're a sharp young fellow', De Niro agrees: '*He's right I am
a smart young fellow*'. This kind of playful response to the text is seen in
other places too. He is thinking about how that thought might manifest
itself in action. The screenplay suggests Fanucci offers him a glass of wine,
and De Niro explores various degrees of refusal that denote his smartness:
'*I refuse with finger, or add water or just don't chink*'. There are philosophical and behavioural attitudes: '*With a sense of delicate curiosity but
never let them know what I'm really thinking*'. There are detailed notes on
costumes and action, and Adlerian preparations as he thinks about where
he has come to and what happened next. As with *Mean Streets*, he tells
himself to '*write a bio of what I was doing as single until now*', and as
with that earlier film again his notes look at the specifics of the financial
relationships he is establishing as a young mafioso:

> *I have collections from owners of crap games who know of me. But these are
> the ones Fanucci had before. Invited these people to come to me to protect them
> from other people like Fanucci & I only take a little money- a third of what
> he was asking for*

De Niro intersperses: '*Did people smoke in those days? Would I smoke*'. And
as he becomes a gangster: '*Humble yet aware of who I am / The way old
times are, the way I fantasise it*'.

He is interested in that point of change, but as an actor he can only
realise it through action and gesture. He is always looking to see how it
will manifest itself in the world, and how his gestures will change as he

becomes more powerful and the world and those around him become subject to his will.

He mingles notes on specific action and gesture—for example, what he should do when he comes home to his wife and baby—with more general philosophical statements that show how Corleone reaches a philosophy and a way of being in the world that we know from the first film, which— in the chronology of events depicted over the two films—is also the subsequent one.

> *BE DOING ONE THING WHILE THINKING ANOTHER. NEVER let people know what really thinking. Especially what feel*
> *Don't lie to cover-up (to be phony) but be straight. part of my strength of character*
>
>
> *say more as cynic and accepter of life than in real surprise It's really nothing new*

The screenplay is part of his journey to a performance, the map, and on its blank spaces and interleaved pages and sheets of notes he inscribes his own discoveries. The map is defined not only by the text but by various paratexts, including the character boundaries established by Brando and the previous film. All of the material that surrounds him is part of his transformation, and is the world over which he exerts increasing domination.

On the reverse of a page about Vito Corleone coming home he makes a list of the evening routine, including detailed notes on preparing the dinner (*'Put gratings on spaghetti'*, *'Making salad no tomatoes oregano salt pepper oil vinegar basil and wine'*) along with thoughts about topics of conversation (*'What did you work tonite'*) and, again, the character's general demeanour (*'Not demonstrative in public'*). He does something similar on one of the interleaved Sicilian-language pages, describing a different sequence, and interpolates a recognition that *'It's my everyday ritual for this scene and all scenes'*. In both of these sequences he carefully notes: *'Wedding ring'*, and in the second makes the more general reminder to *'Show a little more loving color this kind of color when alone'*. As well as emphasising the importance of family to the character, it is as if he is domesticating the screenplay itself, decorating it, finding a way to show a little loving colour and establishing the screenplay as the place where he belongs.

De Niro's script for *The Godfather, Part II* gives a strong sense of the process of transformation from the screenplay to the film, and particularly the journey from the two dimensions of the screenplay to the three dimensions of performance, and the way that the entire world is there for him to interact with. Perhaps this sense of dimensionality is more present because the character's final resting place, in two dimensions on a screen, has already been determined and prescribed by Brando's performance, which De Niro has scrutinised so often. De Niro makes the world of his portion of the script his own, and the entire world around him realised temporarily in three dimensions seems to dissolve into what Walter Gropius called 'the shifting, illusionary space of the imagination'.[84] De Niro's attention to every aspect of the world the young Vito Corleone inhabits has helped to call that space into being and bring it to life.

BIBLIOGRAPHY

ABBREVIATIONS

RDN: Robert De Niro Papers, Harry Ransom Center, University of Texas at Austin.

PRIMARY

Mean Streets (1973), Screenplay by Martin Scorsese, with RDN notes, Folder 93.10, RDN.

The Godfather, Part II (1974), Shooting script, with RDN notes, lacks title page; contains 'old script' and 'new script' pages, with additional script pages and extensive RDN notes re character development, undated, Box 182, RDN.

The Last Tycoon (1976), 11 August 1975, Script Copy 20, with extensive RDN notes, additional mimeo and RDN notes in pocket at front, Box 191, RDN.

SECONDARY

Abel, Marco. 'Becoming-Violent, Becoming-DeNiro', in *Violent Affect: Literature, Cinema, and Critique After Representation* (Lincoln: University of Nebraska Press, 2007), pp. 133–181.

---

[84] Gropius and Wensinger, p. 14.

Auslander, Philip. *Liveness: Performance in a Mediatized Culture*, 2nd ed., London: Routledge, 2008.

Beale, Simon Russell. 'Without Memory or Desire: Acting Shakespeare', Ernest Jones Lecture organised by the Scientific Committee of the British Psychoanalytical Society, 21 June 2009. The British Psychoanalytical Society Archives, London, UK.

Belgrad, Daniel. The *Culture of Spontaneity: Improvisation and the Arts in Postwar America*, Chicago and London: The University of Chicago Press, 1998.

Benjamin, Walter. 'The Work of Art in the Age of Mechanical Reproduction', in Hannah Arendt (ed.), *Illuminations*, trans. Harry Zohn (New York: Schocken, 1969).

Black, Louis. 'Down We Go: Revisiting Renaissance Man Robert Thom's Prolific and Hellish Hollywood Visions', *The Austin Chronicle*, 10 August 2007, https://www.austinchronicle.com/screens/2007-08-10/517929/ [Accessed: 15 May 2020].

Brant, Peter, Colleen Kelsey and Ingrid Sischy, 'A Walk and a Talk with Robert De Niro', *Interview*, 21 March 2012, https://www.interviewmagazine.com/film/new-again-robert-de-niro [Accessed: 15 May 2020].

Cardullo, Bert et al. (ed.), *Playing to the Camera: Film Actors Discuss Their Craft*, New Haven: Yale University Press, 1998.

Conrad, Andreas. 'Wie Robert De Niro per Anhalter durch die DDR reiste', *Die Tagesspiegel*, 11 February 2007, https://www.tagesspiegel.de/kultur/wie-robert-de-niro-per-anhalter-durch-die-ddr-reiste/809516.html [Accessed: 15 May 2020].

Coppola, Francis Ford. *Live Cinema and Its Techniques*, New York: Liveright Publishing Corporation, 2017.

de Balzac, Honore. *Cousin Pons: Part Two of Poor Relations*, trans. Herbert J. Hunt, Harmondsworth: Penguin, 1978.

Denby, David. 'Review: *Bang the Drum Slowly* by John Hancock', *Film Quarterly*, Vol. 27, No. 2 (1973), pp. 49–52.

Dickey, Tina and Helmut Friedel. *Hans Hofmann: Wunder Des Rhythmus und Schönheit Des Raumes* [Catalogue for Exhibition at the Städtische Galerie Im Lenbachaus in Munich, from 23 April to 29 June 1997, Schirn Kunsthalle, Frankfurt, from 12 September to 2 November 1997], New York: Hudson Hills Press, 1998.

Ebert, Roger. 'Reviews: *Bang the Drum Slowly*', *Roger Ebert*, 26 August 1973, https://www.rogerebert.com/reviews/bang-the-drum-slowly-1973 [Accessed: 15 May 2020].

Ebert, Roger. 'Reviews: *Mean Streets*', *Roget Ebert*, 2 October 1973, https://www.rogerebert.com/reviews/mean-streets-1973 [Accessed: 20 May 2020].

Ellis, John. 'The Performance on Television of Sincerely Felt Emotion', *The Annals of the American Academy of Political and Social Science*, Vol. 625, The End of Television? Its Impact on the World (so Far) (2009), pp. 103–115.

Grobel, Lawrence. '*Playboy* Interview: Robert De Niro', *Playboy*, Vol. 36, No. 1 (1989), pp. 69–90, 326.

Gropius, Walter and Arthur S. Wensinger (ed.), *The Theater of the Bauhaus: Oskar Schlemmer, Laszlo Moholy-Nagy, Farkas Molnár*, Middleton, CT: Wesleyan University Press, 1971.

Guerrasio, Jason. 'What It Means to be "Method"', *Tribeca Film Institute*, 19 December 2014, https://www.tfiny.org/blog/detail/what_it_m eans_to_be_method [Accessed: 20 May 2020].

Hirsch, Foster. *A Method to their Madness: A History of the Actors Studio*, New York: Norton, 1984.

Holden, Stephen. 'The Movies That Inspired Martin Scorsese', *The New York Times*, 21 May 1993, https://www.nytimes.com/1993/05/21/movies/the-movies-that-inspired-martin-scorsese.html [Accessed: 20 May 2020].

Horowitz, Frederick A. 'What Josef Albers Taught at Black Mountain College, and What Black Mountain College Taught Albers', *Journal of Black Mountain College Studies*, Vol. 11 (2011), http://www.blackmountainstudiesjour nal.org/volume1/1-9-frederick-a-horowitz/ [Accessed: 20 May 2020].

Horowitz, Frederick A. and Brenda Danilowitz. *Josef Albers: To Open Eyes*, London: Phaidon Press, 2006.

Kael, Pauline. '*Mean Streets*: Everyday Inferno', *Scraps From The Loft*, 11 January 2018, https://scrapsfromtheloft.com/2018/01/11/mean-streets-pauline-kael/ [Accessed: 20 May 2020].

Kael, Pauline. 'Everyday Inferno', *The New Yorker*, October 1973, https://www.newyorker.com/magazine/1973/10/08/everyday-inferno [Accessed: 20 May 2020].

Knopf, R. (ed.), *Theater and Film: A Comparative Anthology*, New York: Yale University Press, 2005.

Levy, Shawn. *De Niro: A Life*, New York: Three Rivers, 2014.

Lowe, Vicky. 'Acting with Feeling: Robert Donat, the "Emotion Chart" and *The Citadel* (1938)', *Film History: An International Journal*, Vol. 19, No. 1 (2007), pp. 73–85.

MoMA documentation for 'An Exhibition of Recent Acquisitions,' Held February 14 Through March 18, 1945, *MoMA*, https://www.moma.org/documents/moma_master-checklist_325455.pdf [Accessed: 15 May 2020].

Murphy, J. J. *Rewriting Indie Cinema: Improvisation, Psychodrama, and the Screenplay*, New York: Columbia University Press, 2019.

Naremore, James. *Acting in the Cinema*. Berkeley: University of California Press, 1988.

'Oral History Interview with John Jr.', 2017 September 28–October 3. Archives of American Art, Smithsonian Institution, https://www.aaa.si.edu/col lections/interviews/oral-history-interview-john-held-jr-17514 [Accessed: 15 May 2020].

Richards, Jeffrey. *The Age of the Dream Palace: Cinema and Society in 1930s Britain*, London; New York: I.B. Tauris, 2010.

Rowin, Michael Joshua. 'Free Radical', *Reverse Shot*, 3 November 2006, http://reverseshot.org/archive/entry/906/hi_mom_depalma [Accessed: 31 May 2020].

Schruers, Fred. 'De Niro' (interview), *Rolling Stone*, 25 August 1988, https://www.rollingstone.com/movies/movie-news/a-rare-talk-with-robert-de-niro-242940/ [Accessed: 15 May 2020].

Sontag, Susan. 'Film and Theatre', *The Tulane Drama Review*, Vol. 11, No. 1 (1966), pp. 24–37.

Stern, Lesley. *The Scorsese Connection*, Indianapolis: Indiana University Press, 1995.

Tait, R. Colin. 'Robert De Niro's *Raging Bull*: The History of a Performance and a Performance of History', *Canadian Journal of Film Studies*, Vol. 20, No. 1 (2011), pp. 20–40.

Tait, R. Colin. 'De Niro and Scorsese: Director-Actor Collaboration in *Mean Streets* (1973) and the Hollywood Renaissance', in Yannis Tzioumakis and Peter Krämer (ed.), *The Hollywood Renaissance: Revisiting American Cinema's Most Celebrated Era* (London: Bloomsbury, 2018), pp. 204–220.

Wilson, Michael Henry. *Scorsese on Scorsese* (Cahiers Du Cinema), Paris: Phaidon Press, 2011.

CHAPTER 4

Taxi Driver

By the time De Niro works on *Taxi Driver* his methods—which we would distinguish from The Method, though they can and do include some Method techniques—have been developed. He has begun to explore collaborative practices with Martin Scorsese on *Mean Streets*, and not only is De Niro now able to combine approaches from theatre and fine art, as well as film performance, he is working with others who are receptive to this approach.

Taxi Driver combines three makers united through their respect for the theory, history and culture of film. If we accept James Naremore's description of De Niro as a theorist, then here he is working with other theorists. Screenwriter Paul Schrader had already written a renowned thesis on *Transcendental Style in Film: Ozu, Bresson, Dreyer* (1972)[1] and his original patron, New Yorker film critic Pauline Kael, was a friend of De Niro's mother Virginia Admiral[2]; while Scorsese's deep knowledge and love of film is perhaps unparalleled in the industry. De Niro's own status had been elevated after winning his first Academy Award for *The Godfather, Part II*, and this allowed him more power as author, with

---

[1] Paul Schrader, *Transcendental Style in Film: Ozu, Bresson, Dreyer* (Berkeley, CA: University of California, 1972).

[2] Lisa Jarnot, *Robert Duncan, The Ambassador from Venus: A Biography* (Berkeley and Los Angeles; London: University of California Press, 2012), p. 48.

© The Author(s) 2020
A. Ganz and S. Price, *Robert De Niro at Work*,
Palgrave Studies in Screenwriting,
https://doi.org/10.1007/978-3-030-47960-2_4

the prestige to help ensure the film would get made. Indeed De Niro's implacable commitment to the film, regardless of the amount he could earn elsewhere, was a major factor in its being made at all.

After Schrader saw the rough cut of *Mean Streets* with producers Michael and Julia Phillips, they were all convinced they had found the actor and director they wanted for *Taxi Driver*. Like De Niro, all were fresh from recent successes, leading to greater power and more opportunities: the Phillipses had produced *The Sting* (1973), Scorsese had directed *Alice Doesn't Live Here Anymore* (1974), and Schrader had co-written *The Yakuza* (1974). It was the Oscar-winning actor De Niro, however, who was under the most pressure. As Schrader pointed out, 'he got thirty or thirty-five thousand to do this film, and he was being offered half a million for something else. He was one of the strongest ones behind it all—absolutely adamant about doing it'.[3] De Niro was returning to work with Scorsese after his experience with Coppola on *The Godfather, Part II*, in which his focus had been realising a version of a character established by Brando and Coppola. Now he was to work on his own embodiment of Schrader's creation, working with a director he knew and trusted.

Taxi Driver exhibits the advantages of an accumulating collaborative history, and of an actor building up a corpus of work. As Leo Braudy puts it, '[f]ilm acting deposits a residual self that snowballs from film to film, creating an image with which the actor, the scriptwriter, and the director can play as they wish', and cites the reported words of one of Schrader's 'transcendental' directors, the Japanese film-maker Yasujiro Ozu: 'I could no more write, not knowing who the actor was to be, than an artist could paint, not knowing what color he was using'.[4] Ozu's comparison of actors to colours intriguingly recalls Josef Albers' visualisation of colours as characters, which we noted in the previous chapter. Braudy suggests that the transfer is all one way, that the actor remains unchanged from one film to the next—that they stay the same colour, to use Ozu's simile; but in fact De Niro's career shows a readiness to learn and change from role to role, and indeed the evidence of the archive is that his biggest motivation

---

[3] Paul Schrader and Richard Thompson, 'Screen writer: *Taxi Driver*'s Paul Schrader' (interview), *Film Comment*, Vol. 12, No. 2 (1976), pp. 11–13.

[4] Leo Braudy, *The World in a Frame: What We See in Films* (Chicago: University of Chicago Press, 1984), p. 198.

is that there should be something to learn, a new aspect of performance or humanity to explore, another director or writer to discover.

By the time De Niro started work on *Taxi Driver* he had devised a methodology drawing on a range of approaches to performance he has encountered: from Bobby Milk, the kid on the Lower East Side, to the young actor who had been studying since he was ten years old, and the emphasis on creativity and performance which were at the heart of both his parents' lives. De Niro learns from Schrader's screenplay and from Scorsese's knowledge of and love of film, but he has found a process of his own which combines the Adlerian building of a character with a critical and collaborative response to Schrader's text, to improvising and constructing scenes with other actors and with the director. His approach to performance includes writing, analysis of character and an immense capacity for painstaking detail, whether in text, costume, interaction, gesture or modes of embodiment of affect.

It is the first time that he has worked with a screenplay that is able to respond to his talent. De Niro's performance in *Bloody Mama* shows his sensitivity to the language of screenwriter Robert Thom, who wrote *Bloody Mama* and three other Corman films including *Death Race 2000* and who graduated from Yale, where he was regarded as a promising poet and playwright; but Thom does not compare to Schrader. And while *The Godfather, Part II* is a tremendous screenplay, De Niro's role is limited. His job was to show how his character became the older Vito Corleone as so memorably portrayed by Marlon Brando, and though De Niro is an astonishing screen presence in the film and his ability to perform in Sicilian dialect and to suggest how Vito Corleone's Godfather evolved is enormously impressive, the parameters for the character and the performance had already been established.

In *Taxi Driver* De Niro is beginning a collaboration between three men at similar points of their careers. When asked at the 40th anniversary screening at Tribeca, all three agreed that at the time they did not talk about what the film meant, or why they were making it. In De Niro's recollection, they '[n]ever had long existential discussions about it', while Scorsese said: 'it just had to be done. That's all. I think Bob and I, we never really spoke about meaning or theory of any kind'.[5] For Schrader, 'that's where serendipity comes in, where three young men at a certain

[5] Josh Grossberg, 'Robert De Niro, Martin Scorsese, Jodie Foster on making *Taxi Driver*' (Interview from Tribeca Film Festival 2016, edited and condensed), *New York*

point in their lives sort of sync up and share a common sort of pathology', and that pathology was also rooted in De Niro's character, Travis Bickle: as the screenwriter put it, 'Bob and Marty and I never really talked much about the script because we knew this guy. We all knew this guy'.[6] The other reason they didn't need to talk about it was because the best way to talk about it was to make the film.

CREATING A BIOGRAPHY

As we have already seen in *Mean Streets*, one of De Niro's methods was to write lengthy notes to himself in the voice of the character. On one of the obverse pages of the De Niro *Taxi Driver* script he writes a character biography:

> *I'm in here for work*
> *I can't sleep just got out of the Marines First came home for about a month but couldn't take that there was nothing there. So I decided to come to NY cause I knew a girl there. But she turned out to just be using me. So now I'm here alone. Don't have any special skills. Have not much $ left. Had a job as a delivery boy for a messenger service but couldn't do it any more, it was the lowest. Got some pills from dealers on the lower east side. So, ive been spending money on that. What little I have. I can't make friends easily. I don't know why.[7]*

This is an extraordinary piece of prose, reminiscent of contemporary New York writers like Sam Shepard or Patti Smith; it could be a Bob Dylan liner note. And yet De Niro is not just expressing the character of Travis Bickle, he is responding to how the screenplay is written by responding to the style of Paul Schrader. Performance involves understanding and embodying the character in the context in which she or he exists. This includes not only the fictional context—the world of the drama where the characters have an imagined physical existence expressed in their clothes

Vulture, 25 April 2016, https://Www.Vulture.Com/2016/04/De-Niro-Scorsese-Foster-Talk-Taxi-Driver-At-40.html [Accessed 30 September 2019].

[6] Grossberg, Ibid.

[7] *Taxi Driver*, Screenplay by Paul Schrader, 29 April 1975, Shooting script with revisions to 29 May 1975; shooting schedule and extensive RDN notes throughout; one page of RDN notes re wolves in back pocket, Box 221, Robert De Niro Papers, Harry Ransom Center, Texas, Austin.

and relationships—but also the context of the fiction, the style and poetics of the world created by the screenwriter. Things happen differently in a world depending on whether it is written by Mamet or Schrader, or the multiple writers of *Meet the Parents*.

De Niro is not simply performing a character, but helping one emerge from one text and become manifest in another. All the preparations he makes are preparations to fuse himself to the text as written by the screenwriter, so that the text as filmed becomes another text in its own right. All actors are co-authors of the film text to some degree; De Niro, with his attention to detail, his sensitivity to language and his ability to represent both the telling detail and the overall understanding, is an exceptional writer in his acting, which simultaneously seizes control of the text and submits to it.

The monologue De Niro writes is particularly interesting in its use of tenses. The 'I' of the character's monologue moves from the past (*'Just got out of the marines'*) to the present (*'She turned out to be using me so now I'm here alone'*). We can see this shift of tense elsewhere in De Niro's annotations. He moves between points of view, expressed variously as 'I' or 'he', and with events as seen by different personae: by his character; by Robert De Niro Junior, New Yorker; and by the imagined audience. Just as he is able to move between the world of fiction and the contemporary New York where the film takes place, he is able to move between reading the script as Travis Bickle or as a textual analyst.

An example of the latter is his commentary on the voice-over on page 57, an extract from Bickle's diary. Schrader has written that Travis is a man 'who wouldn't take it any more, who stood up against the scum, the cunts, the dogs, the filth'. De Niro suggests *'would not'* instead of 'wouldn't', and wonders about changing 'any more' to *'no'* more. Then he adds: *'in this case it's OK or could be opposite. Very formal when writing to self but in conversation informal using improper Eng'*. This has been boxed in for emphasis and the word *'IMP[ortant]'*added. De Niro shifts between writing in character and using a fully external voice; but regardless of whether he is writing from the position of the narrator or from a position entirely within the character, in his commentary as in the monologue he uses a critical precision, with the annotations a kind of pre-performance.

Schrader's description of the genesis of the film is that he had been living, in Los Angeles, very much the kind of life he imagines for Bickle in New York:

I got to wandering around at night; I couldn't sleep because I was so depressed. I'd stay in bed till four or five p.m. then I'd say, 'Well, I can get a drink now.' I'd get up and get a drink and take the bottle with me and start wandering around the streets in my car at night. After the bars closed, I'd go to pornography. I'd do this all night, till morning, and I did it for about three or four weeks, a very destructive syndrome, until I was saved from it by an ulcer: I had not been eating, just drinking. When I got out of the hospital I realized I had to change my life[.][8]

He continues:

That was when the metaphor hit me for *Taxi Driver* [...] the man who will take anybody any place for money; the man who moves through the city like a rat through the sewer; the man who is constantly surrounded by people, yet has no friends. The absolute symbol of urban loneliness. That's the thing I'd been living[.][9]

For Schrader, then, 'The film is about a car as the symbol of urban lone-liness, a metal coffin'.[10] This is echoed in the epigraph Schrader on the title page, from Thomas Wolfe's *God's Lonely Man*:

The whole conviction of my life now
rests upon the belief that loneliness,
far from being a rare and curious
phenomenon, is the central and inevitable
fact of human existence

De Niro here places a note at the top of the page, as if not to disturb the empty space around the Wolfe quotation: '*up to the point I make my decision about death I maybe could be not so sure. After that I know exactly where I'm going and it's simple. (The result is I'm deadly)*'.The decision the character makes, as interpreted by De Niro, is defined as one about death, not about killing; and like the eponymous taxi driver, he changes from being 'not so sure' to being given a destination. By the end of the film 'he knows exactly where he's going'.

---

[8] Quoted in Schrader and Thompson, 'Screen writer', p. 8.

[9] Quoted in Schrader and Thompson, p. 9.

[10] Quoted in Schrader and Thompson, p. 9.

The Concessions Girl Scene

In a relatively inconsequential scene, Travis buys a ticket for the porn cinema and tries to strike up conversation with what the script calls 'the concessions girl'. The scene shows De Niro being 'not so sure': so desperately lonely that he tries to have human contact in a place that is a site only for a commercial transaction. It could easily feel over-expositional. It serves to show Bickle's isolation, and rhymes with two other scenes: when he takes Betsy (Cybill Shepherd), the blonde volunteer for the Pallantine campaign, to a porn film on a date; and when he visits Iris (Jodie Foster), the young prostitute he asks out for breakfast. Just as he takes his date to a porn film, he tries to befriend the girl who works in the porn cinema.

But De Niro's attention to detail, to the rhythms of the scene and to the emotion that makes his character look weaker and more humiliated, shows his commitment to serving the narrative. His annotations make all kinds of suggestions on how the scene might be played. James Naremore observes that actors use posture in the service of characterisation, and that De Niro in particular uses posture in all his roles.[11] This scene offers a fine example (Fig. 4.1): '*Think of self with arm on counter one leg kind of crossed and toe on floor*'.[12] But he also is separating what he does from how he might appear; imagining not what Travis should do, but how he as actor should arrange his body. He is projecting himself into the scene, and ultimately onto the screen. Although we cannot see his feet in the finished film we see his arm on the counter, exactly as he suggested. It manages to combine encroaching in her space with protecting himself as he tries to charm her from behind his shield. Schrader writes: 'He is obviously trying to be friendly—no easy task for him. God knows he needs a friend'. The annotations reveal a great deal about De Niro's concerns and his process: '*Remember try to find my right way to do this. See how will do them, how will it be hard for me*'. This is literally physicalising the action. Schrader has written an attitude to the world ('no easy task for him'), and De Niro is trying to give it corporal form. The idea of 'my right way' suggests a difference between the De Niro who is reading the script, and De Niro the performer who will make his body available for Travis Bickle to inhabit—just as a driver is at the wheel of a taxicab.

---

[11] James Naremore. *Acting in the Cinema* (Berkeley: University of California Press, 1988), p. 49.

[12] *Taxi Driver*, Box 221 [RDN].

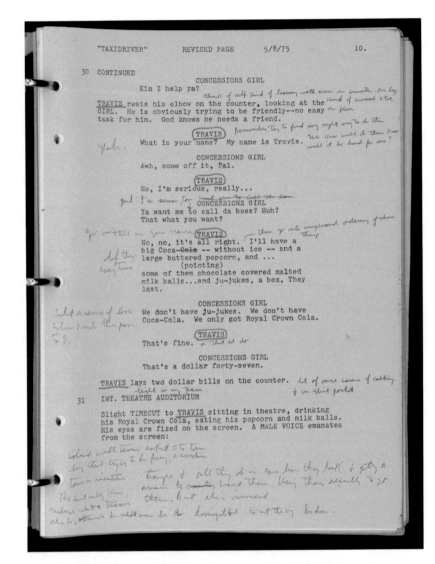

Fig. 4.1 *Taxi Driver* (1976), shooting script, Box 221, RDN, p. 10

De Niro makes suggestions for additional lines, both for him and for the woman behind the counter. He feels, and the execution of the filmed scene seems to confirm, that she gives him too much leeway. She needs to be stronger. Although his precise emendations were not finally used, the scene was indeed extended: in the film as shot, she calls the manager, which immediately forces him to change direction. This is reminiscent of Scorsese's recollections of his cameo role as De Niro's passenger. He recalls that De Niro

> pointed out to me that the first line of dialogue was 'Turn off the meter.' And I did one take, and he said to me, 'When you say, "Turn off the meter," make me turn it off. Just make me turn it off. I'm not going to turn it off until you convince me that you want me to turn off that meter.' So, I learned a lot. He sort of acted with the back of his head, but he encouraged me by not responding to me. And using that tension of the inherent violence, I was able to able to take off and riff some dialogue.[13]

After the Concession Girl threatens him with the manager, the screenplay has a line where Travis orders confectionery. The annotation proposes: '*Then go into impersonal ordering of these things*'. And opposite the list of candy, De Niro has written: '*Diff things every time*'. He is thinking about maintaining the freshness of his performance, and that of the other actor in the scene, with one particularly telling annotation at the end of the scene: '*What a sense of loss...*'

We can see this again and again in the notes: De Niro seems simultaneously to understand the character both as the character understands himself, and as the character is perceived by the audience. As De Niro can be credited with both originating and borrowing material, and with performing himself and inspiring performance in others, part of the genius of his performance is his readiness to occupy both of those positions simultaneously. He inhabits the boundaries between inside and outside, between actor and audience, between acts as they are done and acts as they are perceived.

---

[13] Gregg Kilday, 'Taxi Driver Oral History: De Niro, Scorsese, Foster, Schrader Spill All on 40th Anniversary,' *The Hollywood Reporter*, 7 April 2016, https://www.hollywood reporter.com/features/taxi-driver-oral-history-de-881032 [Accessed 30 September 2019].

Dreaming of Betsy

He also has an understanding of the spaces between characters, both physical and emotional, as the notes on the reverse of the concession scene indicate. On the yellow paper on the back of the new concession scene, De Niro has written a whole page of notes about Travis Bickle's thoughts and attitudes to Betsy, the aide working on the Pallantine campaign (Fig. 4.2). These appear opposite the scene when Bickle sees her for the first time, and act as a kind of visual marker. As the reader leafs through the screenplay the cluster of fantasies on the yellow paper of the new inserted scene stand out vividly. They are a reminder that the script is read many times during the shooting. Each time De Niro flipped through his copy, this desperate cloud of misogynistic longing appeared opposite the white page on which the character as written by Schrader sees the 'very attractive' Betsy 'from a distance, the only way TRAVIS can' among 'America's chosen youth, healthy, energetic, well groomed, attractive, all recruited from the bucolic fields of Massachusetts and Connecticut'. The screenplay continues in a controlled angry prose, with more than a hint of misogyny: 'Her attractions though are more than skin deep. Beneath that Cover Girl facial there is a keen though highly specialised sensibility: her eye scans every man who passes her desk as her mind computes his desirability: political, intellectual sexual, emotional material'.

Schrader remembers that 'Long ago Pauline Kael asked me why I wrote about this character, what it had to do with me. I said, "It is me without any brains"'.[14] Seeing the cool articulacy of Schrader's prose opposite the broken half-poetry that De Niro as Travis Bickle has created shows the complex nature of authorship and interpretation when an actor creates a part from another's writing. The kitsch romantic fantasies about Betsy which De Niro as Bickle conjures up are mingled with suggestions for playing scenes and an analysis of his attitude to her and to himself: '*He'd do everything / she would never have to leave. / He'd cook and shop / walk the dog / we won't need anyone else / I'd go out into the sewer to make $ I don't want her to be contaminated*'. Notable here is the slippage between pronouns, from 'he' and 'she' to 'I' and 'we'. But in this paragraph, at least, Betsy does not become 'you': even in his future fantasy he cannot address her directly.

---

[14] Schrader and Thompson, p. 14.

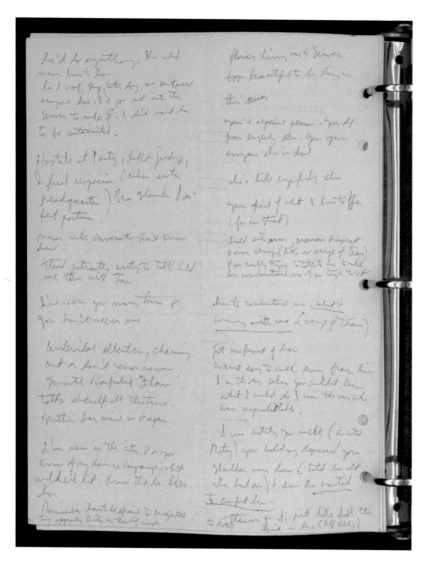

Fig. 4.2 *Taxi Driver* (1976), shooting script, Box 221, RDN, reverse of p. 10

De Niro finds specific places and ways where his sense of self can be expressed. It's complex: De Niro's Bickle doesn't see himself as only an inferior, and again, posture is key to expressing this: '*Hostile at party like a judge, / I feel superior (when enter / headquarters) no slouch. Perfect posture*'. In keeping with Coppola's description of a part inhabiting the actor, it is as if the monologue De Niro writes as Bickle ends up with Bickle offering suggestions to De Niro as actor: '*Never make conversation. Don't know how / Stand patiently waiting to talk / Could use this with Tom*' [the character played by Albert Brooks]. He suggests lines for his situation, introducing again, as with Vito Corleone, the idea of an acted performance, as De Niro imagines what Travis would like to say when he meets her in the future. He is imagining himself into the future both as performer and as character: '*I've seen you many times & / You haven't seen me / Undivided attention charming / not (or doesn't seem) nervous / Smooth and confident flow / Talks about self all the time*'. He mixes in aspects of character biography he might use in the imagined dialogue ('*Mother barmaid in Oregon*') with suggestions for possible chat-up lines: '*I'm new in the city Do you / know of any dance company's / but wouldn't let know that he likes her / remember have to be afraid to be rejected / try approaching Betsy in the chuck* [?] *wagon*'.

The notes are in two columns on the page and, as Scott Balcerzak notes, from the top of the second column the note get darker as Bickle's anger and deep misogyny comes out[15]: '*Flower living in a sewer / Too beautiful to be living in / this sewer / you're a special person your dif / from everybody else you open / everyone*'.[16] The scene becomes another in which De Niro explores the performance of performance ('*Hold with arm / Nervous and upset / Voice change like on verge of tears*'), because for a man like Bickle, to ask a woman out has to be about performance: '*I'm really trying to talk to her to make her understand me / I'm trying to get her to understand me. What's wrong with me / (verge of tears)*'.[17]

---

[15] Scott Balcerzak, *Beyond Method: Stella Adler and the Male Actor* (Detroit: Wayne State University Press, 2019), p. 129.

[16] *Taxi Driver*, Box 221 [RDN], insert opposite p. 21.

[17] *Taxi Driver*, Box 221 [RDN], insert opposite p. 21.

Balcerzak argues convincingly that this sequence evidences Schrader's proposal that the plot structure of *Taxi Driver* is simple:[18] a pathologically lonely man has to choose between two women—Betsy whom he desires but can't have, and Iris who he can have but doesn't desire. Even though he might have a chance with Betsy, who could read him as a poet and a romantic, he drives her away by taking her on the date to the porn movie. Balcerzak shows that there is a clear distinction between De Niro's attitude and Bickle's, and details the specificity with which De Niro is able to summon Bickle's anxiety, rage and delusion.

But De Niro also analyses the scene in light of the possibility that Betsy might fall for him. When they meet in the coffee shop, he stresses:

> *Remember: in this scene there must be enough of a connection for her to be interested in me. So can't be a complete mope. The focus is very important. One thing is my appearance. Makes me more acceptable being young and all. Yet what I think (& certain aspects of behavior) is different.*

Earlier when he asks her out he notes that '*there is something poetic about me & sensitive. To see this in her cause it <u>could</u> be true. It is true*'. When he stands outside the porn cinema, rejected by a furious Betsy who asks 'if you wanted to fuck why didn't you just come out and say it', De Niro's note reads: '<u>*maybe just be still like a stick of dynamite*</u>'.[19] That is both an extraordinary image, and an extraordinary piece of writing—although we need the archive in order to appreciate it. As Balcerzak observes, Bickle then goes on to blame Betsy for the failure of the date.[20] He is unable to take the responsibility or accept the blame, but the actor was able to offer this insight—primarily to himself, and then, perhaps, to everyone who saw his performance.

NOT A DUMB JOB

Jodie Foster has talked in a fascinating interview about working with De Niro on *Taxi Driver*, and how it transformed her idea of what acting was. She had been a child actor from the age of three, so the twelve-year old already felt like the 'veteran'; but just like De Palma when he cast De

---

[18] Balcerzak, p. 128.

[19] *Taxi Driver*, Box 221 [RDN], p. 38.

[20] Balcerzak, p. 132.

Niro in *The Wedding Party* in 1963, she witnessed De Niro's astonishing powers of transformation:

> De Niro took me aside before we started filming. He kept [...] taking me to different diners. The first time he basically didn't say anything. [...] The second time he started to run lines with me [...]. The third time, he ran lines with me again and now I was really bored. The fourth time [...] he started going off on these completely different ideas within the scene, talking about crazy things and asking me to follow in terms of improvisation [...] until that moment I thought being an actor was just acting naturally and saying the lines someone else wrote. Nobody had ever asked me to build a character.[21]

The episode made Foster realise that 'acting was not a dumb job'—and it had certainly never been that for De Niro. His notes on the scene reveal how much attention went on these line readings, and his readiness to explore with the other actor what the scene means and how it can best be expressed. Together they concentrate on finding the beats and energies in these exchanges, which will allow the maximum velocity and trajectory in the major dramatic climaxes.

In the scene in which Travis meets Iris for breakfast and tries to persuade her to go home to her parents, in a scene which precedes his decision to kill, Schrader writes: 'It takes Iris a moment to digest this pure example of negative thinking. "I am loved to the extent that I do not exist"'. De Niro's note to self is, '*Just look at her, you don't know what I'm going to do*'. It is not clear whether this means 'You, the actor Jodie Foster, don't know what I, Robert De Niro, am going to do in this scene', just as the actor paying the concession girl didn't know in what order he was going to name the candy that he wanted; or 'you, Iris, have no idea what I have in mind'. Perhaps there are aspects of both. The scene is mostly shot on Foster, but her interview shows how much she appears to have learned from De Niro as she carries the fierce scrutiny of the camera and De Niro's Travis Bickle. She allows the audience to see her as first a child smearing sugar on her jam, and then as far more mature than Travis, as she deflects his projections about her pimp, Sport (the character played by Harvey Keitel) wanting to kill people.

[21] Cal Fussman. 'Robert De Niro: What I've Learned', *Esquire*, 14 December 2010, https://www.esquire.com/entertainment/interviews/a9087/robert-de-niro-quo tes-0111/ [Accessed 22 May 2020].

PREPARATION AND PROJECTION

Schrader describes the moment when the character makes his own decision to kill as follows:

> TRAVIS is again writing at the table. His western shirt is again open, exposing his bare chest.
> A note of despair and doom has entered Travis' normally monotone narration voice:
> This will be the last entry in his diary. ·
>
>
> TRAVIS (V.O.)
> My whole life has pointed in one direction
> I see that now. There has never been any choice
> for me.[22]

De Niro's annotation: '*this could be done with little sense of the dramatic or cadence, or sense that what I'm saying is developing into something imp. (in a crescendo)*'. This shows an analytical awareness not just of what he should do, but of how it might be perceived. De Niro's attention is on his delivery of the lines, but also on how this reading might be interpreted. It offers a possible way to express the moment where the character becomes certain of the route he has chosen. As an actor he needs to find a way to perform this, but the Travis Bickle De Niro is preparing to portray cannot yet access that sureness. The actor offers an extremely articulate interpretation of Bickle's coming moment of certainty, but Bickle cannot yet own the certainty his character does not yet possess. The annotations are not in the voice of the character, but they represent the insights the character can have at that moment.

If in the voice-over De Niro is inserting himself over the written text, elsewhere he imagines how he will be seen in the finished film. When he considers Schrader's description of the dénouement, as Travis goes on his killing spree, De Niro responds with an image: '*Have image of walking upright [...] into the killing the two guns hanging at my side. ready but hanging*'. This ability to imagine himself both within the character and how he will appear on film is one of the things that makes De Niro so impressive: his ability to inhabit this intertextuality as actor and character,

---

[22] *Taxi Driver* (1976), (Box 221, HRC, Texas, Austin), p. 90.

performer and observer, means he can both assume the character as envisioned by the writer, and in collaboration with the director foresee how he will appear on film. Just as the screenplay is a site where he can work on the text, his body becomes a site where the text works on him. He projects the text into a future where it will become three-dimensional through his body, and beyond that to a more distant one where it will appear on screen.

We can think about the word 'projection' in a number of different ways in addition to the idea of cinema projection, such as projection into the future, and the architect's drawing or a cartographic principle involving the representation of three dimensions in two. Among the many definitions of 'projection' in the *Oxford English Dictionary* are the following:

> 2a. The drawing [...] of a map or plan of a surface, or of a two-dimensional diagram of a three-dimensional object;
>
> 2b. A representation of a figure on a surface according to a particular system of correspondence between its points and the points of the surface;
>
> 5a. An image or representation of an object formed on a surface (originally esp. the retina) from elsewhere; the action of forming such an image [...] the process of projecting an image on a film, slide, etc., on to a screen for viewing.
>
> 6a. The process of causing thoughts, ideas, or emotions to exist, or appear to exist, in the external world [...] a mental image visualized or regarded as a reality.
>
> 6d. The action of conveying a particular image or impression to others; the ability to impress one's presence on others, or to communicate one's character or personality;
>
> 9. The action of forecasting or estimating future events.

'Projection' also has definitions that involve alchemical transmutation, the throwing or casting of an ingredient into a crucible, and transmutation into gold or silver. These ideas of transformation via imagination, into the future and across dimensions, and even across matter, are useful in thinking about what an actor does when she or he works on a screenplay. They must imagine the words of the text as appearing three-dimensionally through their performing body, and—rather like the cartographical use of the term—they must also imagine their three-dimensional performing self being mapped in two dimensions by the camera, before being finally projected on to the screen. We have seen too the way that De Niro identifies data points that allow him to inhabit a character and project him into the future, such as moneys owed, as in *Mean Streets* or daily domestic rituals, as in *The Godfather, Part II*. We think of the work of the actor as happening in front of the camera, but much of it must happen in the close reading of the text and the first imaginative creation of the work in the mind of the performer.

We can see part of this process in the note De Niro adds to the script just before the climax as his character Travis prepares for the kill: '*In better shape, pacing like a wolf*'. This simile is a product of research, with the *Taxi Driver* file containing notes De Niro made from observing wolves in the New York zoo. As Balcerzak observes, this is part of an Adlerian approach to building a character. Observing an animal was an exercise that helped with characterisation, because it helps to 'break the human inhibition'.[23] There is a pleasing play here on the name of Thomas Wolfe, whose paragraph on loneliness was used by Schrader as a metonym for the screenplay. As Balcerzak point out, 'the exercise is primarily employed to consider new ways to approach Bickle's physicality'[24]; but as he adds, De Niro is also using it as a broader way to approach characterisation. De Niro's numbered list of observed characteristics is as follows:

Wolves

1. *Walks similar to what I do.*
2. *Head chin resting good maybe for when looking at her from cab.*
3. *Way pick up head and peek to side when hear something. Certain quality to it.*
4. *Certain way of stealthily walking which is good.*
5. *Way they curl up to sleep resting on chin good.*
6. *Way heart (?) goes when resting is good.*
7. *Lick myself, my wounds.*

For Balcerzak, this last observation 'considers the vulnerability [...] that defines a predatory person'.[25] In performance terms '*Lick myself, my*

---

[23] Balcerzak, p. 124.
[24] Balcerzak, p. 125.
[25] Balcerzak, p. 125.

wounds' is not a description of a vulpine action that DeNiro can incorporate in his performance; it is an attitude to self that De Niro can remember. Usually language must be expressed in action or gesture, whether specifically referenced in the script or not, but De Niro finds equivalences that can emerge in behaviours, with himself or other characters. We may observe Travis walking stealthily, but we probably won't consciously recognise the attitude De Niro embodies. He is trying to present a way of being in the world that is not necessarily specifically manifested in a particular gesture, but is something more akin to a philosophy.[26]

The screenplay is not just the story as expressed by the writer in marks on paper, but the place where that story begins to be expressed in action, speech and gesture. De Niro's use of Adler's method is clearly important, but it is informed by a range of other tools, as Balcerzak notes:

> De Niro deconstructs the direct given circumstances and recognises their larger cultural contexts, especially regarding Travis as a gendered subject. The actor acknowledges the psychosexual pathology of the character as a product of a culture of paranoia and misogyny [...] De Niro understands the ending of the film must reflect the nihilism that runs through the rest of the script.[27]

De Niro uses Adlerian research methods of textual analysis, with metaphor and a concordance of a character's motivations; but he draws also on his own theoretical approach, which combines various forms of embodied knowledge, his knowledge of the character, and his increasing experience of performing on film.

He constructs his performances using three main foundations: the character's understanding of himself, which we could call *internal*; the creator's version of the character—*authorial* or *analytical*; and the perspective of the future film audience—*cinematic*. It is this ability to inhabit all of those positions simultaneously that makes De Niro at his best such a great actor, and ensures that his performances have power and precision as well as emotion. The annotations in the archives enable

---

[26] De Niro has often said the creature that he had in mind when creating Bickle was a crab. See for example Lawrence Grobel, '*Playboy* Interview: Robert De Niro', *Playboy* 36.1 (January 1989), p. 76.

[27] Balcerzak, pp. 134–135.

us to trace some of the choices he made, but also to understand how and when both the actor and the character reached these decisions. For example, when he is '*getting ready to kill these motherfuckers down-town* <u>*Eyes Wild*</u> *(you know what I mean)*' to the time of his arrival at the doorway where Sport stands, he has previously written another diary passage on the obverse page of the screenplay summarizing Travis's state of mind:

> *I decided maybe it not such a good idea to kill Pallantine. Maybe to let it go a bit. Don't do it tomorrow [illegible] I'll help her first.*
> *We're in the same neighbourhood / It's the next day around one o clock / We met and I saw her go out with Sport / He's a greaser. He takes advantage / I'm on the verge of doing something to somebody. / [illegible] of people like her, a kid. / That's why with Sport I'll kill him in a second. / Probably has control over her / Sexual control*

As De Niro reflects on the staging of Travis' arrival at the house where Sport lives, he proposes a number of actions which adds specificity to this character's diary and explores how the attitudes he has outlined will be explored in action and gesture. The action expressed in the screenplay text is: 'TRAVIS'S taxi screeches to a stop and parks obliquely against the curb'. De Niro expounds this both in terms of action ('*Maybe have the door open fast*') and as a reiteration of De Niro's analysis of Travis's thought process and affective state: '*I'm ready to die and anxious to take them all with me' / Deliberate animal walk to him / 'Think of the ugliest thing this person can be' / 'Maybe a real long Ehhhhhhhy Sport*'. This gives us four different ways the actor can think about the character: (1) his state of mind ('*I'm ready to die and anxious to take them all with me*'); (2) how he moves ('*Deliberate animal walk to him*'); (3) what he thinks at a particular moment ('*Think of the ugliest thing this person can be*') and (4) what he might say or do ('*Maybe a real long Ehhhhhhhy Sport*'). As the screenplay moves towards its bloody climax De Niro's annotations explore a dream-like quality, which some have commented on in the final film. For example, Schrader describes that the old man he has stabbed should 'scream in pain'. In an annotation De Niro wonders '*how bout no pain*', while later in the same sequence as he kills Sport he refers to '*the whole sexual thing coming out*', which he identified previously, and adds: '*final build up, with the image to this*'. Do we know what '*the image to this*' means? We know De Niro has an image in his mind of the killing, but because so many of the annotations are so clear it is a shock to be reminded that they were not written for public consumption. The only person who needed to understand them was the actor himself. In the anniversary interview De Niro emphasises the seriousness of the moment:

> it's funny when you do those kinds of terrible, gruesome scenes, everybody kind of jokes. And that made me think about people who are in those types of situations for real, probably have no choice but to joke about it. And that's kind of what we were doing [...] because it's just so gruesome that, you know, you make jokes about it. Even though it wasn't real, it was real enough for us in any case.[28]

What makes the moment so powerful is that it comes out of a precisely observed and delineated set of naturalistic and closely argued actions and intentions. In the final annotation, after the '*funny and exaggerated face*' he suggests he should make when the police arrive after the blood-bath, and the conclusion where Betsy watches him drive down the street in his cab, De Niro gives an assessment of what he thinks the ending means, and what kind of feeling the audience should take from it. This is another moment where De Niro's ability to prepare a performance, and simultaneously analyse how the audience should interpret it, is impressive:

> *Should be ambiguous that's the real truth of it. That nothing's written and life goes on and we're all lonely from the start again yet look at what we did before which means nothing now. In my case it was about killing Pallantine and then really killing the others. & for what?*[29]

We can understand the conclusion as both 'real' and 'fantastic', and De Niro's annotations clearly indicate that this ambiguity is part of his inten-tion. In an interview with De Niro Xan Brooks raised the question of whether Travis actually dies at the end of *Taxi Driver*, suggesting that 'the hazy closing sequence (the killer as hero, back behind the wheel) is just his fantasy of the afterlife.' De Niro responds: 'You mean the end of the movie? Well, that's an interesting theory. I know that was not the

---

[28] Grossberg, 'Robert De Niro, Martin Scorsese, Jodie Foster'.

[29] *Taxi Driver*, Box 221 [RDN], p. 105.

intention, but it's as valid as anything'.[30] And yet Schrader said in an interview not long after the film was made,

> It pretends to be a realistic film, but it takes all kinds of license. The whole film takes place inside that man's head; [...] I think the ending is thematically immaculate and poetically satisfying. [...] He's just about to do the act [of killing Pallantine] which will totally remove him from our sympathy. That's when the realism of the script starts to fade; it moves into a poetic level.[31]

'A Character like Travis Bickle'

The ground-breaking nature of the performance was recognised at the time. Pauline Kael, Schrader's mentor, wrote in her review that 'Robert De Niro is in almost every frame: thin-faced, as handsome as Robert Taylor one moment and cagey, ferrety, like Cagney, the next', and distinguishes his performance from 'the peasant courtliness of his Vito Corleone in *The Godfather, Part II*. [...] Travis is dangerous in a different, cumulative way'. Kael analyses why she considers his performance distinctive: 'Some actors are said to be empty vessels who are filled by the roles they play, but that's not what appears to be happening here with De Niro. He's gone the other way. He's used his emptiness—he's reached down into his own anomie', and she perceptively identifies the sexual quality to the performance that De Niro too has referenced: 'In its own way, this movie [...] has an erotic aura. [...] The fact that we experience Travis's need for an explosion viscerally, and that the explosion itself has the quality of consummation, makes *Taxi Driver* one of the few truly modern horror films'.[32] Tom Shone, in an article to commemorate the film's 40th anniversary, suggests that

> Travis is no mere character, subject to the plot of *Taxi Driver*: he is the plot. 'Someday a real rain will come and wash all this scum off the streets,'

---

[30] Robert De Niro and Xan Brooks, 'I'd like to see where Travis Bickle is today' (interview), *The Guardian*, 14 November 2013, https://www.theguardian.com/film/2013/nov/14/robert-de-niro-travis-bickle-taxi-driver [Accessed 20 May 2020].

[31] Schrader and Thompson, 'Screen writer', p. 14.

[32] Pauline Kael, 'Underground Man: Martin Scorsese's *Taxi Driver*', *The New Yorker*, 2 February 1976, https://www.newyorker.com/magazine/1976/02/09/underground-man [Accessed 20 May 2020].

he says in voiceover, in the flat, pedantic tone of someone reading aloud a letter of complaint about drainage to their local council. It is the tone of autodidacts, sociopaths and bores, and Travis is all three.[33]

It is the apparent absence of performance that is so compelling and so distinctive, and for which all of De Niro's prior experience as well as his specific formulations for this role had prepared him. Shone cites Leonardo DiCaprio as claiming that 'Playing a character like Travis Bickle is every young actor's wet dream'.[34] But there was no character like Travis Bickle until De Niro. The archive is a testament to the articulacy with which he produces the inarticulacy of Bickle, and it reveals De Niro's fluency across language, gesture and costume as means of expression. The HRC houses the jacket and boots worn by De Niro as Travis Bickle; the carapace of their fused creation belongs in the Texas archive, alongside the screenplay and annotations that inspired it. The boots and jacket originally belonged to Schrader, while the hairstyle was devised by De Niro and Scorsese:

> [T]he mohawk was something that Marty and I came up with. A friend of his who was in special forces [...] showed us a picture of he and his outfit and a couple guys had mohawks [...] And we said, 'That's great. Let's use that. Let's try and do it.' [...] I was about to do *The Last Tycoon* after, and my hair was all bushy and everything. So I remember Marty and I [...] met at Gallagher's Steakhouse [...] and we decided to get Dick Smith to do a test [...] and it worked.[35]

If Scorsese and De Niro came up with the iconic image of the mohawk, which we can also see as a reference to Akira Kurosawa's *Seven Samurai* in which *ronin* Kambe cuts his hair before going to rescue a child from a criminal, the 'you talkin to me?' sequence is De Niro's own creation. At the fortieth anniversary screening, Schrader said: 'Bob called me and said, "Well, in the script, it says that he pulls out the gun, looks at himself, talks to himself. Well, what's he saying?" I said, "Just make up stuff"'. As Scorsese recalled, 'We were running behind schedule, and I knew Bob would have to say something to himself in the mirror, and I honestly

---

[33] Tom Shone, 'How *Taxi Driver* Ruined Acting', *The Economist 1843*, 6 May 2016, https://www.1843magazine.com/culture/the-daily/how-taxi-driver-ruined-acting [Accessed 20 May 2020].

[34] Shone, ibid.

[35] Grossberg, 'Robert De Niro, Martin Scorsese, Jodie Foster'.

didn't know what it would be [...] I was sitting at Bob's feet, and then he just started talking to himself. De Niro said that the 'mirror thing was just something that I improvised that felt right. Marty was always good and easy about trying things'. Scorsese described it as 'like a jazz riff. Just like a solo'.[36] And as Schrader said on another occasion, 'To me, it's the best thing in the movie. And I didn't write it'.[37] It remains the most iconic moment of the film: 'Every day for 40 fucking years', De Niro said when he introduced it at the Tribeca reunion, 'at least one of you has come up to me and said—what do you think—"*You talkin' to me?*"'[38]

Steve Wilson, Curator of Film at the HRC, has analysed the screenplay in detail. He notes that at this iconic moment the script just proposes: 'Mirror thing here?' De Niro concentrates on the physicalisation of the action with the various weapons, and as Wilson notes, he 'merges these external actions with the character's motivations and objectives to create the performance':

> the [...] phrase, 'he sees nothing but himself,' seems to be what inspired Scorsese and De Niro to stage the scene in front of a mirror. De Niro's famous line, 'You talkin' to me?', ostensibly directed at an imagined antagonist, reaches another level of meaning when directed at himself.[39]

Travis Bickle cannot be separated from De Niro's performance. According to Schrader:

> Bobby had once wanted to write an assassination story [...] about a kid who carried a gun around New York. He was lonely. He fantasized about using it.[...] Bobby said he was never able to write that script [...], but when he read *Taxi Driver*, he saw all the things he wanted to do with it. I told him, 'You know what the gun is, don't you Bobby? It's your talent. At that time in your life you felt you were carrying that huge talent around and you didn't know what to do with it. [...] You knew that if you

[36] Kilday, 'Taxi Driver Oral History'.

[37] Schrader and Thompson, p. 11.

[38] Grossberg, 'Robert De Niro, Martin Scorsese, Jodie Foster'.

[39] Steve Wilson, 'You talkin' to me?', *Ransom Center Magazine*, 13 October 2016, https://sites.utexas.edu/ransomcentermagazine/2016/10/13/you-talkin-to-me/#more-17749 [Accessed 20 May 2020].

ever had a chance to take it out and shoot it, people would realize how important you were, and you would be acknowledged.'[40]

After *Taxi Driver*, no one would ever doubt his talent again.

BIBLIOGRAPHY

ABBREVIATIONS

RDN: Robert De Niro Papers, Harry Ransom Center, University of Texas at Austin.

PRIMARY

Taxi Driver (1976), Screenplay by Paul Schrader, 29 April 1975, Shooting script with revisions to 29 May 1975; shooting schedule and extensive RDN notes throughout; one page of RDN notes re wolves in back pocket, Box 221, RDN.

SECONDARY

Balcerzak, Scott. *Beyond Method: Stella Adler and the Male Actor*, Detroit: Wayne State University Press, 2019.
Braudy, Leo. *The World in a Frame: What We See in Films*, Chicago: University of Chicago Press, 1984.
De Niro, Robert and Xan Brooks, 'I'd Like to See Where Travis Bickle Is Today' (interview), *The Guardian*, 14 November 2013, https://www.theguardian.com/film/2013/nov/14/robert-de-niro-travis-bickle-taxi-driver [Accessed 20 May 2020].
Fussman, Cal. 'Robert De Niro: What I've Learned', *Esquire*, 14 December 2010, https://www.esquire.com/entertainment/interviews/a9087/robert-de-niro-quotes-0111/ [Accessed 22 May 2020].
Grobel, Lawrence. '*Playboy* Interview: Robert De Niro', *Playboy*, Vol. 36, No. 1 (1989), pp. 69–90, 326.
Grossberg, Josh. 'Robert De Niro, Martin Scorsese, Jodie Foster on making *Taxi Driver*' (Interview from Tribeca Film Festival 2016, edited and condensed), *New York Vulture*, 25 April 2016, https://www.vulture.com/2016/04/de-niro-scorsese-foster-talk-taxi-Driver-At-40.html [Accessed 30 September 2019].

[40] Schrader and Thompson, p. 19.

Jarnot, Lisa. *Robert Duncan, The Ambassador from Venus: A Biography*, Berkeley, Los Angeles, and London: University of California Press, 2012.

Kael, Pauline. 'Everyday Inferno', *The New Yorker*, October 1973, https://www.newyorker.com/magazine/1973/10/08/everyday-inferno [Accessed 20 May 2020].

Kilday, Gregg. 'Taxi Driver Oral History: De Niro, Scorsese, Foster, Schrader Spill All on 40th Anniversary,' *The Hollywood Reporter*, 7 April 2016, https://www.hollywoodreporter.com/features/taxi-driver-oral-history-de-881032 [Accessed 30 September 2019].

Naremore, James. *Acting in the Cinema*. Berkeley: University of California Press, 1988.

Schrader, Paul. *Transcendental Style in Film: Ozu, Bresson, Dreyer*, Berkeley, CA: University of California, 2018.

Schrader, Paul and Richard Thompson, 'Screen writer: *Taxi Driver*'s Paul Schrader' (interview), *Film Comment*, Vol. 12, No. 2 (1976), pp. 6–19.

Shone, Tom. 'How *Taxi Driver* Ruined Acting', *The Economist 1843*, 6 May 2016, https://www.1843magazine.com/culture/the-daily/how-taxi-dri ver-ruined-acting [Accessed 20 May 2020].

Wilson, Steven. 'You Talkin' to Me?', *Ransom Center Magazine*, 13 October 2016, https://sites.utexas.edu/ransomcentermagazine/2016/10/ 13/you-talkin-to-me/ [Accessed 20 May 2020].

CHAPTER 5

The Last Tycoon

The Last Tycoon (1976) is not widely regarded as a significant moment in De Niro's career. The film was an adaptation of F. Scott Fitzgerald's last novel, which was left incomplete when, in an unnerving echo (or anticipation) of the fate that would befall his protagonist, Fitzgerald died suddenly of a heart attack on 21 December 1940, with barely a third of the projected work fully drafted. That protagonist, whom De Niro would portray, was Monroe Stahr, a Hollywood producer clearly based on Irving Thalberg, who fifty years earlier had made the same journey from New York to Hollywood as De Niro.

Thalberg was a phenomenon: by the age of twenty he was running Universal studios, where he famously fired Erich von Stroheim, a decision that Roland Flamini, one of Thalberg's biographers, said 'asserted the primacy of the studio over any director',[1] and forever altered the balance of power in the movie industry. The Thalberg we encounter in *The Last Tycoon*, refracted through the persona of Stahr, is working in 1935 at a studio apparently based on MGM and with the character of Stahr's boss, Pat Brady (played by Robert Mitchum in the film), seemingly modelled on Louis B. Mayer. Stahr, like Thalberg, is destined to die young through a combination of illness, frailty and extreme overwork; in

---

[1] Roland Flamini, *Thalberg: The Last Tycoon and the World of M-G-M* (New York: Crown Publishers, 1994), p. 36.

© The Author(s) 2020
A. Ganz and S. Price, *Robert De Niro at Work*,
Palgrave Studies in Screenwriting,
https://doi.org/10.1007/978-3-030-47960-2_5

117

the rather bifurcated novel the workaholic aspect of Stahr's character co-exists with a romantic storyline that becomes predominant in the film, in which Stahr, whose wife Minna has died before the narrative begins, falls in love with the inscrutable Kathleen Moore.

The Last Tycoon is a period piece, in many senses: it is a nostalgic look back from the 1970s to the classical Hollywood of the mid-1930s, and it exploits the then-current vogue for Fitzgerald in the wake of a commercially successful 1974 adaptation of Fitzgerald's earlier novel *The Great Gatsby* that had been written by Francis Ford Coppola, who had recently directed De Niro's Oscar-winning performance in *The Godfather: Part II*, and produced by Robert Evans, who was to become one of the real-life models on which De Niro would draw in developing the Stahr character: in one of the actor's innumerable notes to self he reminds himself to '*Watch, just to see how [Robert] Evans deals with people and ask him how he's diplomatic*'.[2]

Even in 1940 Fitzgerald's book has a strongly elegiac tone, an ambivalent celebration of the doomed, totemic producer in mourning for his lost wife, but also in the process of being eased out of the way by the money men who lack his principles and essential if enigmatic decency. Much about the production itself, however, was not so much nostalgic as dated, even at the time. The project had originated with the veteran Hollywood producer Sam Spiegel, who had worked in Hollywood as early as 1927, although most of his best-known movies dated from the 1950s and early 1960s. The director, Elia Kazan, had won an Academy Award for the Spiegel-produced *On the Waterfront* (1954), but by the 1970s he was in semi-retirement after a number of flops and the continuing fallout of having named names to the House Un-American Activities Committee.

It was Kazan who recruited De Niro for *The Last Tycoon* after sending him a copy of Harold Pinter's screenplay in the fall on 1974,[3] and Kazan who also rather pressured Spiegel into accepting him.[4] De Niro was currently unavailable, and working on a Neil Simon-scripted, Mike Nichols-directed production of *Bogart Slept Here*; but after this fell through, suddenly he was able to move swiftly from *Taxi Driver* to a

[2] *The Last Tycoon* (1976), 11 August 1975, Script Copy 20, with extensive RDN notes, additional mimeo and RDN notes in pocket at front, Box 191, RDN.

[3] Shawn Levy, *Robert De Niro: A Life* (New York: Three Rivers Press, 2014), p. 188.

[4] William Baer (ed.), *Elia Kazan: Interviews* (Jackson, MI: University Press of Mississippi, 2001), p. 201.

commitment to *The Last Tycoon*. After spending so long immersed in the harrowing role of Travis Bickle, he was enthused by the prospect of playing Monroe Stahr and working with these iconic figures: 'It was like going from the darkest depths to light and inspiration; from black to white; from total angst to being with Kazan and Sam Spiegel. It was a whole other thing'.[5] In a development that would come to typify De Niro's chameleon-like determination to take on new challenges and avoid repetition, this film would be radically unlike those on which he had spent the last several years, with the opportunity to play a very different kind of role from the gangsters and contemporary New Yorkers that had preoccupied him in the early 1970s.

WORKING WITH KAZAN

The opportunity to work with Elia Kazan proved an irresistible lure for De Niro. Kazan was one of the most influential figures in the development of American performance, having begun his career in the 1930s acting with the Group Theatre, co-founded by De Niro's early mentor Stella Adler. But although Kazan achieved some recognition as an actor, his greater interest proved to be in directing: he went on to co-found the Actors Studio in 1947, the year in which he directed the premiere of Tennessee Williams' *A Streetcar Named Desire* (1947), as he would for its subsequent film adaptation in 1951, both starring Marlon Brando.

Kazan, then, was a very different kind of director from those De Niro had worked with beforehand, all of whom were primarily film-makers. Kazan was a theatre-maker as well, and was regarded as the actor's director par excellence. De Niro admired him tremendously: 'he is a wonderful director and he knows the theatre and the movies, and works well in both. He gives you all the support that you need in a professional way—like a coach, you know'.[6] The admiration was mutual: when asked about the oft-mooted comparison with Brando, Kazan replied that De Niro was 'more meticulous and more hardworking. He's very imaginative. He's very precise. He figures everything out both inside and outside. He has good emotion. He's a character actor: everything he does

---

[5] Lawrence Grobel, '*Playboy* Interview: Robert De Niro', *Playboy* (January 1989), p. 76.

[6] 'Dialogue on Film: Robert De Niro' (interview), *American Film*, 6.5 (1981), p. 40.

he calculates. In a good way [...] He's the hardest working actor I ever met'.[7]

Nowhere is the truth of this statement more evident than in De Niro's voluminous research and script annotation for *The Last Tycoon*. Kazan describes the relationship between the screenplay and the finished film using some of the metaphors that one often encounters in screenwriting manuals: as an architectural structure, as a framework fleshed out in the production of the film itself. In a speech he delivered in 1973, shortly before commencing work on *The Last Tycoon*, Kazan remarks: 'A screenplay's worth has to be measured less by its language than by its architecture and how that dramatises the theme. A screenplay, we directors soon enough learn, is not a piece of writing as much as it is a construction. We learn to feel for the skeleton under the skin of words'.[8] We can certainly see De Niro's annotations as searching for the embodiment of the character, but also as a skin, his handwritten notes being literally situated on top of the skeleton of the screenplay text.

Some of this work involved a very different kind of collaboration than De Niro had followed with Scorsese. Kazan was independently working up an analysis of the character that he discussed with De Niro, both in rehearsal and on paper. Some of this analysis has been published in Kazan's diary,[9] and De Niro retained in his archive extensive correspondence from Kazan about Monroe Stahr, including Kazan's construction of a detailed backstory for the character, and an analysis of his motivations.[10] In Kazan's description of the process of working with De Niro,

> I would tell him a lot of things. But with a good actor, you can tell him a lot and you have to watch what he latches on to and what he does not latch on to. He picked from what I told him; 'cause I can talk about that character a long time. He picked out the right things; he worked hard on them, and I would say he contributed an awful lot. I'm a director who does work with actors. So, I did contribute, but I would say that anything anyone might praise me for, they should first mention Bobby because it's

[7] Baer, p. 210.

[8] Elia Kazan, *Kazan on Directing* (New York: Knopf, 2009), p. 237.

[9] Kazan, pp. 228–231.

[10] *The Last Tycoon* (1976), Production materials, notes and correspondence from Elia Kazan re Stahr character, Box 89.2 [RDN].

Bobby's performance. He 'takes on' a character. You know that old cliché about how an actor becomes the person.[11]

The admiration is clearly mutual, and De Niro actively wanted to work with a director who took this approach to scripts, character development and working with an actor; but it appears that what Kazan saw was De Niro selecting from ideas that the director would give him, and not director and actor collaborating equally in the creation of the role. As De Niro put it later, Kazan 'had done a lot of thinking for me, sometimes too much thinking'.[12]

This does not mean that De Niro had no agency, of course. His fulsome notes on the screenplay and the supporting materials in the HRC show him approaching the project with at least as much dedication as to his earlier roles. These materials offer an unparalleled insight into De Niro's process at a particular historical moment, and how working on this film affected his understanding of both what screen acting is and what it might become. Because he is playing the part of a film producer, his research encompasses film history and film theory as well as film performance, learning from a great director about how to interpret the work of another great writer, Harold Pinter.

De Niro's experience on the film also forced him to learn the limits of interpretation. The overwhelming sense after reading his pages of diligent neatly written notes on the screenplay and in the substantial supporting material, and on looking at the finished film, is that it is while doing this work that he comes to understand the work of representation and the relationship between text and performance in a different way, which he will explore during the next phase of his career. It is as if he tests the pure Adlerian and Method approach to character research to destruction, and finds the shortcomings of the idea that a cerebral knowing of the character can define a performance—though it can certainly help.

For De Niro *The Last Tycoon* meant an encounter with a producer who doubted him, and a director who wrote that the film's climax 'said more about me and my feelings than it did about the film's hero'.[13] This leaves De Niro rather isolated, a feeling that emerges within the film in the form

---

[11] Baer, p. 211.

[12] Robert De Niro in *Elia Kazan: An Outsider*, 35 mm film, directed by Annie Tresgot. France: Argos Films, 1982.

[13] Elia Kazan, *Elia Kazan: A Life* (New York: Da Capo, 1997), p. 781.

of an actor who stands almost alone in representing a particular mode of performance. James Naremore has pointed out that *The King of Comedy*, which we shall examine in the next chapter, 'involves an unusually self-conscious mix of acting *styles*', and that 'the film seems to be using [Jerry] Lewis to suggest a difference between generations'.[14] Very similar observations can be made of *The Last Tycoon* (and indeed of the 1974 *Gatsby* due to the involvement of Coppola and Evans). Kazan's movie *was* a variation on the all-star vehicle as a form of contemporary commercial blockbuster, bringing together celebrated actors from different eras and nations, that had been part of the attraction of *The Towering Inferno* and *Airport 1975*, two of the big hits of 1974, the year in which Kazan sent De Niro Pinter's script for *The Last Tycoon*. On the latter's release in 1976 audiences would therefore have been unsurprised to see De Niro and Jack Nicholson, two of the most critically acclaimed of the younger generation of 'New Hollywood' actors, appearing alongside familiar icons of 1940s and 1950s Hollywood like Robert Mitchum, Ray Milland, Tony Curtis, Dana Andrews and John Carradine, as well as Jeanne Moreau, star of so many films of the French 'nouvelle vague' that had inspired Coppola and Scorsese as well as De Niro's generation of actors. The contrasting styles make it relatively easy to concentrate on the performances of individual actors instead of seeing them as part of an ensemble, but it is also striking that De Niro's performance as the literally buttoned-up Monroe is radically different again from that of Nicholson, his contemporary.

WORKING WITH A LITERARY TEXT

Fitzgerald was part of the canon, as arguably was Pinter; for the first time De Niro was working on a film adapted from what might be called a 'literary' text, as opposed to a popular bestseller like Mario Puzo's *The Godfather*, or an original screenplay like *Taxi Driver*. *The Last Tycoon* was also the first occasion on which De Niro would be working on a full-blown Hollywood production of the post-classical era, with everything that went along with it, including a package of perhaps irreconcilable talents and the demands of a role that required him—again for the first time—to play a character who was not just a serious, introspective film producer but also the romantic leading man. Despite De Niro's best

---

[14] James Naremore, *Acting in the Cinema* (Berkeley: University of California Press, 1988), pp. 263, 282; emphasis in the original.

efforts, Kazan was ultimately unable satisfactorily to bring either of these two aspects of the character or the story fully to life. This is partly a condition of Fitzgerald's novel, which keeps prompting the thought that the characters and the world they inhabit are somehow not fully alive, but already victims of the past. In the last line of *The Great Gatsby* the narrator Nick Carraway had reflected: 'So we beat on, boats against the current, borne back ceaselessly into the past'.[15] The film critic David Thomson detects a similar note in *The Last Tycoon*:

> *The Great Gatsby* takes place in 1925, and something central has gone wrong. American energy is betrayed already. The past has been lost, or escaped. But that liberty is a greater loss. Imagine that tone of voice drawing the covers up over the bodies of *The Last Tycoon*—imagine it a woman's voice, dry and tough, but broken—and you see how it might have been an extraordinary novel. The notes that Fitzgerald left for the book have Cecilia telling the rest of the story as she dies in a tuberculosis sanitarium, with Stahr dead and her father remarried.[16]

The absence of a proper ending to the novel is one that Pinter's screenplay addresses ingeniously, as we shall see. But this elegiac quality is endemic both to the story world and to the production of Kazan's film. Pinter's screenplay does not stray significantly beyond the confines of the chapters that Fitzgerald had fully drafted, and the script does not directly make use of the notes and fragmentary plot sketches that the critic Edmund Wilson, the novel's first editor, appended to the text. Fitzgerald's early death was not, then, the only way in which the novelist's own circumstances uncannily repeated those of his protagonist; both Stahr and Fitzgerald lived, in a sense, half a life, and the condition of the papers Fitzgerald left means that this is true of the book itself: editors—and screenwriters and actors—must conduct research and exercise their imaginations to complete the work.

It was the literary status of the screenwriter, however, that posed De Niro the greater problem as he worked on developing his role. Spiegel had commissioned Harold Pinter to write the screenplay, expressly for

---

[15] F. Scott Fitzgerald, *The Great Gatsby*, ed. Ruth Prigozy (Oxford: Oxford University Press, 1998), p. 144.

[16] David Thomson, *The Whole Equation: A History of Hollywood* (London: Abacus, 2006), p. 47.

Mike Nichols to direct; but 'after some months work on the script'[17] Nichols withdrew, to be replaced by Kazan. This did not affect the screenplay, however, because Pinter had a long-standing, and virtually unique, contractual arrangement that his screenplays could not be altered during production without his written permission. Kazan reports that 'it wasn't Fitzgerald that I was reverential towards, it was Harold', and that he 'swore' to Pinter 'that I wouldn't change any of his dialogue. And I didn't change one syllable of it. I found a way to stage it all'.[18] One of those ways was via the casting of De Niro, which Robert Sklar suggests represented Kazan's attempt to assert authorship over the material, in a manner that rather contradicted what the director had told Pinter: 'With De Niro [...] Kazan aimed at putting on screen the book that Fitzgerald had been in the midst of writing as much as, or more than Pinter's screenplay adaptation'.[19]

This contractual situation would, however, pose serious difficulties for De Niro, whose recent experiences with Scorsese on *Mean Streets* and *Taxi Driver* had been with a director who had encouraged a fluid, improvisational approach to working with the script, while even Coppola had given De Niro licence to re-write parts of *The Godfather, Part II*, coming to rely on the actor for assistance with the Sicilian-language scenes. An unalterable screenplay was inimical to the actor, who observed that 'with Kazan we stuck very much to the script, practically word for word, because Kazan promised Harold Pinter that he wouldn't change anything. I frankly think that a script should be changed; you have to make the adjustments. [...] or it becomes something rigid'.[20]

The film was simultaneously De Niro's first encounter with overtly 'literary' source material, and the first time he had made what was identifiably a 'Hollywood' studio movie as opposed to a low-budget independent film, or a work such as *The Godfather, Part II* that was associated with a writer-director who was in some sense defined in opposition to the

---

[17] Harold Pinter, 'Introduction' to *Collected Screenplays One* (London: Faber, 2000), p. x.

[18] Baer, p. 214.

[19] Robert Sklar, 'Filming an Unfinished Novel: *The Last Tycoon*', in R. Barton Palmer, ed., *Twentieth-Century American Fiction on Screen* (Cambridge: Cambridge University Press, 2010), p. 20.

[20] 'Dialogue on Film: Robert De Niro', p. 46.

studio that was nevertheless funding the film. *The Last Tycoon* also resembled the old-fashioned 'classical' Hollywood in taking the screenplay as a blueprint for the film (albeit for the decidedly un-classical reason that the screenwriter had right of veto), instead of allowing De Niro and others freedom to adapt the work throughout the film-making process. On *The Last Tycoon*, not only is De Niro unable to adapt Pinter's script, even his director is working on something on which he has had no input. In this sense the screenplay text is, paradoxically, radically separated from the subsequent film text, because it has not been shaped for the screen by any members of the production team other than the writer. Rarely can the separation between the two kinds of texts be more clearly delineated than in this film about Hollywood written by an Englishman in London. Indeed, Pinter's agent Emmanuel Wax wrote to Keith Turner on 14 January 1974 that 'Harold can only write scripts the way he sees them and finds it impossible to write do [sic] directions whether producer's or director's or anyone else, although he is very willing to listen to suggestions'. His contract made provision for extra payment if he appeared on set, though Wax adds: 'He makes a major contribution by being there at odd times during the shooting'.[21]

And yet for these very reasons this encounter tells us a great deal about De Niro's practice. By this stage in his career he knows considerably more about the process of film-making, and certainly American film-making, than Pinter, who had not previously worked in Hollywood; but he is not able to work with the writer as he had been able to work with Schrader or Coppola. If *The Last Tycoon* is a film about power and powerlessness in Hollywood in its heyday, De Niro was nevertheless linked to his character of Monroe Stahr for exactly these reasons, albeit in an entirely different production context.

De Niro's annotations on this script show the different ways in which he attempted to wrestle with the shackles that constrain him. With Stahr, one of the tasks with which De Niro—and, as we shall see, Pinter—was confronted was building up a backstory and a persona to a character, and the relationships into which that character enters, that Fitzgerald had left, both purposely and accidentally, vague and unknowable. De Niro's research covers the character Stahr, the historical figure Thalberg, and the working lives of the classical Hollywood producers. His comments on the

---

[21] Correspondence from Emmanuel Wax to Keith Turner, 14 January 1974, GB 58 Add MS 88880/6/27, Harold Pinter Archive, British Library Manuscripts, London, UK.

script are even more intense than on any of the other screenplays in the archive, and read like memos from a studio head; not coincidentally, Thalberg and especially David O. Selznick were famous for the detail of their memos. De Niro comments not just on what has happened, but what he thinks it means, while the handwriting itself seems to be not only *about* the character, but *in* character: it is smaller, neater, more controlled and more consistently in full sentences than in his annotations for both earlier and later films, and is noticeably different from (for example) the wild gesticulatory analyses of *Goodfellas*, or the acute but generally taciturn observations of *Taxi Driver*.

THE TITLE PAGE

At the very top of the title page of his copy of Pinter's 11 August 1975 script (Fig. 5.1),[22] De Niro has underlined, as a kind of epigraph, his summary of Stahr's dominant attitude: '*Give orders. Don't worry about not being liked. There's too much involved. You're the boss!*' This is presumably either De Niro's own independent observation, or a record of a conversation with Kazan at which actor and director have agreed on this approach to the character. Below this headline remark is a quotation: '*5000 people work at International [W]orld [F]ilms*', an observation derived from Fitzgerald's novel.

Following this comes a series of epigrammatic quotations from the sources De Niro has consulted. The archive retains over a dozen historical, critical and biographical works on Fitzgerald, Thalberg and the Hollywood of this era, and De Niro's handwritten annotations are to be found on his copies of Samuel Marx's *Mayer and Thalberg: The Make-Believe Saints* (1975)[23] and Bob Thomas's *Thalberg: Life and Legend* (1969),[24] as well as King Vidor's *A Tree Is a Tree* (1953).[25] De Niro carefully places quotation marks around words to indicate that they are not spoken in the voice of either De Niro the actor or Stahr the character, but are derived from these secondary works: '*I said "once a Star always a*

---

[22] *The Last Tycoon*, Box 191 [RDN].

[23] Samuel Marx, *Mayer and Thalberg: The Make-Believe Saints* (1975), annotated by RDN, BV 193 [RDN].

[24] Bob Thomas, *Thalberg: Life and Legend* (1969), annotated by RDN, BV 199 [RDN].

[25] King Vidor, *A Tree Is a Tree* (1953), annotated by RDN, BV 201 [RDN].

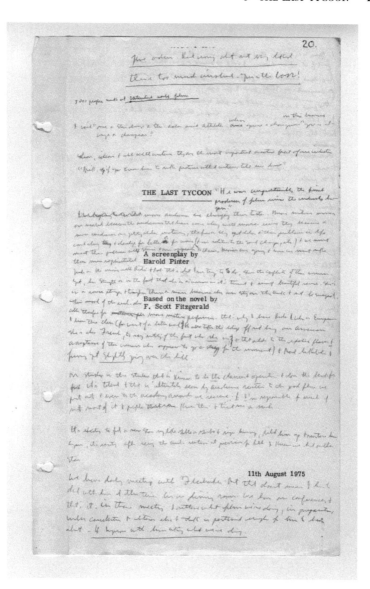

Fig. 5.1   *The Last Tycoon*, Box 191, RDN, title page

Star. Actors aren't athletes. When you're a champion in this business you're always a champion'.[26] '*Ideas, ideas + all with writers. They are the most important creative facet of our industry. "Nick, if you know how to make pictures without writers tell me how"'*[27]; and then, in different ink from the preceding and following material, and therefore presumably added at a different time: '"*He was unquestionably the finest producer of films since the industry began*"'.[28]

From here until the bottom of the page there are no further quotation marks, and De Niro now seems to be writing as Thalberg/Stahr:

> *Movie audiences are changing their tastes. More writers movies are needed because the audiences that have come along with movies since they became a mass medium are getting older, maturing, therefore they get older + their problems in life come along + develop for better or for worse (+ in relation to the social change, etc.) + we must meet these problems with stories + an approach to them. Movies are young + now we must make them more sophisticated.*

Although these sentences draw on De Niro's research, it is as if he now enters into a kind of free indirect speech, the factual information merging with the voice of Stahr before it does so explicitly ('*we must meet these problems*'). Yet the style remains detached, analytical; it is the voice of Stahr as the studio executive, writing to himself about the changing situation in Hollywood at this time, using a style that approximates the preferred mode used by Thalberg, Selznick and other producers of this era—the memo from the all-powerful executive.

At this point De Niro moves from outlining this wide-ranging historical approach to Stahr to an exploration of how his character approaches the first episode in the screenplay. Pinter chooses to open by dramatising a filmed scene between the imported French star Didi (Jeanne Moreau) and her husband Rodriguez (Tony Curtis). De Niro writes:

---

[26] The quotation derives from Samuel Marx, *Mayer and Thalberg*, p. 149.

[27] The statement (by Thalberg) is quoted in Alice Goldfarb Marquis. *Hopes and Ashes: Birth of Modern Times, 1929–1939* (Macmillan, 1987), p. 63. We were unable to trace the original source.

[28] This last quotation appears to derive from Howard Dietz, 'A Positive Personal Force, Says Dietz', *Motion Picture Herald* 124 (19 September 1936), p. 18.

Just as the movie with Didi + [?] That's what I'm trying to do. Show the conflicts of this woman. Yet, her strength is in the fact that she is a woman in its truest + most beautiful sense. She is in a sense stronger + tougher than a man because she can stay on the track + not be swayed. This mood of the aud[ience] also calls therefore for more mature performers. That's why I have Didi (who is European + has the class (for want of a better word) to take the edge off not being an American. She is also French, to say nothing of the fact [of] who <u>she</u> is, + that adds to the exotic flavor + acceptance of this woman, who appears to go astray for the moment) + [?] likeable + funny yet <u>slightly</u> going over the hill.

This is Stahr's perspective on why he has brought this French actor to Hollywood, and what are the strengths and weaknesses of the position.

Then De Niro as Stahr connects these observations about Didi's 'class' to the status of the studio for which he himself works:

Our studio is the studio that is known to be <u>the</u> classiest operator and does the best for its talent + that is ultimately seen by audience reaction to the good films we put out + even to the [A]cademy [A]wards we receive. + <u>I'm</u> responsible for much if not most of it + people know this + trust me as <u>such</u>.

It's exciting to find a new star say like Gable or Garbo + sign him up + restore him again, it's exciting after seeing the aud[ience] reaction at previous for both & knew we had another star.

And then he moves from the self-reflection and self-evaluation the Didi scene has occasioned to a more straightforwardly professional account of, and perhaps preparation for, part of his daily routine. This highlights the aspect of Stahr that dominates the novel but is rather underplayed in the film: the brisk, businesslike way in which he organises himself in a world that makes incessant calls on his time:

We have daily meetings with Fleischacker. But that doesn't mean I have to deal with him at other times. As in dining room. We have our conferences + that's it. In these meetings I outline what films we're doing, in preparation, under consideration + whatever else I think is pertinent enough for him to hear about. <u>It happens with him asking what we're doing.</u>

The analysis continues on the verso, in which De Niro as Stahr goes into considerable detail about the financial negotiations he is conducting with Fleischacker—once again showing De Niro's concern with the precise calculations about money as an insight into character, just as he had earlier done in reckoning exactly how much money Johnny Boy owes in *Mean Streets*. On this page of *The Last Tycoon* we see De Niro thinking about exactly what kind of deals Stahr is engaged in, how much Stahr knows about the finances of each film, and how the money is to be distributed. In short, De Niro is thinking himself into quite precise evaluations of the money-oriented aspects of Stahr's job, even though the detail of this is largely invisible within Pinter's screenplay.

BUILDING A CHARACTER

Throughout his annotations we can see the range of sources De Niro has drawn upon in order to explore every aspect of the character. His customary diligence in exploring and extending the character and the story world prompted the marginal notes and paratexts that he habitually added to the screenplay. The form the actor's preparatory work takes here echoes, coincidentally or otherwise, a property of the novel. Fitzgerald's death left his book in an unfinished, fragmentary condition, with six fully drafted chapters along with Fitzgerald's own marginalia and additional notes and outlines, at the centre of which is the enigmatic, half-formed character that De Niro was now required to portray. Perhaps it was not just by accident of circumstance that Stahr came to exist in fragments, however; like Stahr, Fitzgerald's earlier creation Jay Gatsby is purposely presented as an enigma, seemingly the product of a past that is glimpsed yet is essentially unknowable. Towards the end of *The Great Gatsby* the eponymous hero's father unearths a note his son scrawled into a book in his childhood. Much like De Niro's habitual numbered series of tasks and character observations, Gatsby has broken down his self-analysis into a 'SCHEDULE' itemising the actions he must perform during the day, followed by a list of six 'GENERAL RESOLVES':

> No wasting time at Shafters or [a name, indecipherable]
> No more smoking [sic] or chewing
> Bath every other day
> Read one improving book or magazine per week
> Save $5.00 [crossed out] $3.00 per week
> Be better to parents[29]

---

[29] Fitzgerald, *The Great Gatsby*, p. 138.

Gatsby is creating his own character through itemizing a list of tasks
and resolutions that collectively will form a persona, much as the American 'self-made man' had done ever since the *Autobiography* of Benjamin
Franklin. It captures precisely the paradox of the creation of character—to
get to the heart of the self by, quite literally, making it up. The resem-
blance between Gatsby's approach and De Niro's is uncanny—right down
to the occasional illegibility of the notes.

Among the copious paratexts that De Niro assembled in preparing
for the role is some specially made notepaper with the printed header
'From the desk of: Monroe Stahr'. (Figure 5.2) On this paper De Niro
has carefully itemised a series of props:

1. *Pens. My pen filled*
2. *Pad cover*
3. *Lamp*
4. *Gallies*
5. *Slips of paper*
6. *Glasses*
7. *Mail on desk*

   Memos
   letters to be signed after I
   dictated them.

In what feels like De Niro's appreciation of the ironic complexity of
the situation, he uses the prop of the headed notepaper to list what he
thinks would truly be on the desk of Monroe Stahr: so the memo headed
'from the desk of Monroe Stahr' describes itself. Perhaps we can link this
to De Niro, who can also be said to be in some sense describing his
own contents and who will, like the desk, have to assume a materiality
in the fictional world. The imitation studio memo seems to represent
De Niro's own predicament, which feels like a crisis of authenticity as
he works phenomenally hard to create a simulacrum of Monroe Stahr
while also negotiating the multiple identities that coalesce into the first
person 'I'.

De Niro's annotations, not only on the script but also on secondary
sources, including Bob Thomas' biography of Thalberg, show him trying
to synthesise the character he will be playing through mingling a number
of different identities: the 'I' of the character and the 'I' of the actor will

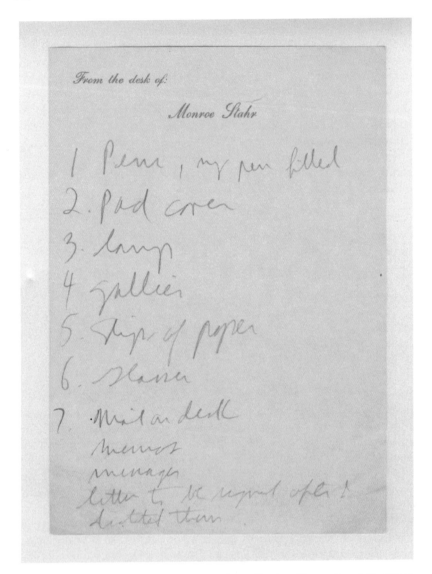

Fig. 5.2 'From the Desk of Monroe Stahr', *The Last Tycoon*, Box 191, RDN

incorporate elements of De Niro himself, the fictional character of Stahr, and the historical figure of Thalberg. At some points De Niro emphasises the difference between the three identities. '*Exactly what voice will I have? Because I think I'm not really like Thalberg in terms of the Jewishness. But certainly can be. It would be fun*'. Here the 'I' is clearly De Niro, but elsewhere 'I' is the character he will be playing: '*I have my mother's sensibilities. The sensibilities of a woman*'. But he is also thinking about how as an actor to achieve these effects: '*Remember in all scenes (one with Rodrigues comes to mind). Rehearse rehearse, familiarise, rehearse*'; '*Soft voice, assured Very Limp. But absolutely not ingenuine*'. There are also notes where the identification is with the 'I' of Thalberg, as well as Stahr: '*Would like to see some of my greats, "Ben Hur"* etc.'; '*Go look at my office at MGM*'. But he is also making research notes for himself. One reads, baldly: '*talk to Adolph Zukor*'. Astonishingly Zukor, founder of Paramount and producer of the very first American feature-length film, was still alive at 102 years old, and had been in his 60s during Thalberg's heyday.

This complexity of identity is key. De Niro is the physical point where multiple sources and interpretations intersect, and through which they have to be expressed. He has to navigate his way between Thalberg as a real person, mediated by the various primary and secondary sources De Niro is consulting; Fitzgerald's fictionalisation of Thalberg in the persona of Stahr; Pinter's adaptation, and De Niro's own conceptualisation of what the job involves. He researches what it would feel like to do the work, and speculates on what analogies might be helpful, but above all there is a focus on materiality: each of these understandings will need to be revealed through physical action and gesture. One of De Niro's tasks in creating the performance is to assemble a concordance of the character according to all of these sources, which will of necessity be sometimes contradictory, or redundant. He needs to find a system for taking those decisions.

STAHR'S RELATIONSHIP WITH KATHLEEN

There was another, and again in a sense generational, issue surrounding casting that impacted on De Niro's performance. Natasha Fraser-Cavassoni, in her biography of Sam Spiegel, notes that it was the producer who insisted upon the casting of the younger female roles: Kathleen (played by Ingrid Boulting), with whom Monroe Stahr is in love, and

Cecilia (Theresa Russell), the daughter of studio executive Pat Brady. For each of these actors *The Last Tycoon* would be her first major film role, and in each case the casting was due to Spiegel attempting to exploit his powerful relationship to exert pressure over a young female actor.[30] In the light of contemporary revelations about Harvey Weinstein and the open secrets surrounding the #MeToo movement, a barely concealed subtext of *The Last Tycoon* appears to be the sexual exploitation of women in the film industry. Indeed, this seems to have led to a certain tension between Pinter and Kazan: as recalled by Donald Pleasance, who in the film plays the novelist-screenwriter Boxley, 'Kazan was after a sexually very explicit film and Harold would never go for that'.[31]

In the present context it is important to note that Spiegel's insistence on casting Boulton meant that, in Pinter's understated words, the film was 'disappointing' because it was 'too romantic and the casting of the central female role was underpowered' (by contrast, Pinter found De Niro 'impressive').[32] Fraser-Cavassoni quotes Pinter as saying that though he found Boulting delightful she 'did not cut the mustard',[33] and Fraser-Cavassoni describes her as 'woefully wooden on camera'.[34] *Variety*'s reviewer remarked of the 'handsome but lethargic' film that 'Ingrid Boulting is the elusive charmer who penetrates somewhat into De Niro's interior, but since her own expressions are limited in scope, we don't really know what she finds there'.[35]

Amidst this nightmare, where powerful old men were demanding the right to harass young women, De Niro was focused on his research for the film, while Tony Curtis complained about the time De Niro took

---

[30] Natasha Fraser-Cavassoni, *Sam Spiegel* (New York: Little, Brown, 2003), p. 352. In an interview with Roger Ebert many years later, Russell stated that Spiegel had sexually assaulted her (Roger Ebert, 'Interview with Theresa Russell', *Roger Ebert*, 21 September 1988, https://www.rogerebert.com/interviews/interview-with-theresa-russell, [Accessed 22 September 2019]).

[31] Quoted in Michael Billington, *Harold Pinter* (London: Faber, 2007), p. 241.

[32] Pinter, *Collected Screenplays One*, p. xi.

[33] Fraser-Cavassoni, p. 352.

[34] Fraser-Cavassoni, p. 352.

[35] Variety Staff, '*The Last Tycoon*' (review), *Variety*, 31 December 1975, https://variety.com/1975/film/reviews/the-last-tycoon-2-1200423612/ [Accessed 20 May 2020].

'interpreting and analysing his character almost line by line'.[36] It is symp-tomatic of De Niro's relative lack of authority in the production of *The Last Tycoon* that in a film that saw him for the first time taking on, in however qualified a sense, the role of a romantic leading man, he was forced to perform the scenes in which this aspect of the character comes to the forefront while playing opposite a partner whose performance was ineffectual, and is largely an absence in their scenes together, because she was a victim imposed on the production by Spiegel.

Faced with this intractable problem, and another in having to work with an unchangeable script, De Niro concentrates on those things that he can bring to a scene. For example, he analyses the prehistory of the relationship with Kathleen, while working through the potentially infinite sets of choices in terms of action and gesture that can make the nuances of the relationship filmable. In an extraordinary list of 23 annotations written on the screenplay he discusses how he will be sitting in a scene in the office with Kathleen (Fig. 5.3):

9. *All 3 buttons of jacket closed. I'm serious and not a swinger and in some ways pride myself on it. I have more imp. things to do.*

10. *I think of myself throughout speaking very softly.*

11. *We have a signal, my secretary and I that when I'm with someone other than a very imp. person and even then, she is [to] interrupt me for my next appt. Do improv and have understanding with her before scene.*

12. *Every time I get up I'm going somewhere important and I have an important thing to do. I have no casual moments. I don't know how to be casual. I can't be casual.*

13. *Find when I can look at my secretary and she automatically [illeg-ible] she has all my appointments.*

14. *Find things I can do to loosen up within nature of situation and character, I do everything fully.*

The 23 points combine specifics ('*all 3 buttons closed*') with the reasons why that decision has been arrived at, and how else it might manifest itself. The actor is at the nexus between the character's thought processes,

---

[36] Aubrey Malone, *The Defiant One: A Biography of Tony Curtis* (Jefferson, NC: McFarland, 2013), p. 159.

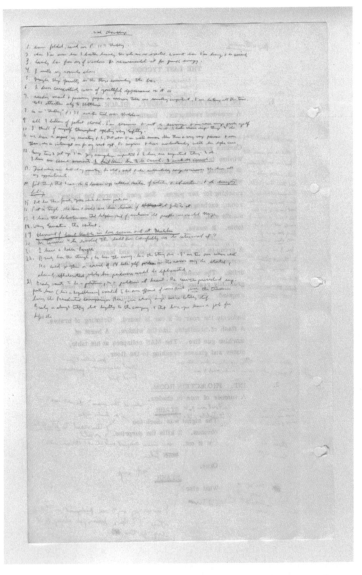

Fig. 5.3 *The Last Tycoon*, Box 191, RDN, notes on character and scene

habits, state of mind and what the other characters around him may be thinking or wanting. De Niro is exploring the character's reasons and motivations, how these can be translated into things that are filmable, and whether these things are purely descriptive or instead can inform the tone or rhythm or attitude or other longitudinal quality of the performance. He is exploring who he believes Monroe Stahr to be, and how the character would behave in each situation.

The relationship with Kathleen should form the emotional centre of the film at some level, but De Niro is trying to realise a scene that cannot work for the aforementioned reasons, which are beyond his control. He is putting in an abundance of annotation onto a script that cannot talk back to him, or give anything back, because it cannot change in response; and similarly, but for different reasons, he can get no real response from Boulting to the work he is putting into the scene, because she cannot provide the level of performance required.

Lacking a reaction from either Boulting or Pinter, another approach De Niro takes is to look to the novel for glosses on the script. An example is in his annotations on the scene with Kathleen on page 72: '*We've just made love but probably didn't speak all the way back. I feel empty, lost?*' He quotes the novel to explore his state of mind, even though the screenplay is substantially different ('I can't stop looking at you'). In the margin, De Niro has written: '*Serious and passionate and direct*'. The sequence is a delicate one, where Stahr is attracted to Kathleen but unable to move towards her. The facts of the difference between them act as obstacles— expressed, for example, in the fact that Stahr's home doesn't have an address, 'Just Bel-Air; there's no number'. De Niro's gloss is that this is '*A fact, not to be distant, really just explaining it*'. At the top of the page he has written: '*On the one hand I don't want to get involved, on the other I do*', but he also quotes Fitzgerald's text at length: '*He refused to let the aloofness communicate itself. He kept looking at her and moved his head from side to side in her own gesture, saying without words "you know what's happened to me"*'. This flows straight onto his own adaptation of Fitzgerald's text: '*She comes in my arms and is mine totally again then "Before anything could change I whispered good nite (sic) and went to my car"*.' In a larger hand he adds: '*a total rejoicing welcome*'. De Niro is moving between Fitzgerald's narrator and his own 'I', and draws on both equally to prepare the script for performance.

Not surprisingly, the scene also provides some outstanding illustrations of De Niro's facility with close textual analysis. Immediately beneath the line 'I don't want to lose you' he adds an instruction: *'lift her head before'*. De Niro is combining attitude, thought and action to perform the sequence, but more striking still is his reading of the line itself, which he has parsed as follows: *'yet (but) can't (don't want) commit to her yet'*. (Figure 5.4) As so often, he expresses in the very form of his notes an essential aspect of the character's response. The parentheses and multiple subtextual qualifications in this annotation brilliantly express the character's misgivings about pursuing the relationship, not least because it is haunted by the image of Stahr's dead wife Minna. (In the novel, Stahr sees in Kathleen 'the face of his dead wife, identical even to the expression'.[37]) The tortured syntax of De Niro's note—even the omission of the 'to' before 'commit' is possibly intentional, with the emotional meaning clear but the grammar cloudy—represents a further intensification of Stahr's anxieties and self-doubt. It is a sign of the actor's ambition and commitment that he aims to express all of these unspoken meanings in the line, while retaining its superficially straightforward meaning for the benefit of Kathleen. Even then De Niro has not exhausted its potential: as we shall see below, Pinter re-introduces the line at the end of the film in a different context, prompting yet further analysis from De Niro of what it can reveal about his character.

Another key moment in the story surrounds a letter Kathleen has written to Stahr, which has gone missing but which he now possesses. At this point we do not know its content, but wonder if in it she is ending the relationship, or is confessing to another one. De Niro writes: *'One way is to look at it and think should I open it now or wait'*. He accordingly surrounds the moment in the screenplay with questions, observations and specifics about what will be on the envelope, or the order in which things will occur. *'Did she leave it there purposely, to find later'*? Elsewhere: *'I'll wait- it might be negative. Thinking I shouldn't open because I would like to ask her. Things have changed'*. And soon: *'It's nice to have a letter from her unexpectedly even I don't know when A xxxx [illegible]'*. ('It was nice to have a letter' comes from Fitzgerald's novel.) And then: *'Thoughtful hand to face thinking what was she trying to do, she must have written this before she knew what we'd do?'*

We can see in these annotations De Niro putting himself in the mind of the anxious lover: debating whether to open a letter that may contain

---

[37] Fitzgerald, *The Great Gatsby*, p. 33.

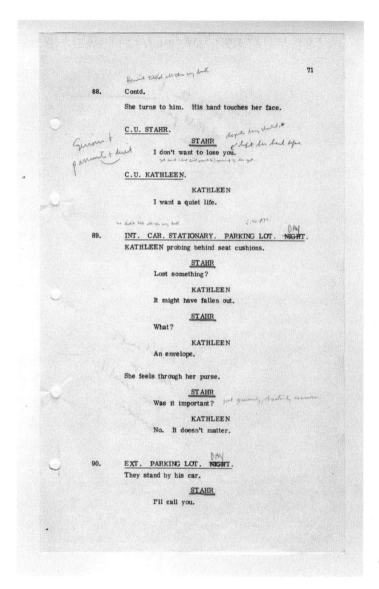

Fig. 5.4 *The Last Tycoon*, Box 191, RDN, p. 71

disastrous news or good, wondering if it is better to talk to Kathleen without ever opening it, restlessly questioning the motives of the beloved. De Niro's annotations also follow Pinter's script in counterpointing these thoughts and actions with more mundane displacement activities, taking advantage of the distractions of work. The screenplay reads: 'STAHR looks at the letter in his hand. It is addressed to himself. He starts to open it, stops, puts it down. He picks up a script from a pile of scripts, a pencil, and starts to read the script'. De Niro draws on the novel, the screenplay, his own research, and conversations with Kazan to propose specific gestures or interpretations (which are not always acted on); there are other gestures, like his smelling the letter, which form part of the action without being mentioned in the script or in De Niro's adaptation. What we see in the film is De Niro in character as Monroe Stahr embodying and making visible the moments as Stahr prepares for the dénouement of discovering the content of the letter. Each moment has to be read not only as a succession of incidents in themselves but as a culmination of the previous scenes, building to Stahr's realisation that he is alone.

It is striking that De Niro spends so much time exploring Stahr's response to the letter. At one level, of course, it shows him entering into the thought processes of a man fearful that the loved one is about to reject him. At the same time, the situation of a man asking himself questions because he cannot receive answers from the ostensible addressee re-enacts his situation in preparing to make the film: for different reasons, neither the screenplay nor the woman playing Kathleen is fully able to answer the questions he has.

THE BOXLEY SCENE

Perhaps the most widely commented-upon episode in both the novel and the film is the scene in which Stahr gives an object lesson in screenwriting to George Boxley, a novelist who has been brought to Hollywood as a dialogue writer but is suffering the frustrations of being teamed with 'two hacks' who 'seem to have a vocabulary of about a hundred words'.[38] Stahr asks Boxley to forget about dialogue for a moment and to picture a scene. He is to imagine himself sitting silently in his office when a young woman

---

[38] F. Scott Fitzgerald, *The Last Tycoon*, ed. Edmund Wilson (Harmondsworth: Penguin, 1974), p. 40.

enters and, without noticing him, empties the contents of her purse onto a table: two dimes, a nickel and a matchbox. She puts the two dimes back into her purse, goes over to a stove, places her black gloves inside and begins to set fire to them. She is interrupted by the phone ringing: an unheard voice speaks, she replies 'I've never owned a pair of black gloves in my life', replaces the receiver, and starts to light the match. Just then the Boxley figure is to notice that there is a second man in the room, watching the woman … 'What happens?', asks Boxley. Stahr replies: 'I don't know. I was just making pictures'.

David Bordwell describes the episode in Fitzgerald's novel as 'an exemplary scene, showing how good Stahr is at his job. He subtly steers Mr. Boxley, the East Coast littérateur, towards returning to the screenplay. But he also tutors Mr. Boxley, and us, in a deeper awareness of how classical Hollywood aimed to tell its stories' in 'clean, straight storytelling'. It isn't full of spectacular action; instead, '[w]hat we have is plot and character fused in a *situation*. The scene creates, out of mundane materials, a crisis'.[39]

Importantly, however, it is not a crisis that Stahr is required to resolve—what we have is, indeed, a situation, but not a *story*, and certainly not a completed story. Stahr is able to sidestep the question not only of what the story is and how it ends, but even of 'what happens next?' As Thomson remarks, Thalberg 'had learned enough about movies to see how a certain thing shown provocatively plus information withheld equaled suspense', and yet Stahr 'knows it is a trick, as opposed to profundity, and he has begun to worry over that gap'.[40] The Boxley scene gives us part of the equation of what a classical Hollywood story can look like, but it is a very long way from being the whole equation; while it appears to be about plot, the scene is more precisely about the activities of writing and cinematic storytelling themselves. This is also true of the book, screenplay and film: the novel is a goldmine of tantalising information, but it lacks the conclusion and structure that Fitzgerald might have provided had he lived. One way of thinking about De Niro's annotations on the *Last Tycoon* screenplay, which are exceptionally expansive even by

[39] David Bordwell, 'How to tell a movie story: Mr. Stahr will see you now', *Observations on Film Art* (website), 5 January 2014, http://www.davidbordwell.net/blog/2014/01/05/how-to-tell-a-movie-story-mr-stahr-will-see-you-now/ [Accessed 24 May 2020]; emphasis added.

[40] Thomson, *The Whole Equation*, p. 29.

his standards, is as an attempt to fill that gap, to propose to it questions that once again, ultimately, it cannot finally answer; but in the Boxley scene in particular (on which Kazan also wrote a long memo), they are also an attempt to discover the actions that will best express the activity of cinematic storytelling as Stahr perceives it.

For Bordwell, the scene misrepresents the novel:

> Apart from adding unnecessary lines, it's an exercise in ham, with other characters watching Boxley's discomfiture and a smug Stahr (Robert De Niro) dashing about the room and pantomiming the action. Kazan's Stahr burlesques the story situation he invokes, whereas I take the novel's scene as a playful but sincere object lesson.[41]

Pinter's script goes a long way towards verifying this observation, as it specifies both the movements and the pantomimic quality, with Pinter noting on no fewer than four occasions in the short scene that Stahr 'mimes' the woman's actions. There is, however, no strong reason to doubt Stahr's sincerity in wishing to help Boxley, and Donald Pleasance's facial expressions in the film reveal that the frustrated writer is feeling progressively less discomfited and instead is becoming both more involved in Stahr's story and more impressed by the producer's acuity. If Bordwell's evaluation of the episode in the film is right, the fault would seem to lie more with how the screenwriter has rewritten Fitzgerald than with how either the actor or the director has chosen to interpret the action.

But it is also important to stress that in the Boxley scene De Niro is portraying not an actor—and not a writer, either—but a male producer who is pantomiming how a female actor might go about portraying the imaginary performance of a cinematic scene that the producer is extemporising, for the benefit of a writer who appears to have little to no idea of how cinematic storytelling, either in writing or in performing, actually works. This presents challenges that do not confront Fitzgerald, who as a novelist can write the episode simply as dialogue. De Niro's enactment of the scene, by contrast, is a performance of a performance: he is portraying a character who is not himself an actor, but is attempting to pantomime the meaning of screen performance.

Thomson notes that the moment when the woman empties her purse 'needs a close-up […] we want to see—it won't take long before we walk

---

[41] Bordwell, 'How to tell a movie story'.

out if we don't see the information, the thing itself, that is being referred to'.[42] Yet in staging the scene as it is portrayed in the novel—that is, as an interaction between Stahr and Boxley—the film is unable to provide the shots for which the description so obviously calls. As both Thomson and Bordwell point out, we know nothing about the woman—she 'has no history, or backstory. She is less a person or a character than a presence, waiting for texture, a lie calling for explication'.[43] Yet it is that provision of texture, that obsession with finding out who a character is, that drives both De Niro and Kazan. Indeed, De Niro specifically mentions '*back story*' in his notes for the scene, which show evidence of his improvisation with Kazan to find out what had happened beforehand: '*Establishing that this is his first meeting of the day, that he's feeling good and the back story with Boxley*', namely that '*I've brought him here to Hollywood to work on this project*'.

Finding the backstory to the characters might have been one way of completing the story Stahr tells in the Boxley scene, just as finding out what makes Stahr tick is crucial to De Niro. Presented with a similar problem in relation to Fitzgerald's novel—how to complete an incomplete story—but seemingly unwilling to invent episodes that the novelist had not fully drafted, Pinter ended his screenplay by dramatising and re-telling the Boxley scene, reworked so that the purposely inconclusive story Stahr tells Boxley is refashioned as a means by which to conclude, or at least suggest a conclusion to, the enigma of Monroe Stahr. Towards the end of the film he is ousted by studio executives, who are then driven away in limousines as Stahr walks through an empty, silent studio and through the open door of a sound stage, 'into the blackness', as the soundtrack echoes to his footsteps and to the line Stahr has earlier said to Kathleen at his Malibu house: 'I don't want to lose you'.

Between the banishment and this concluding darkness comes the revisitation of the Boxley scene, which is now seemingly a projection of Stahr's imagination or unconscious, with the role of the anonymous woman taken by Kathleen. After Stahr's line 'I was just making pictures' is heard in voice-over, Kathleen looks into the camera, which now adopted the position of the Man in the scene. The Man's hand touches her face; Stahr looks into the camera and, in another call-back, says: 'I don't want to

[42] Thomson, p. 108.

[43] Thomson, p. 10.

lose you'. As De Niro's annotation insists, this enigmatic line, delivered to camera, is '*Very IMP[ORTANT]*'. While he had completely covered some of the white spaces of the first Boxley scene with handwritten commentary, on the script for the re-imagined scene he confines himself to a wonderfully terse and lucid explication of its multiple possible meanings in this new context, in which the 'you' that might be lost is variously:

1. *Kathleen*
2. *my life*
3. *my job, position*
4. *the audience*

'Audience' is pointedly underlined, indicating that the relationship to the spectator implied by the look into the camera is arguably the most important relationship in screen acting. It is Pinter's script that makes these possibilities available—the Boxley scene in Fitzgerald's novel does not really prompt any similar reflections—but it is De Niro's skill as a critic that unpacks them, and his ambition as an actor that prompts the desire to find a way of expressing all of them simultaneously. De Niro's note recognises that Stahr's final line in Pinter's text represents the nodal point of the uncannily elegiac quality of *The Last Tycoon*, with the woman in the story representing Kathleen, just as Kathleen represents the lost Minna, while Stahr—and the actor—must finally and inevitably lose even the consolation of being perceived by the spectator, as his life, his career and the film descend into darkness.

BIBLIOGRAPHY

ABBREVIATIONS

RDN: Robert De Niro Papers, Harry Ransom Center, University of Texas at Austin.

PRIMARY

A Tree Is a Tree (1953), Vidor, King, annotated by RDN, BV 201, RDN.
The Last Tycoon (1976), 11 August 1975, Script Copy 20, with extensive RDN notes, additional mimeo and RDN notes in pocket at front, Box 191, RDN.

The Last Tycoon (1976), Production materials, notes and correspondence from Elia Kazan re Stahr character, Box 89.2, RDN.

Mayer and Thalberg: The Make-Believe Saints (1975), by Marx, Samuel, annotated by RDN, BV 193, RDN.

Thalberg: Life and Legend (1969), Thomas, Bob, annotated by RDN, BV 199, RDN.

SECONDARY

'Dialogue on Film: Robert De Niro' (interview), *American Film*, Vol. VI, No. 5 (1981), p. 40.

Baer, William (ed.), *Elia Kazan: Interviews*, Jackson, MS: University Press of Mississippi, 2001.

Billington, Michael. *Harold Pinter*, London: Faber, 2007.

Bordwell, David. 'How to Tell a Movie Story: Mr. Stahr Will See You Now', *Observations on Film Art* (website), 5 January 2014, http://www.davidb ordwell.net/blog/2014/01/05/how-to-tell-a-movie-story-mr-stahr-will-see-you-now/ [Accessed 24 May 2020].

Dietz, Howard. 'A Positive Personal Force, Says Dietz', *Motion Picture Herald*, Vol. 124 (1936).

Ebert, Roger. 'Interview with Theresa Russell', *Roger Ebert*, 21 September 1988, https://www.rogerebert.com/interviews/interview-with-theresa-rus sell [Accessed 22 September 2019].

Fitzgerald, F. Scott. *The Last Tycoon*, ed. Edmund Wilson, Harmondsworth: Penguin, 1974.

Fitzgerald, F. Scott. *The Great Gatsby*, ed. Ruth Prigozy, Oxford: Oxford University Press, 1998.

Flamini, Roland. *Thalberg: The Last Tycoon and the World of M-G-M*, New York: Crown, 1994.

Fraser-Cavassoni, Natasha. *Sam Spiegel*, New York: Little, Brown, 2003.

Goldfarb Marquis, Alice. *Hopes and Ashes: Birth of Modern Times, 1929–39*, New York: Macmillan, 1987.

Grobel, Lawrence. '*Playboy* Interview: Robert De Niro', *Playboy*, Vol. 36, No. 1 (1989), pp. 69–90, 326.

Kazan, Elia. *Elia Kazan: A Life*, New York: Da Capo, 1997.

Kazan, Elia. *Kazan on Directing*, New York: Knopf, 2009.

Levy, Shawn. *De Niro: A Life*, New York: Three Rivers, 2014.

Malone, Aubrey. *The Defiant One: A Biography of Tony Curtis*, Jefferson, NC: McFarland, 2013.

Naremore, James. *Acting in the Cinema*, Berkeley: University of California Press, 1988.

Pinter, Harold. *Collected Screenplays One*, London: Faber, 2000.

Sklar, Robert. 'Filming an Unfinished Novel: *The Last Tycoon*', in R. Barton Palmer (ed.), *Twentieth-Century American Fiction on Screen* (Cambridge: Cambridge University Press, 2010), pp. 8–25.

'*The Last Tycoon*' (review), *Variety*, 31 December 1975, https://variety.com/1975/film/reviews/the-last-tycoon-2-1200423612/ [Accessed 20 May 2020].

Thomson, David. 'The Director as Ranging Bull: Why Can't a Woman Be More Like a Photograph?', *Film Comment*, Vol. 17, No. 1 (1981), pp. 9–15.

CHAPTER 6

Improv(e)

Among the many notes on *The King of Comedy* script is one reading **IMPROV** in large soft grey pencil, underlined for emphasis. Very faintly DeNiro has added an extra E, so it now also reads **IMPROV**E. It is an indicator, perhaps, of some of the renewed emphases in his work after *The Last Tycoon*, a film in which the script could not be changed. At that point De Niro went back to working with Martin Scorsese on what we might call the performance trilogy: *New York, New York* (1977), *Raging Bull* (1980) and *The King of Comedy* (1982), a sequence interrupted only by Michael Cimino's *The Deer Hunter* (1978). Each of the three films is about performers and performance: De Niro plays variously a saxophone player, a boxer and an aspiring comedian, and in each case his performance explores the liminal area between screenplay and film.

In this chapter we examine De Niro's transformed approach to performance, the relationship between screenplay text and filmed text, and his techniques for exploring and prototyping what will appear on screen, as well as his systems for notation and his range of tools of textual embodiment. We will also see how he incorporates various forms of authorship, including improvisation, into his practice. In each of these films De Niro is central not only to the film's performance, but to its existence; indeed, in both *Raging Bull* and *The King of Comedy* he was the driving force in bringing the project to the screen, and in *Raging Bull* he co-wrote the final shooting script.

© The Author(s) 2020
A. Ganz and S. Price, *Robert De Niro at Work*,
Palgrave Studies in Screenwriting,
https://doi.org/10.1007/978-3-030-47960-2_6

New York, New York (1977)

The mixed reception and weak box office that greeted *New York, New York* on release have sometimes seen it placed alongside *The Last Tycoon* and *1900* (Bernardo Bertolucci 1976) as a sequence of at least relative failures that briefly interrupted De Niro's otherwise unbroken series of masterpieces from *Bang the Drum Slowly* to *Raging Bull*, although few reviewers felt that the problems with any of these films lay in De Niro's own performance. Superficially, Scorsese's new film had some other resemblances to *The Last Tycoon*: each is a 1970s movie starring De Niro in a film about the classical-era Hollywood of the 1930s and 1940s, in which the predominant approaches to acting were very different from those De Niro had grown up with.

In *New York, New York* De Niro plays Jimmy Doyle, a jazz saxophonist and (later) band leader, whose talent and fame are ultimately eclipsed by those of the singer Francine Evans (Liza Minnelli), their marriage falling apart as Jimmy fails to come to terms either with Francine's success or with her desire to have a child. The archive shows that, as with *The Last Tycoon*, the actor threw himself into the project with an enthusiastic commitment to the film and to the extension of his range. And while *The Last Tycoon* suffers from the compromised source material and from a mélange of incompatible elements, *New York, New York* was a much more integrated project from the beginning.

This was not always acknowledged even by Scorsese himself, with some of the director's own subsequent comments contributing to a widespread critical view that the extensive improvisation ultimately resulted in a film that lacked focus and coherence: 'a mess', as Scorsese once remarked,[1] or 'too much, too much', in the words of a recent biographer of De Niro.[2] In 1990, for example, Scorsese remarked:

> we made it up as we went along. We had a pretty good script by Earl Mac Rauch and didn't pay any attention to it. The two methods of filmmaking—the improvisatory style and the old studio style, where you build sets—didn't blend. You're wasting money that way, because the set was

---

[1] Martin Scorsese, quoted in Shawn Levy, *De Niro: A Life* (New York: Three Rivers Press, 2014), p. 196.

[2] Levy, p. 206.

built, and you would improvise yourself into another scene. Then you'd
have to reimprovise yourself back into that set. It was crazy.[3]

Later, the director—like many critics—would come to see *New York, New
York* more favourably, and to recognise that far from compromising the
film, the improvisatory approach successfully realised Scorsese's intention
of finding a contemporary way of reimagining the classical-era Hollywood
musicals of the thirties and forties, and of discovering how the actors
should perform within it.

As the director put it in an interview for a DVD release in 2005: 'when
I went to Hollywood in the seventies, what I saw of the old Hollywood
was dying away; and the films that I saw in the late forties and throughout
the fifties [...] have the stamp of a Hollywood studio on [them]'. Yet the
'artifice' of these films, such as 'the obvious sets' that sometimes 'look
painted', presented 'a different kind of reality, a parallel universe':

> there's a codification, there's a code that occurs: the happy endings that
> weren't quite realistic, that weren't true, there was something else going
> on emotionally in these films that were very true to the human condition.
> And I tried to bring that out in *New York, New York* but place it against,
> and upon, the old template.[4]

Scorsese, then, was 'trying to come to terms with the reality that I sensed
from these movies', and 'I decided that the way to handle *New York,
New York* would be to deal with the artifice right up front, at a time in
the seventies when that sort of thing wasn't happening; that was gone'.[5]

Improvisation was key in trying to get at this particular reality.
Contrary to the impression of chaos that he suggested in earlier interviews, by 2005 Scorsese was eager to point out that the improvisations
were 'based on the script by the way—it isn't always just made up as you
get there'. As the director notes, he and De Niro had previously tried a
more restricted improvisatory approach to certain scenes in each of their

---

[3] Martin Scorsese, quoted in Anthony De Curtis, 'Martin Scorsese: The Rolling
Stone Interview', *Rolling Stone*, 1 November 1990, https://www.rollingstone.com/
movies/movie-features/martin-scorsese-the-rolling-stone-interview-192568/ [Accessed 20
May 2020].

[4] Martin Scorsese, 'Introduction' to *New York, New York*, DVD (special edition)
(California: Metro-Goldwyn-Mayer, 2005).

[5] Scorsese, ibid.

previous films together, *Mean Streets* and *Taxi Driver*. Although Scorsese recalled that *Taxi Driver* had a script with 'nothing to alter', in fact, as we saw in Chapter 4, some of its most telling scenes depended on De Niro's improvisatory skills. But as Scorsese explained in 2005,

> By the time I got to *New York, New York* I wanted [...] to push the improvisation more. The very fact, too, that you wouldn't normally feel actors behaving that way, *looking* that way, looking that way with that style, with the make-up just a little heavy, the shoulder pads on the men that were just a little bigger. The tension was a kind of naturalistic behaviour of the actors within the confines of an artificial-looking film. I wanted to put the two styles together: as I say, the artifice and truth. [...] The idea was to on the one hand embrace the artifice, in a good sense, the artifice and the beauty of the old Hollywood with room enough for a new way of looking at life, a new way of looking at emotions, a new way of examining emotions, a new way of examining lives of creative people, and putting the two together and seeing if they could stay together, or feel comfortable together in the frame.[6]

This contemporary, 'new way of examining emotions' that post-dated the acting style of the original Hollywood musicals was exactly what De Niro was committed to exploring in his preparations for the film. It can only have helped that the old studio style was exactly what he had been working on with Kazan for *The Last Tycoon* before coming to *New York, New York*, and he approaches the idea of improvisation with enthusiasm.

The logistical factors in working this way on an expensive production with elaborate sets were 'a factor in the film taking twenty-two rather than the scheduled fourteen weeks to shoot'.[7] Contemporary news reports of the turmoil surrounding the production negatively impacted both its immediate and its subsequent reception, but in retrospect the artistic success is easier to recognise. David Thomson, for example, even goes so far as to say that *New York, New York*,

> seems to me Scorsese's best film. It is a self-portrait, and a pained study of how obsession breaks all ties, of how bullishness ends alone. De Niro has never been better, because his demon and his charm have never been

---

[6] Scorsese, ibid.

[7] Leigh Grist, *The Films of Martin Scorsese, 1963–77: Authorship and Context* (New York: Palgrave Macmillan, 2013), p. 162.

harder to tell from the other. It is also the closest Scorsese has come to a real woman character, though he fell short of what I take to be the intention—to make Liza Minnelli as forceful, wilful, and selfish as De Niro.[8]

It is not at all clear that this was the intention, though, and in at least in one important respect Minnelli's Francine Evans does ultimately eclipse De Niro's Jimmy Doyle, in that—rather following the template of the classical Hollywood musical itself—the final quarter of the film is largely devoted to lengthy production numbers that showcase Francine's elevation to Hollywood superstar, a status that excludes Jimmy, who disappears from the screen during these sequences. A later cut would remove some of this material, restoring the balance between the characters if thereby fundamentally altering the meaning of the film.

There is a positive, creative tension between the talents the two lead actors brought to the project. Minnelli was in her element, having four years earlier won an Oscar for her show-stopping turn as Sally Bowles in *Cabaret* (1972), and she literally takes centre stage during her numbers, with the physically marginalised De Niro often expressing Jimmy's frustration in musically inappropriate interpolations on the sax. But De Niro was determined to bring not verisimilitude in mimicking, but an aptitude in actually performing, the saxophonist's part so that he could credibly rival Minnelli as a musical performer and thereby help to dramatise effectively the central dynamic between two creative personalities. Instead of letting the director use edited close-ups to conceal his inability to play the notes, De Niro took lessons from Georgie Auld, the veteran tenor saxophonist who in the film takes on the role of Frankie Harte, the bandleader Jimmy will displace in the course of the story. As De Niro explained, 'I wanted it to look like my horn, that it belonged to me. I didn't want to look like some schmuck up there. You can do that, you can get away with that. But what's the point?' Auld concurred: 'The kid plays a good tenor sax, and I mean it, and he learned it in three months'.[9]

If Minnelli held the upper hand over De Niro in musical ability, De Niro was on home turf in working again with Scorsese, with the two men keen to push the limits of De Niro's proficiency in improvisation, while

---

[8] David Thomson, 'The Director as Raging Bull: Why Can't a Woman Be More Like a Photograph?' *Film Comment*, Vol. 17, No. 1 (1981), p. 15.

[9] Quoted in Levy, p. 198.

she came from a very different tradition. As with the musical collaboration, however, the creative tension between the ingénue trying to go toe-to-toe with an Oscar-winning actor and seasoned improvisor proved highly productive. Scorsese begun production by shooting Minnelli's spectacular 'Happy Endings' sequence, a Hollywood-style and necessarily improvisation-free musical montage. Here Minnelli was in her element, working in the traditions of her parents, director Vincente Minnelli and actress and singer Judy Garland. Next he turned to what would be the first encounter between Jimmy and Francine at a nightclub on V-J Day. In rehearsing the dialogue '[De Niro] would throw something at her', Scorsese said, 'and she'd keep coming back. There was no stopping her'.[10] The sequence perfectly captures what the director was aiming for: the wisecracking dialogue successfully references the stylised verbal sparring of classical-era musicals and screwball comedies, while the improvisation gives De Niro's performance in particular a naturalistic feel more akin to what he and Scorsese had captured in their earlier collaborations. Scorsese came to regard this successful first attempt as unfortunate, because it made him over-confident in continuing to shoot in this fashion, but in fact it established the basis for a consistently productive dynamic between the two leads that persists throughout the film, even if, as a result, '[t]he script ballooned into a crayon box of color-coded pages written and rewritten virtually the night before each day's shoot and then altered once again on the set'.[11]

Perhaps the progressive marginalisation of the De Niro character in Scorsese's original cut is another reason why this role is less widely celebrated than those of *Taxi Driver*'s Travis Bickle, *The Deer Hunter*'s Michael Vronsky or *Raging Bull*'s Jake LaMotta. Instead of taking the lead role as in these other films, in *New York, New York* De Niro is half of a double act with Minnelli, although Jimmy's structural eclipse by Francine allows De Niro once again to explore the limits of male frustration and its propensity to erupt into extreme violence. In a climactic argument between the two characters in the claustrophobic confines of Jimmy's car, 'De Niro worked himself into such a frenzy that he wound up needing medical attention'.[12] As the actor recalled: 'I thought it would

[10] Quoted in Levy, p. 196.

[11] Levy, p. 196.

[12] Levy, p. 199.

be funny to show, out of complete rage, an insane absurdity, where you get so nutty that you become funny, hopping mad. I saw that the roof of the car was low, and I hit it with my head, then I hit it with my hand. Liza got hurt, and I think I hurt my hand'.[13]

De Niro was able to exploit his character's profession as a saxophonist to extend his emotional range and means of expression. In *The Conversation* (1973), the film Francis Ford Coppola made before working with De Niro on *The Godfather, Part II*, Coppola and lead actor Gene Hackman had already explored the potential of the solo saxophone as an instrument for externalising a character's inner confusion and frustration. But in *New York, New York*, as a saxophonist temperamentally drawn to soloing and incapable of submitting wholly to the discipline of playing as part of a big band ensemble, improvisation is ingrained within Jimmy's very character. This is the case musically, with De Niro having to express Jimmy's inability to function fully as a team player in a traditional big band, his jealous anger at any challenge to his authority as band leader, and his improvisatory skills as a soloist, including his visible relief and delight at the greater autonomy he enjoys in playing the modern jazz of the Harlem band. But this is also integrated with a kind of emotional improvisation, when for example he blows the heavily pregnant Francine off-stage after she tries to join him for a number, as their marriage collapses beyond repair.

De Niro's script annotations reveal how extensively his rapid musical training and his commitment to seeing the character from the inside has translated itself into his writing.[14] They have a different quality to those on earlier scripts. Not only is each of the films considered in this chapter about performance, De Niro's practice in annotating the text draws from the particular performance practice he has been learning. For example (perhaps as a result of learning the saxophone well enough to be able to appear to play on screen), in the very first annotation at the top of the first page he makes reference to the rhythm of his performance explicitly where he encourages himself to consider '*the rhythm of language*'—underlined twice. It is as if after the detailed parsing of Pinter's dialogue in *The Last Tycoon* under Kazan's guidance to research character and significance,

---

[13] Lawrence Grobel, '*Playboy* Interview: Robert De Niro', *Playboy*, Vol. 36, No. 1 (January 1989), p. 80.

[14] *New York, New York* (1977), Shooting script, with script revisions and RDN notes; production material laid in, Box 215 [RDN].

he is now exploring performance in a different way, thinking less about the written and its conceptual meaning, more about other elements—rhythm, affect, desire—using musical qualities to define his approach to the role, while alongside his annotations, as so often before, there is a numbered list of notes, questions and observations.

As important both for his performance in *New York, New York* and subsequently is what else his exposure to music taught him. His performance encourages him to think about musicality and rhythm in a different way, both in terms of the kinds of annotations and in a different and less verbal approach to performance itself. The annotations pick up on aspects of rhythm, and they also start to make use of visual equivalences for notations. This is a technique De Niro develops and refines, which we can call an attempt to find ways to notate affect. The more considered and cerebral methods of his process on *The Last Tycoon*, which were strongly influenced by the methods of Kazan and the Actors Studio, are replaced by a practice which put the physical performer at the heart of his interpretation.

Kathryn Millard, in her study of *Screenwriting in a Digital Era*, comments on the use of the term 'compose' across the arts, and how the word creates a common link between the visual and the musical:

> Composers invent and work with materials drawn from their own experience, and from the history of their art form. In the arts, the term emphasises the way artists interact with their materials, arranging shapes, lines, colours and textures to create meaning and visual experience. In screen media, composition refers primarily to how the director and cinematographer frame events in front of the camera, often building on aesthetic strategies drawn from painting and photography. Yet, as pens, cameras and audio recorders merge, as writing becomes a process that involves creating and combining images, sound and words, the practice of composing becomes more and more relevant to screenwriting and filmmaking.[15]

An actor has to understand the rhythmic aspects of the film, which is, like music, a time-based medium. She or he also needs to understand basic principles of composition, how they will contribute to the photographed images through which the audience will understand the story; but they

---

[15] Kathryn Millard, *Screenwriting in a Digital Era* (Basingstoke: Palgrave, 2014), p. 137.

also need to compose themselves, a process which literally incorporates the rhythmic and the visual in the actor's body.

De Niro uses a number of techniques to denote these qualities of embodied harmony or dissonance. For example, he echoes a lyrical response to the script using musical terms and scat lyrics as modes of expression: '*I'm only looking to get at you baby oh baby oh hey*'. He also starts to use precise placement of comments as a form of annotation of affect. He amends the line 'I'm from Jersey, Jersey City' by adding the word '*man*' below 'Jersey' and before 'Jersey City'. By placing the word 'man' at an uncomfortable distance from the printed dialogue it comments on it, and in omitting any drawn line or arrow connecting the missing word to its place in the sentence De Niro evokes a feeling of detachment that seems entirely appropriate to the stoned anomie of the character, so that the word 'man', drifting away from 'Jersey' and 'Jersey City', becomes a powerful visual representation of Jimmy's rootlessness.

De Niro may have been musically trained for the role by Georgie Auld, but he drew on a still more famous saxophonist in shaping the character. On his list of things to do is: '*Go to Jersey City and Hoboken and see how they talk*'. Whether or not De Niro conducted this field research, in the event New Jersey came to him, because the important role of Cecil Powell, who fronts the Harlem band that provides Jimmy with a creative outlet for his facility with musical improvisation, was played by Clarence Clemons, a member of Bruce Springsteen's E-Street Band that was based in New Jersey and was now world-famous in the aftermath of Springsteen's breakthrough 1975 album *Born to Run*.

The screenplay pages in which Jimmy shares space with Cecil Powell are among the most densely annotated in the whole script. In an extreme contrast to what De Niro was able to do on *The Last Tycoon*, but in keeping with his uncredited role as co-writer on *Taxi Driver* and, still more so, his forthcoming work on *Raging Bull*, De Niro either writes or transcribes from filmed recordings of the improvised recordings not only his own dialogue but also that of Powell/Clemons, in the most minute detail. On a single page in scene 8, for example, among dozens of deletions, substitutions and suggestions he alters (or glosses) Powell's awkward welcoming description of Jimmy as 'Mr. Hep Notation' to 'he can really blow', and completely rewrites the following exchange:

TYPESCRIPT	*DE NIRO*
CECIL POWELL Hi, my man. Where you been? JIMMY DOYLE World War II. CECIL POWELL I don't think I'd seen you around. JIMMY DOYLE Is this what's been happening? Fantastic. Never heard it like that! ... If you need a white guy –	CECIL POWELL Hey, my man. Where are the old cats? JIMMY DOYLE Man I'm them. I'm ready to start blowing. CECIL POWELL Man that shit must a been something else. JIMMY DOYLE Is this it? What's been going on? Never heard too much sound like that. If you need an ofay –

In keeping with the spirit of improvisation, many of De Niro's suggestions have a tentative quality. Jimmy's final lines in the above exchange, for example, seem to prompt the actor also to suggest multiple alternatives: '*Why wasn't I onto this*', '*What's been a-happening*'. In many places it is unclear whether a particular note indicates a proposed alteration of the line or an interpretive gloss upon it, but the overall effect is something much more colloquial, truer to the rhythms and idiom of the musicians with whom De Niro was interacting, more ready to accept the simultaneously respectful yet racially charged language of Jimmy and Cecil's interactions, than the rather stilted, grammatically precise syntax of the typescript. The scenes with Clemons remained genuinely improvisatory, with the dialogue never staying faithful either to the typescript or to the handwritten emendations, but the success of the method can be seen in the relaxed, naturalistic affect of Clemons' performance, which fully captures his expertise as a musician without ever suggesting any level of discomfort as an untrained actor.

Here De Niro is less fascinated by research into historical precedent than he was on *The Last Tycoon*. Admittedly Jimmy cannot be so clearly identified as a historical figure in the way Monroe Stahr could be with Irving Thalberg, but it seems that De Niro's focus has changed. He now appears more interested in the ideas that preoccupy a character, rather than the exploration of specific histories or physical gestures. As he observes in his numbered lists, he is asking questions or making general statements or general analyses. As Scorsese concluded in 1990, via these unique preparations 'I think we got some real good stuff out of it—and some real truth about that world and relationships between creative people'.[16] His suggestion at this date that the film could have been short-ened, with less music, is reflected in the various releases in which the concluding part of the film was alternately condensed and expanded, but Scorsese captures the essential dialogue between De Niro's improvisatory approach and the dramatic storyline in observing that 'The repetition of scenes between the couple was really more like *life*, where a scene repeats itself and repeats itself and repeats itself'.[17]

Although awed by his pupil's dedication and progress in learning the saxophone, Georgie Auld discovered that for the tutor, it had a down-side: 'He asked me ten million questions a day. It got to be a pain in the ass'.[18] This was not an unusual experience; as Susan Brady notes, while working with the actor on *The Godfather, Part II*, 'Francis Ford Coppola was reportedly shocked by all the questions De Niro kept hammering him with'.[19] De Niro's process is often through questioning, but he has good reason to need an answer. No-one is more accountable than the film actor: his or her answers are always visible; it is the actor above all, in collaboration with the director, who has to be responsible for maintaining the coherence of the character from the individual fragments of perfor-mance recorded over different days and weeks. As well as finding some kind of internal logical consistency, he or she has to find the dramatic peaks and troughs, and ensure the character assumes an understandable whole from the agglomeration of scenes often shot out of chronological order on disparate sets and locations.

Raging Bull

At the same time as De Niro was acting in *New York, New York*, he was also furthering preparations for *Raging Bull*. In an extreme contrast to *The Last Tycoon*, and perhaps in direct response to his experiences on that film, De Niro would originate and consistently reshape the idea and script for *Raging Bull* while placing the body of the actor centre stage in playing the boxer Jake LaMotta, a figure who is the polar opposite

---

[16] Quoted in De Curtis, 'Martin Scorsese'.

[17] Quoted in De Curtis, 'Martin Scorsese'.

[18] Quoted in Levy, p. 198.

[19] Susan Braudy, 'Robert De Niro—The Return of the Silent Star', *The New York Times*, 6 March 1977, https://www.nytimes.com/1977/03/06/archives/robert-de-niro-the-ret urn-of-the-silent-screen-star-robert-de-niro.html [Accessed 20 May 2020].

of the literally buttoned-up Monroe Stahr. De Niro pitched the idea for *Raging Bull* to a reluctant Scorsese in 1974, the same year as he first received Pinter's script for *The Last Tycoon*, subsequently acquiring the film rights to LaMotta's autobiography in 1976. Several different writers including Pete Savage, Mardik Martin and Paul Schrader worked from LaMotta's autobiography to develop different versions of the script, but the final version of the screenplay[20] only came together when De Niro and Scorsese retired for three weeks to the Caribbean island of St. Martin, before a script with only De Niro's initials attached was delivered early in 1979.[21] Although others, especially Schrader, undoubtedly made major contributions, De Niro had initiated the project, was at least significantly responsible for the final draft, and continued to make important hand-written revisions to the screenplay that further influenced the words and actions in the finished film. Producer Irving Winkler clearly identified De Niro as the author: 'It was Bob's film', he said. [22] De Niro's role as author is discernible throughout the various drafts, and he is always intervening as a performer, thinking about how LaMotta will play on film from the very moment that he reads the boxer's autobiography.

De Niro's annotations to his copy give an insight into the genesis and development of the project, and show him continuing his notion of the concordance, and curating the audience's understanding of the emotional state of the character.[23] What is different is that in stark contrast to the repressed, verbal, cerebral performance of *The Last Tycoon*, and after the musical improvisation underlying his role in *New York, New York*, De Niro has put the embodied self at the very heart of the film, which is dependent on De Niro's use of his own body to evoke the body of Jake LaMotta and to inspire an affective response to that body in the bodies of the audience.

LaMotta personally dedicates De Niro's copy of the book to the actor, and the inscription is perhaps as good a way as any of looking at what De Niro is attempting:

---

[20] *Raging Bull* (1980), 'Final Script,' Box 126.4 [RDN].

[21] Levy, pp. 232–233.

[22] Quoted in Richard Schickel, 'Brutal Attraction: The Making of Raging Bull', *Vanity Fair*, 22 February 2010, https://www.vanityfair.com/news/2010/03/raging-bull-201003 [Accessed 15 May 2020].

[23] *Raging Bull* (1980), Shooting script, with RDN notes, Box 229 [RDN].

To Bob De Niro
According to Pete - the only actor that could play my crazy "whackedout"
life and make it come alive again

With love
Jake LaMotta.[24]

Notably, LaMotta invites De Niro to play not his character, but his 'life'. From the very beginning De Niro is thinking in terms of image and performance, and the process of arriving at a screenplay through a process of visualising and condensing the role—of playing not the character but the life—is something that DeNiro will develop and refine over this next phase of his career.

On the very first page of his copy of LaMotta's autobiography, De Niro writes: '*Page 1 Young clean strong healthy. First image looking sharp*'. De Niro also annotates the pictures in the book. He frames a shot of LaMotta flanked by his father and brother as he leaves the Courtroom after testifying, draws a box close up around LaMotta's head to emphasise how it would appear in a close-up frame, and writes: '*Curly med hair is good and way shirt is buttoned*'.

It is possible, of course, that these notes were made closer to shooting, and that De Niro is not responding directly to the book. But the other comments on the drafts show that he is thinking visually, and always about how scenes can play and how he can play them. He is also involved in the process of assembling a concordance of the character. For example on page 68 of the Schrader version of the screenplay he is simultaneously writing down suggestions about changed lines or line readings while at the same time suggesting that other lines need to change for consistency.[25] The script offers the line: 'did you ever fuck my wife?' De Niro proposes instead: '*you know what I heard. I heard you fucked my wife*'. This has the sense of the boxer Jake LaMotta sparring with his brother Joey: it is no longer a direct question but a declarative sentence, a proposition. He also suggests that his brother's line should read '*You've gotta go in the ring in a week*' rather than 'in a month' as written, because '*if*

[24] Jake LaMotta, with Joseph Carter and Peter Savage. *Raging Bull: My Story* (1970), inscribed by LaMotta to RDN, and annotated by RDN, BV 235 [RDN].

[25] *Raging Bull* (1980), undated screenplay by Paul Schrader; with RDN notes, Box 125.3 [RDN].

it was a month I could still get my weight down or do this scene last or give me a few days to do other stuff before this whole last sequence so I can blow up'. He is continuing to think not only about how his unfitness has manifested itself but about the different materialities of performance each timespan would entail. If he were as much as a month away from going in the ring he would need to be visibly more unfit, because otherwise Joey wouldn't comment on it. He is thinking, then, not only about the relationship between the brothers and his character's mental and physical state, but also how this could be realised under the exigencies of the shooting schedule.

In the event, the filmed version opts for 'a week' and not 'a month', and although there are substantial changes between this version of the screenplay and the filmed version (De Niro as Jake LaMotta in fact says 'did you fuck my wife'), the film has a much longer moment of sparring while De Niro looks at his brother and takes a different looping approach to LaMotta's paranoid jealousy. But it is De Niro who proposes the alternative line reading, and he is also thinking about the timescale for LaMotta's training and how that is going to be integrated with his own getting into shape—or out of shape—for the character.

The shift from a more cerebral form of 'knowing' a character such as Monroe Stahr to the embodiment which De Niro undertakes in the roles of Jimmy Doyle, Jake LaMotta and Rupert Pupkin leads him to explore a very different form of performance practice, in which his use of the body is much more central. The apotheosis of this is *Raging Bull*, in which he transformed his body twice: once in order to play LaMotta the boxer and then to play the character later, aging and overweight. Much has been written about De Niro's decision to break the shooting schedule so he could put on the sixty pounds necessary to play an out of shape LaMotta. Some were critical or troubled by it: Kevin Esch quotes the adverse reactions of Pauline Kael and Andrew Sarris, two of the most prominent American film critics at the time. For Kael, 'What De Niro does in this picture isn't acting, exactly [...] I'm not sure what it is. Though it may at some level be awesome, it definitely isn't pleasurable',[26] while for Sarris

---

[26] Pauline Kael, '*Raging Bull*: Religious Pulp, or the Incredible Hulk', in *For Keeps: 30 Years at the Movies* (New York: Dutton, 1994), p. 874; quoted in Kevin Esch, '"I Don't See Any Method At All": The Problem of Actorly Transformation', *Journal of Film and Video*, Vol. 58, No. 1–2 (2006), p. 95.

De Niro outdoes Lon Chaney 'in wreaking havoc on one's metabolism for the sake of shocking and depressing [his] audience'.[27]

Esch himself examines De Niro's transformation in the contemporary context of the growing phenomenon of the bodybuilder as actor, citing the examples of Arnold Schwarzenegger and Sylvester Stallone. *Rocky* (1976) had not only launched Stallone's stardom and pipped *Taxi Driver* to win the Academy Award for Best Picture, with Stallone and De Niro both being nominated for Best Actor; it also set the template for an ongoing sub-genre of boxing movies that forms part of the context for *Raging Bull*, the release of which was sandwiched between Stallone's *Rocky II* (1979) and *Rocky III* (1982). Irwin Winkler, co-producer of the *Rocky* series, was also the producer of both *New York, New York* and *Raging Bull*. De Niro's performance as the real-life boxer Jake LaMotta is therefore intimately bound up with Stallone's as the fictional Rocky Balboa, but the very names of the characters in the films (Rocky's opponent is 'Apollo Creed') help to demonstrate that the apparent similarity masks a fundamental difference. 'Actorly transformation' aims at 'greater fidelity of performance', in Esch's words,[28] and De Niro's punishing dedication quite literally embodies such notions of fidelity and authenticity by effacing the actor in the process of attempting physically and in every other way to become LaMotta, to enact his 'life' and not his 'character'. By contrast, the body-building of Schwarzenegger and Stallone within action movies has the quite different aim of presenting the performer's physique as 'a site of spectacle within the bombast of the film':

> since action cinema has been the primary domain where actors have dramatized their bodies in this way, these transformations are not discussed in 'actorly' terms—as signs of dedication to the craft of acting. Instead, these performances and films have been viewed symptomatically, as examples of Reaganite ideology or reactions to undermined masculinity in a postindustrial economy.[29]

Esch also points out that, following De Niro's performance in *Raging Bull*, weight gain and loss became increasingly common as a technique in

---

[27] Andrew Sarris, 'Mean Fighter from Mean Streets', *Village Voice*, 19 November 1980, p. 55; quoted in Esch, p. 95.

[28] Esch, p. 96.

[29] Esch, p. 97.

Hollywood acting, with 'Twenty-seven actors [being] nominated for or received Oscars in leading or supporting roles that advertised weight gain or loss or other bodily transformation' between 1980 and 2004.[30]

Esch sees De Niro's performance in *Raging Bull* as exemplifying a 'new turn in Method acting', and cites several professionals who take a contrary view regarding the need for the actor to go to such lengths to achieve this kind of authenticity. Most famously, Laurence Olivier responded to Dustin Hoffman's decision to deprive himself of sleep in preparation for playing the insomnia-plagued character Babe in *Marathon Man* (1976) by languidly suggesting, 'Why don't you try acting, dear boy?' Similarly, actor and teacher Lindsay Crouse tells her students, 'you're either an actor or you're not [...] For the most part, going to that extreme is bull, that's someone who is not an actor. You don't have to cut your leg off at the hip to play a paraplegic'.[31] And to give one final example, Eli Wallach, who was a founding member of the Actors Studio yet seems less prepared to dismiss De Niro's kind of work as being that of someone who is 'not an actor', nonetheless draws essentially the same distinction:

> One does it literally, the other imagines, and I fit into the latter group, the imagining-what-it's-like. I've just been reading about De Niro, who's a wonderful actor, but he's been playing this catatonic [*Awakenings*, 1990], spending three months in this hospital and two months in that one. And that's where all the hype and the publicity is.[32]

All of these actors, especially Olivier and Crouse, express two major reservations about the kind of work that De Niro performs. First, they see an explicit contrast between acting and not-acting, with De Niro falling on the wrong side of that line. Second, and only slightly more sympathetically, there is a tendency to think of De Niro's practice as a kind of obsession, and that there is a correct amount of performance that an actor should do. As Esch puts it in summarising Wallach's position: 'De Niro seems to stand for something larger: a tendency toward overvaluing performances of physically or psychologically damaged or

---

[30] Esch, p. 98.

[31] Quoted in Esch, p. 97.

[32] Esch, pp. 97–98.

otherwise marginal characters, in large part due to the demands of physical fidelity undertaken by the actor for the role'.[33]

Yet we can see De Niro's physical transformation differently: in terms not of simulation or fidelity, but of *embodiment*. De Niro's fascination with LaMotta's story is a fascination with the extremes of performance. To understand and perform the role of LaMotta De Niro needs to understand what it means to inhabit the world from the body of a boxer, trained to react violently and to withstand enormous amounts of pain. As an actor, like a boxer, he has to rely on his own body—both as the location of the conflicting desires and passions of the character, and as the means by which these are expressed and communicated on film. Indeed, his injunction on the first page of the shooting script is to '*[a]lways think of ways to express self thru [sic] body*'.[34] It was through training with LaMotta, and apparently enduring around a thousand boxing bouts, that De Niro reached an embodied understanding of what it means to go through life fighting for a living.

A professional athlete's relationship with his or her body is very different from that relationship for an ordinary member of the public; and, probably more than any other performer, a boxer uses their body as their instrument. Both athlete and actor are linked by the word 'performance', of which the multiple definitions in the *Oxford English Dictionary* include the following: 'The accomplishment or carrying out of something commanded or undertaken; the doing of an action or operation'; 'The quality of execution of such an action, operation, or process; the competence or effectiveness of a person or thing in performing an action; *spec.* the capabilities, productivity, or success of a machine, product, or person when measured against a standard' and, specifically, 'The action of performing a play, piece of music, ceremony, etc.'.

The most extreme form of performance assessment must be that of a boxer, which is in part determined on whether they have hit their opponent more often and more effectively than they have been hit. In taking on the role of a boxer De Niro has to rely on his body both to undergo the extremes that are the essence of the profession, and to make it sufficiently boxer-like to convince the audience. But he also has to understand what it means to inhabit the world in a boxer's body; and, perhaps as

---

[33] Esch, p. 98.

[34] *Raging Bull* (1980), Box 229 [RDN].

important, what it means to be the same person, yet to have lost that body. De Niro's weight gain has been seen as an indicator of extreme commitment and at the same time as somehow a gimmick or a fad, as indicated by Kael's review and in Wallach's dismissal of De Niro's preparations as 'hype'. David Thomson describes De Niro's weight gain in preparation for playing the older LaMotta as 'much touted and very disturbing'.[35] But if it is disturbing for the audience to see that transformation, how much more disturbing must that transformation have been for the character, for the real LaMotta—from inhabiting a body that won him a World Championship performance to one that is capable of any kind of performance at all.

Nowhere is this contrast brought home more strongly than in the concluding scene, which returns us to the dressing room with which the film commenced. That opening sequence began with an establishing shot of an advertising poster outside a New York theatre in 1964, announcing 'An Evening with Jake LaMotta'; a cut to the bottom the hoarding states the time of the performance, before another cut transitions to the dressing room where the aging LaMotta rehearses his nightclub routine. The establishing shot of the theatre at the end of the film, however, omits the cut and instead pans down to show the whole of the hoarding: now we see that the 'Evening with Jake LaMotta' will feature 'the works of Paddy Chayefsky, Rod Serling, Shakespeare, Budd Schulberg [and] Tennessee Williams'.

At first it seems an incongruous list. In the opening scene we watched LaMotta rehearse a less literary, comic stand-up act: 'That's Entertainment!', as he announces in the sound bridge that takes us from 1964 to the punishing bout with Jimmy Reeves in 1941. The unedited establishing shot before the final scene has something of the quality of a stand-up's 'call-back' gag—the payoff punchline to what the audience only now recognises as a set-up earlier in the film. While the first scene appears to show LaMotta struggling to remember a series of gags and personal anecdotes, the last reveals these to be merely one element of an evening that will show LaMotta trying to recall and perform not just his own words, but famous speeches scripted by others, Shakespeare

---

[35] Thomson, p. 12.

appearing to fit oddly within an inventory of otherwise exclusively American writers who were in their heyday in the 1950s, as LaMotta's boxing career was coming to an end.

What connects at least four of these writers, however, is an association with Marlon Brando, whose stage and screen breakthroughs came in productions of Williams' *A Streetcar Named Desire*. Brando was nominated for an Academy Award for *Julius Caesar* in 1953, and received the award for his performance as Terry Malloy in the following year's *On the Waterfront*, which was written by Schulberg. Serling, meanwhile, was an uncredited writer on *One-Eyed Jacks* (1961), the only film directed by Brando, who also starred. Chayefsky's connection is more tangential, although he also worked closely with Elia Kazan and his first broadcast script was a teleplay of Schulberg's *What Makes Sammy Run?* In any case, the camera pauses as it pans down the list of writers, first holding Chayefsky and Serling in the frame and then, as it moves down, cutting them out so that only Shakespeare, Schulberg and Williams—the three most obviously connected to Brando—are visible, before Scorsese cuts to the dressing room.

The immediate effect of this establishing shot prior to the final scene of *Raging Bull*, then, is to connect physical and vocal performance and improvisation to written scripts; and then, as the scene unfolds, to connect De Niro/LaMotta to Brando. The decision by Scorsese and De Niro to have LaMotta render a slightly scrambled rendition of Terry Malloy's 'I could have been a contender' speech, which was originally delivered by Brando just after Terry's brother Charlie has reminded him that he is now too overweight to box competitively, sees Robert De Niro playing Jake LaMotta playing Marlon Brando playing Terry Malloy in *On the Waterfront*—who, arguably, is momentarily playing LaMotta, since the source of Terry's anguish in this 1954 movie is 'that night in the Garden' when Charlie told Terry he had to throw a fight, just as LaMotta had come under immediate suspicion of doing in his 1947 Madison Square Garden bout against Billy Fox (as both LaMotta's autobiography and *Raging Bull* confirm). This final scene of *Raging Bull*, then, opens up a dizzying series of intertextual connections, at the heart of which lies confirmation that a central aspect of the film is a meditation on performance.

De Niro had already, in a sense, played the young Brando in *The Godfather, Part II*. This further intertextual connection between the two men prompts the recognition that the visible differences between the younger and the older Brando, the younger and the older Vito Corleone and the younger and the older Jake LaMotta are most strikingly expressed in weight gain—the aspect of De Niro's performance in *Raging Bull* that attracted the most immediate attention. De Niro's embodiment of the overweight LaMotta thereby forms a direct reference to Brando, who had already been linked to De Niro as his predecessor in both the acting pantheon generally and in *The Godfather* films specifically. As Shawn Levy notes, in *Raging Bull* 'for the second time in a half dozen years, De Niro will literally repeat dialogue first spoken by Brando in an Oscar-winning role in an Oscar-winning role of his own'.[36]

The role of Terry Malloy, meanwhile, refers in multiple ways to F. Scott Fitzgerald's *The Last Tycoon*, in which De Niro would perform in what was to be Elia Kazan's last movie. *On the Waterfront* is often seen as Kazan's greatest and most personal film, in which he justifies his naming names of fellow-Communists to the House Un-American Activities Committee. As noted, it was written by Budd Schulberg, who was identified by Fitzgerald as the co-inspiration of the character of Cecilia in *The Last Tycoon*,[37] and Schulberg's Hollywood novel *What Makes Sammy Run?* was based on the life of his father, Hollywood producer B. P. Schulberg, just as *The Last Tycoon* was based on the life of another producer, Irving Thalberg.

So in choosing in *Raging Bull* to perform a speech directed by Kazan, written by Schulberg and realised by Brando, De Niro is making a statement about performance. As the film ends with De Niro alone in a dressing room, trying to remember his lines in front of a mirror like the one where he famously improvised the most famous lines of Travis Bickle in *Taxi Driver*, he is asserting his own agency and corporeality as an actor. Just before he goes out to perform, he tells himself: 'Go get 'em, champ', and then his body erupts into a physicality far more expressive than his deliberately flat, and slightly hesitant and garbled, readings of Schulberg's lines.

In the screenplay this speech lacks the contextualisation that De Niro as LaMotta offers in the finished film, in which he explicitly names both the actor and the film he is quoting from: 'Some people aren't that lucky, like the one that Marlon Brando played in *On the Waterfront*.

---

[36] Levy, p. 247.

[37] Matthew J. Bruccoli, 'Introduction' to F. Scott Fitzgerald, *The Love of the Last Tycoon: A Western*, ed. Matthew J. Bruccoli (Cambridge: Cambridge University Press, 1993), p. xxvii.

An up-and-comer who's now a down-and-outer. Do you remember that scene in the back of the car with his brother Charlie, a small-time racket guy and it went something like this ...' True to the improvisatory spirit that animates De Niro's approach to scripting the film, Malloy's speech is *something* like, but not exactly the same as, LaMotta's rendition. A comparison of the two performances reveals additional dialogue delivered in the finished film by De Niro as LaMotta that does not feature in Brando's original performance. These additional lines are written word for word in De Niro's hand in the screenplay: '*I was never no good after that night Charlie*' in the right-hand margin, and '*It was like a peak you reach and then it's downhill. It was you Charlie*' in the left. The two pieces are linked to each other with one great swooping arrow from right to left, while another from the bottom of the page connects them to the point in the text they should appear, after the words 'a one way ticket to Palookaville'. There is, perhaps, another kind of performance being enacted on the page: we might read these two additions as a right hook and a left-handed uppercut.

The effect of De Niro's amendments to the final speech is to make it more apposite to LaMotta's situation, and to underline that LaMotta is accusing not just his own brother but also himself, because unlike Brando in *On the Waterfront*, De Niro does not speak these lines to another actor playing his brother: in *Raging Bull* the words are spoken to himself in the mirror, echoing his lines to himself in *Taxi Driver*. The performance shows a point where the character appears also to lose it, to forget his lines before miraculously regaining his place by the skin of his teeth, just as De Niro himself miraculously regains the sympathy of the audience for LaMotta by his reminder here that what we have encountered is performance, with the film at its conclusion explicitly referring to its own status as fiction.

In a magnificent coda, not present in the screenplay, De Niro's physicality reasserts itself. After his halting speech is over and he has been addressed by an off-camera stagehand (played by Scorsese), he bends down to the mirror to quietly intone 'go get 'em champ' before punching at air, at an imaginary opponent. Firstly, a hesitant one-two is followed by a flurry of punches, and he speaks the mantra 'I'm the Boss, I'm the Boss, I'm the Boss, I'm the Boss, I'm the Boss', before finally repeating the energetic flurry of punches and the accompanying grunts. It is a reminder of his identity as a boxer, but it also serves to unite the fat, aging LaMotta to the younger man in tip-top shape, and to remind us that De Niro has managed to become both of them. This final shot perfectly captures the embodiment of the real boxer LaMotta in the shape of the real actor De Niro: the older LaMotta was once the younger, and the actor made himself big enough to inhabit them both.

There is also an intensely physical quality to the scene in a second sense. De Niro/LaMotta first punches the air as he faces the mirror directly; he then wanders off-screen left, returns, and is seen punching the air towards screen right. He then disappears to the left again and is heard grunting and punching once more—we are presumably to imagine that now he is punching towards the left. With memories of the brutality of the film's fight scenes freshly revived, subliminally the audience is surely fearful that now LaMotta will come back into shot and start punching in the only direction he has left—at the camera; at *us*. The whole scene is a startling reminder that film spectatorship involves more than simply watching. Vivian Sobchack has written about the 'cinesthetic subject', who

> both touches and is touched by the screen—able to commute seeing to touching and back again *without a thought* and, through sensual and cross-modal activity, able to experience the movie as both here and there rather than clearly locating the site of cinematic experience as onscreen or offscreen. As a lived body and a film viewer, the cinesthetic subject subverts the prevalent objectification of vision that would reduce sensorial experience at the movies to an impoverished "cinematic sight" [.][38]

If the audience experiences the film as an embodied and sensory experience, this is still more true for the actor. It is the actor's body, after all, exists in three dimensions, which has to travel both within the space of the frame and the duration of the film, and above all which has to inspire and carry those sensations in the audience. But it is also surely true that De Niro's performance in *Raging Bull* aims to create something more than an experience that is simply seen or heard; along with the sound mix and editing it also generates a visceral response to the events while also engaging with the visibly 'lived', aged and fattened, body De Niro presents on screen. It is through both those bodies that we experience what it was like to be LaMotta.

---

[38] Vivian Sobchack, *Carnal Thoughts: Embodiment and Moving Image Culture* (Berkeley: University of California Press, 2004), p. 71; emphasis in the original.

For Sobchack, the sensual experience of watching a film can be in some ways more intense than the sensation of the thing in real life:

> Certainly, this feeling and the sense I have of sensing at the movies is in some ways *reduced* in comparison with direct sensual experience—this because of my only partially fulfilled sensual grasp of my cinematic object of desire. But just as certainly, in other ways, the sense I have of sensing when I watch a film is also *enhanced* in comparison with much direct sensual experience—this because my only partially fulfilled sensual grasp of the original cinematic object is completed not in the realization of that object but through my own body, where my sensual grasp is reflexively doubled since, in this rebound from the screen, I have become not only the toucher but also the touched.[39]

We could add that the objects have been moved into a symbolic and metaphorical world where their sensations are stronger because of their attached meanings; and perhaps the more powerful the sensations are in the lived body of the spectator, the better we may consider the film—or the performance. This perhaps is De Niro's genius. If we accept Sobchack's thesis that there is a powerful connection of sensation between the audience and the subject, then the role of the actor is crucial in enabling us to feel what their character is feeling—and the only instrument they have is their body.

In *Raging Bull* De Niro's process from the inception has been to find those moments of corporeal affect in LaMotta's autobiography; to distil them, working in collaboration with the screenwriters, Scorsese and LaMotta himself; and to make them part of his own body. This process is simultaneously intensely physical and intensely cerebral: De Niro's impassioned improvisations show his ability both to comprehend a character and to bring them to physical expression, while his annotations on LaMotta's autobiography show how he is always imagining he character not only in terms of good dramatic scenes but in terms of bodily presence. Consequently, although the annotations and improvisations reveal many different facets to De Niro's understanding of the character, ultimately these can only be expressed in the ways in which he physically personifies the figure of LaMotta. The achievement is that, far from being a mere gimmick, 'bull' or 'hype', the embodiment challenges the commonplace

---

[39] Sobchack, p. 77; emphasis in the original.

distinctions between acting and not-acting raised earlier in our discussion of this film. Sobchak notes something similar in relation to fiction and nonfiction films:

> it is relatively rare when *distinctions between fiction and documentary are purposefully and "really" confused* in the film object itself and the two representational forms so complexly interwoven that they confound the spectator's capacity to discriminate precisely between them, resulting in a rich, if unsettling, epistemological ambiguity.[40]

It is perhaps precisely this ambiguity that can lead spectators such as David Thomson to experience De Niro's performance as 'very disturbing', since it enacts a troubling state somewhere between the representational and the real.

The actor Simon Russell Beale has similarly written about the potential desirability of such states of confusion and ambiguity:

> The mind of the actor has to be open, relaxed and receptive; and by that I mean receptive not only to the idea of ill-defined states of mind, but also to the possibility that no decision is final, that details, certainly, but fundamental components, too, can change in performance. [...] [A]nything that we say or think about our acting is just a blueprint for live performance, which is by its nature unpredictable. The decisions that an actor may make can be very wrong, of course, but nothing he or she does is ever absolutely right or correct or the whole answer.[41]

Russell Beale is talking about performing Shakespeare on stage rather than acting for the screen, but both are dependent on embodiment: ideas expressed through performance. The difference is that for the film actor the iterations are not over a period of time but in the different takes. As Scorsese recalls:

> Bobby and I explored all the different ways of delivering the lines, and we did at least twenty takes. The most interesting one, the one we kept, is the simplest, the least expressive. A plain voice, that's all. Bobby would

---

[40] Sobchack, p. 265; emphasis in the original.

[41] Simon Russell Beale, 'Without Memory or Desire: Acting Shakespeare', Ernest Jones Lecture organised by the Scientific Committee of the British Psychoanalytical Society, 21 June 2009. The British Psychoanalytical Society Archives, London, UK.

<u>like to have used three different takes, one after the other, but the most</u>
<u>monotone was the best. [...] I find it all the more touching if the face or</u>
<u>the voice betrays no emotion.</u>[42]

Sobchack observes that skin is an immensely important organ of sensation, and several different kinds of skin are being written and acted upon in *Raging Bull*. De Niro's skin becomes a proxy for this metaphorical skin of the audience. In Anne Rutherford's words, 'Cinema is not only about telling a story; it's about creating an affect, an event, a moment which lodges itself under the skin of the spectator'.[43] As Russell Beale remarks in quoting director Roger Michell, 'When you have to deliver a soliloquy, always cast the audience in a role'.[44]

Second, De Niro's skin is the organ on which his own suffering is inscribed; it is exposed and beaten. The audience can read the marks on the skin, but they are dependent on the skill of the writer, director and actor to enable them to detect the emotional pain that lies beneath it. As De Niro comments on an early draft of the screenplay, '*Reference to emotional pain rather than physical and how physical is much easier to take*'.[45] The marks of the physical pain are visible, but the emotional pain happens elsewhere.

And, finally, we can see the screenplay itself as a kind of skin, with De Niro's hand leaving annotations as marks upon it, just as the boxer's hand leaves marks upon the opponent. We have previously suggested that the two comments on the 'contender' speech, one in each margin connected together by a swinging arrow, resembles a one-two boxing combination. But more generally, despite the numerous iterations through which it had already passed, the script that De Niro is working on is still sketchy at this point, openly asking for completion: '*Then Jake talks about "Jealousy" he quotes from Othello. (this part of the routine to be researched.)*' Screenwriter Mardik Martin writes in a note that De Niro kept in his file: 'Most

---

[42] Michael Henry Wilson, *Scorsese on Scorsese* (Cahiers du Cinéma) (Paris: Phaidon Press, 2011), p. 107.

[43] Anne Rutherford, 'Cinema and Embodied Affect', *Senses of Cinema*, 25 March 2003, http://sensesofcinema.com/2003/feature-articles/embodied_affect/ [Accessed 15 August 2019].

[44] Russell Beale, 'Without Memory or Desire'.

[45] *Raging Bull* (1980), untitled, undated, rough first draft in three acts; typescript with notes by RDN and Mardik Martin, Box 124.6 [RDN].

scenes are still basically unrefined, especially the last third of the script where the discussion ended at our last meeting'.[46] De Niro's approach to such refinement is not via the usual screenwriter's method of marks on the script, the type- and hand-written alterations that will be effectively erased once the new version has been professionally typecast into another completed draft for circulation to the production team. Instead, his hand-written changes remain as visible marks on the unique script from which he himself will work.

THE KING OF COMEDY

The final film in this performance trilogy is *The King of Comedy* (1982), in which De Niro plays would-be comedian Rupert Pupkin. Along with his fellow deranged celebrity-stalker, Masha (Sandra Bernhardt), Pupkin hatches a desperate plan to kidnap their idol Jerry Langford (Jerry Lewis) to force the network to allow Pupkin to deliver his stand-up routine on Langford's show. The film emerged directly from De Niro and Scorsese's collaboration on *Raging Bull*. De Niro's interest in both projects went back to 1974, the year in which his attention had been caught by an unpublished novel by Paul Zimmerman, in which the Pupkin character already combines the roles of obsessive autograph hunter, would-be comedian and television celebrity. As with *Raging Bull*, too, *The King of Comedy* was essentially De Niro's film, Scorsese confirming that 'it was more Bob's project than mine'.[47]

As the director tells it, De Niro had originally intended that the film would be directed by Michael Cimino, with whom he had worked on *The Deer Hunter* (1978), but this plan fell by the wayside when Cimino decided instead to direct *Heaven's Gate*. By this point Scorsese and De Niro were 'working on Jake La Motta's speeches in *Raging Bull* and we were having fun like two crazy kids. In that mood of euphoria and mutual understanding, Bobby suddenly asked me to reread Zimmerman's script. This time I understood it. The characters began to come to life'.[48] De Niro actively drove the writing, working from the novel and two previous

---

[46] Mardik Martin, ibid.

[47] Quoted in Levy, p. 278.

[48] Quoted in Wilson, p. 114.

screenplay adaptations of it to create a new iteration with Scorsese for which, yet again, neither man chose to take credit.

De Niro's script annotations for *The King of Comedy* reveal different attempts to explore performance: '*Try different ways, this line. Calm, suspicious, calm, suspicious*'.[49] And the film was, again, a radical departure, with a tone that is deliberately uncomfortable, in many ways. At several moments it is uncertain whether or not an event is 'really' happening or is instead a projection of Pupkin's imagination, which straddles the borderline between reality and fantasy. Sometimes the distinction is clear: when, in an early sequence in a restaurant, Langford asks Pupkin to stand in for him on the show, the audience immediately recognises this as imaginary because the restaurant shots are intercut with others of Pupkin acting out the same dialogue and events in his basement. But as the film proceeds the basement comes more and more to represent not just the confines of his domestic world but the expansion of his delusional creativity, leaving us uncertain, for example, whether or not Pupkin's mother, with whom he apparently lives and who is heard but never seen, is wholly, partially or not at all a figment of his imagination. The lines are blurred further because she is played by Catherine Scorsese, the director's mother.

Pupkin's imagination, of course, is dependent on De Niro's. At the beginning of the film De Niro is drawing on his own experience of being the target of fans and autograph hunters like Pupkin:

[handwritten margin note: → do terrifying things to prep for self film]

> He was fascinated most of all by the Rupert Pupkins he had to deal with every day, the intrusive people who relentlessly pursue him. [...] On *The King of Comedy* Bobby had developed a technique: role reversal! He would set about chasing autograph-hunters, stalking them, terrifying them by asking them tons of questions.[50]

There is a wittily metafictional dimension to this, as when De Niro's Pupkin rehearses his routines in his mocked-up basement studio, where he projects himself as a chat show star flanked by cut-outs of Liza Minnelli, De Niro's co-star in *New York, New York*, on one side, and of Jerry Lewis as Jerry Langford on the other. When, at the climax of the film, Pupkin finally performs his stand-up routine on the show, the question is not only whether or not the performance is 'funny', but also whether or

[49] *The King of Comedy* (1983), Undated script, with RDN notes, Box 235.2 [RDN].

[50] Scorsese in *Scorsese on Scorsese*, pp. 114–115.

not Robert De Niro—the famously serious actor who had not previously performed a major role in a film comedy and is an often reluctant and sometimes awkward interviewee—is actually being funny too. This uncertainty was part of the planning for the film from the outset. As Scorsese recalls:

> During the second week of the shoot, I told Bobby, 'What I really liked the first time I read the *The King of Comedy* was the monologue'. It was neither good nor bad; you couldn't draw any conclusions about Rupert's possible talent. It was a brilliant idea. Bobby replied, 'That's exactly what you said when you gave me the script.'[51]

Pupkin remains inscrutable, and his talent is irrelevant; what matters is his performance, and this structural ambivalence about how the audience is to read the performances of both Rupert Pupkin and Robert De Niro is central to the film's affect. As the British comedian and game show host Bob Monkhouse used to joke, 'they all laughed when I said I was going to be a comedian. They're not laughing now'.[52]

Finally getting his chance to appear on television, Pupkin gives a seven-minute performance that is the culmination of his ambition, very unlike the faded boxer Jake LaMotta's hesitant backstage rehearsal for the stand-up routine that forms a comment on his decline at the end of *Raging Bull*. Yet although we are to imagine that Pupkin performs in front of the Langford show's audience, there is a problem: just as with Pupkin's mother, we hear, but do not see, the spectators. Instead we see Pupkin watching his own performance afterwards on a television screen in a bar, in another attempt to impress Rita Keene, the barmaid who is the object of his unrequited love. As in *Raging Bull*, then, the recognition that the figure performing the monologue is both De Niro and/or Pupkin prompts questions of interpretation that are inextricable from the multiple audiences that perceive the performance: the spectator of *The King of Comedy*; the audience in the Langford studio; Langford, who after escaping from Masha sees Pupkin's routine replayed on multiple screens in the window of a television showroom; Rita, who is played by

---

[51] Ibid., p. 114.

[52] Bob Monkhouse, 'They're Not Laughing Now...', *The Guardian*, 29 December 2003, https://www.theguardian.com/uk/2003/dec/29/arts.artsnews1 [Accessed 30 May 2020].

Diahnne Abbott, to whom De Niro was married at the time; and Pupkin himself.

Yet as with *Raging Bull*, too, the giddying layers of this metacinematic representation of a performance co-exists with the recognition that the monologue itself forms a climactically painful moment of self-revelation for the character. Everything Pupkin says, about his parents wanting to return him as defective, his alcoholic mother, his father beating him in the stomach, or being hit so often at school that kids got extra credit for it, is extraordinarily painful, until he finally segues into another form of truth by joking that Lewis is tied up at the moment—'and I'm the one who tied him. I know you think I'm joking but believe me that's the only way I could break into showbusiness'. It is another performance of pain. The pain on the inside that De Niro mentions in his annotation in *Raging Bull* is delivered in *The King of Comedy* with a smile, but it is no less horrifying—indeed, as it comes from the lightweight figure of Pupkin who is, like LaMotta, victoriously performing through his anguish, it is in some ways more disturbing.

If *Raging Bull* is about the actor's embodied presence, *The King of Comedy* is also about the actor's aura, the set of expectations that surround them, and the ways in which they make themselves impenetrable. In *Raging Bull* the body and its fragility are visible: the vulnerable half-naked image of LaMotta in the ring is the location of his pain and the means by which he inflicts pain on others, and there is a limit to the amount of protection the body can offer. In *The King of Comedy*, by contrast, we only see Pupkin's constructed self; his costume and hair are the invisible armour of celebrity, which makes him untouchable.

De Niro's previous process of conducting research to inhabit the character becomes a metaphor: like Rupert Pupkin, the stalker of celebrities, he researches the character he wishes to become, tracks him down, and then replaces him on screen. As De Niro comments in one of his annotations on the scene where Pupkin and Rita turn up at Langford's mansion, '*One more thing (of course) is that I know practically everything that one could know from the outside about Jerry's life*'. One can see Pupkin's stalking of Langford as a dramatisation of De Niro's process on *The Last Tycoon*: that somehow study alone can teach you what you need to become the character. To perform his own character of Pupkin, however, he needs to do something more radical. De Niro's transformation from the dutiful performer of *The Last Tycoon*, who was realising a character whose parameters were determined by others, has become transformed into a full role in co-creating the film text, in collaboration with the script, the other performers, and the director.

Central to this is the dynamic between De Niro, Lewis and Bernhardt. Lewis was a live performer and television star, who as Langford was playing a version of his own persona, one that had come into being in interacting with others, initially on stage as part of a double act with Dean Martin. Ironically Lewis, the ultimate showbiz figure, was in some ways the most avant-garde of all the performers De Niro had worked with to this point, with improvisation being just as much at the heart of his process as it was as that of, say, John Cassavetes. In 2013 Lewis remarked of his experiences on *The King of Comedy*:

> When you get a script, you see openings where you can do specific things. That's what happened; we found wonderful places where Bobby and I could be from the top of our heads. The entire scene in my home, there was nothing rehearsed. When I come back with the golf club, all of that was ad-libbed, the whole seven or nine minutes.[53]

Lewis, then, was used to collaboration and improvisation, albeit of different kinds to those that had previously been developed by Scorsese and De Niro, and Scorsese recalls that 'It was a remarkable and moving experience to watch him at work, improvising with Bob De Niro and the other actors'.[54]

Lewis also brought with him something of the impermeability of the star persona, and as well as being a film and stage actor of long standing he was also a successful television director; indeed, Scorsese notes that Lewis 'knew his way around live television so well that I asked him to direct some of the actual on-air sequences for The Jerry Langford Show'. Nevertheless, the proximity of Jerry Langford to Lewis himself presented the actor with its own challenges:

[53] Scott Macaulay, 'Scorsese, De Niro, Lewis and Bernhard Recall *The King of Comedy*', *Filmmaker*, 1 May 2013, https://filmmakermagazine.com/69894-scorsese-de-niro-lewis-and-bernhard-recall-king-of-comedy/#.XtPISlB7mYV [Accessed 31 May 2020].

[54] Martin Scorsese, 'Martin Scorsese on Jerry Lewis: "It Was Like Watching a Virtuoso Pianist at the Keyboard"', *The Guardian*, 1 September 2017, https://www.theguardian.com/film/2017/sep/01/jerry-lewis-martin-scorsese-king-comedy-nutty-professor [Accessed 31 May 2020].

Jerry Langford was an uncomfortable role for him to play, because he was skirting the edges of his own life in absolutely every scene. Sometimes it went beyond that: he was wearing his own clothes, he was playing scenes where he was often expressing his own feelings about showbusiness and celebrity, and at times you didn't know if you were seeing Jerry Langford or Jerry Lewis.[55]

Similarly, Bernhardt recalls that 'Masha was very close to the character I was at that time, in terms of, like, my craziness and my ability to just kind of take it all the way out there. It just dovetailed perfectly with the role'.[56]

If Lewis represented the past of comedy performance, Bernhard represented the future; and between them is De Niro. When their two energies meet, as Bernhard/Masha ties up the kidnapped Lewis/Langford, De Niro's Pupkin is steering an apparently calm and controlled route between their two personae, as can be seen in De Niro's screenplay notes on the speech in which he explains to Langford why he has had no choice but to kidnap him ('Why didn't you just listen to the tape when I asked you? [...] A few minutes of your time to listen to something I'd worked on my whole life?'). The annotations show how De Niro navigates a path through this tragicomic dynamic of the moment: on the one hand, '*Really Sincere in this. Only way this works*', but on the other, '*Remember whole attitude is colored by it being a fake gun*'. Opposite the second half of the speech he adds a regretful comment directed at Langford: '*it hurt me as much as it hurt you*'. When Langford proposes in response that he and Pupkin go over to his office right away, De Niro continues this tone of baffled hurt: '*If I don't believe him I just carry on and say "I don't know if I believe you Jerry" and keep on until I make him convince him*' (sic). Further down the page he adds, '*This is so interesting cause it's calm. I'm just laying it out to him*'. De Niro uses the focused clarity of his written lines to contrast to both the wilder energy of Lewis's improvisation and Bernhard's performance of self. His character is an absence of self, defined by his ambition for his career.

[55] Scorsese, 'Martin Scorsese on Jerry Lewis'.

[56] Keith Phipps, 'Sandra Bernhardt Remembers *The King of Comedy*', *The Dissolve*, 30 January 2014, https://thedissolve.com/features/movie-of-the-week/389-sandra-bernhard-remembers-the-king-of-comedy/ [Accessed 31 May 2020].

Among the papers is an advertisement from 'Contemporary Comedy, a company that provides jokes for chat show hosts',[57] which insists:

> To be consistently funny everyone needs help. Even the superjocks.
> That's the kind of help I'm offering you. Consistently funny material to get you to the top or to stay there. The very same material the superjocks use.

It is not clear whether this document, which has a phone number scrawled on it in ballpoint, has been kept because De Niro used the company, because he thought it would seem consistent with his other practical research for *New York, New York, Raging Bull* or *Taxi Driver*, or because it represents a tone and attitude to the world that seems to sum up Rupert Pupkin, determined to get to the top or to stay there. For a character like this, content and meaning are subordinate to ambition. It is the same unshakeable attitude which has motivated Pupkin throughout the film, and whatever provoked the decision to leave this advert in the archive, it belongs as a testimony both to the thoroughness of De Niro's process and to the various ways he build a character:

> I'm confident Contemporary Comedy will help you!
> So confident in fact, I guarantee it!

Pupkin is a salesman: irrepressible, impermeable and ultimately irresistible, because there is nothing he will not do to get what he wants. And that perhaps is why his character has become so much more influential since the film was made.

BIBLIOGRAPHY

ABBREVIATION

RDN: Robert De Niro Papers, Harry Ransom Center, University of Texas at Austin.

---

[57] *The King of Comedy* (1983), Box 235.2 [RDN]; *The King of Comedy* (1983), Production materials (Character and script notes, list of scenes, lyrics for 'Come Rain or Come Shine', and script fragments), Box 88.1 [RDN].

PRIMARY

The King of Comedy (1983), Production materials (Character and script notes, list of scenes, lyrics for 'Come Rain or Come Shine', and script fragments), Box 88.1, RDN.

The King of Comedy (1983), Undated script, with RDN notes, Box 235.2, RDN.

New York, New York (1977), Shooting script, with script revisions and RDN notes; production material laid in, Box 215, RDN.

Raging Bull: My Story (1970), LaMotta, Jake, with Joseph Carter and Peter Savage. inscribed by LaMotta to RDN, and annotated by RDN, BV 235, RDN.

Raging Bull (1980), 'Final Script,' Box 126.4, RDN.

Raging Bull (1980), Shooting script, with RDN notes, Box 229, RDN.

Raging Bull (1980), undated screenplay by Paul Schrader; with RDN notes, Box 125.3, RDN.

Raging Bull (1980), untitled, undated, rough first draft in three acts; typescript with notes by RDN and Mardik Martin, Box 124.6, RDN.

SECONDARY

Beale, Simon Russell. 'Without Memory or Desire: Acting Shakespeare', Ernest Jones Lecture organised by the Scientific Committee of the British Psychoanalytical Society, 21 June 2009. The British Psychoanalytical Society Archives, London, UK.

Braudy, Susan. 'Robert De Niro—The Return of the Silent Star', *The New York Times*, 6 March 1977, https://www.nytimes.com/1977/03/06/arc hives/robert-de-niro-the-return-of-the-silent-screen-star-robert-de-niro.html [Accessed 20 May 2020].

Bruccoli, Matthew J. (ed.). *The Love of the Last Tycoon: A Western*, ed. Matthew J. Bruccoli, Cambridge: Cambridge University Press, 1993.

De Curtis, Anthony. 'Martin Scorsese: The Rolling Stone Interview', *Rolling Stone*, 1 November 1990, https://www.rollingstone.com/movies/movie-fea tures/martin-scorsese-the-rolling-stone-interview-192568/ [Accessed 20 May 2020].

Esch, Kevin. '"I Don't See Any Method at All": The Problem of Actorly Transformation', *Journal of Film and Video*, Vol. 58, No. 1–2 (2006), pp. 95–107.

Grist, Leigh. *The Films of Martin Scorsese, 1963–77: Authorship and Context*, New York: Palgrave Macmillan, 2013.

Grobel, Lawrence. '*Playboy* Interview: Robert De Niro', *Playboy*, Vol. 36, No. 1 (1989), pp. 69–90, 326.

Kael, Pauline. *For Keeps: 30 Years at the Movies*, New York: Dutton, 1994.

Levy, Shawn. *De Niro: A Life*, New York: Three Rivers, 2014.

Macaulay, Scott. 'Scorsese, De Niro, Lewis and Bernhard recall *The King of Comedy*', *Filmmaker*, 1 May 2013, https://filmmakermagazine.com/69894-scorsese-de-niro-lewis-and-bernhard-recall-king-of-comedy/#.XtPISlB7mYV [Accessed 31 May 2020].

Millard, Kathryn. *Screenwriting in a Digital Era*, Basingstoke: Palgrave, 2014.

Monkhouse, Bob. 'They're Not Laughing Now...', *The Guardian*, 29 December 2003, https://www.theguardian.com/uk/2003/dec/29/arts.artsnews1 [Accessed 30 May 2020].

Murphy, Kathleen. Martin Scorsese and Gavin Smith, 'Made Men', *Film Comment*, Vol. 26, No. 5 (1993).

Phipps, Keith. 'Sandra Bernhardt Remembers *The King of Comedy*', *The Dissolve*, 30 January 2014, https://thedissolve.com/features/movie-of-the-week/389-sandra-bernhard-remembers-the-king-of-comedy/ [Accessed 31 May 2020].

Rutherford, Anne. 'Cinema and Embodied Affect', *Senses of Cinema*, 25 March 2003, http://sensesofcinema.com/2003/feature-articles/embodied_affect/ [Accessed 15 August 2019].

Scorsese, Martin. 'Martin Scorsese on Jerry Lewis: "It Was Like Watching a Virtuoso Pianist at the Keyboard"', *The Guardian*, 1 September 2017, https://www.theguardian.com/film/2017/sep/01/jerry-lewis-martin-scorsese-king-comedy-nutty-professor [Accessed 31 May 2020].

Sobchack, Vivian. *Carnal Thoughts: Embodiment and Moving Image Culture*, Berkeley: University of California Press, 2004.

Stern, Lesley. *The Scorsese Connection*, Indianapolis: Indiana University Press, 1995.

Thomson, David. 'The Director as Ranging Bull: Why Can't a Woman Be More Like a Photograph?', *Film Comment*, Vol. 17, No. 1 (1981), pp. 9–15.

Thomson, David and Ian Christie (ed.), *Scorsese on Scorsese*, London and Boston: Faber & Faber, 1989.

Wilson, Michael Henry. *Scorsese on Scorsese* [Cahiers Du Cinema], Paris: Phaidon Press, 2011.

CHAPTER 7

Character

In almost every film we have discussed so far De Niro plays the lead role, especially in the ones he chose after his Oscar success with *The Godfather, Part II* in 1974. In the mid-1980s, however, his ambitions seemed to change discernibly. Shawn Levy connects this to a change in representation, when De Niro signed a contract with the new, powerful Creative Artists Agency. Following the success of *The Untouchables* (1987) he was now a bankable star willing to work in 'marketing-driven, studio-funded film[s] of the cookie-cutter sort', as Levy unfairly characterises *Midnight Run* (1988), which was certainly a commercial success but also an excellent film, and perhaps De Niro's outstanding performance in a comedy. Levy suggests that around this time the actor developed 'a taste for work that wasn't necessarily grueling or stone-serious', and that 'he was shopping around for lighter parts'.[1]

It is certainly true that during this period De Niro was happy no longer to be expected to carry a film as the lead actor, and that he started to select smaller roles; and also that in many cases the script annotation is somewhat less extensive than is found on earlier screenplays. It is important to remember, though, that the unprecedented levels of work he put into films like *Taxi Driver* and *Raging Bull* meant that he had now mastered certain approaches to preparation that he had been exploring earlier in his

---

[1] Shawn Levy, *De Niro: A Life* (New York: Three Rivers, 2014), p. 335.

© The Author(s) 2020
A. Ganz and S. Price, *Robert De Niro at Work*,
Palgrave Studies in Screenwriting,
https://doi.org/10.1007/978-3-030-47960-2_7

181

career, and that some kinds of script annotation can be correspondingly reduced. His work on the later films can now be informed by the use of improvisation and by his understanding and consolidation of everything he has learned.

In this chapter we look at two such films in which he does not play the lead: Al Capone in Brian De Palma's *The Untouchables* (1987) and James Conway in the Scorsese-directed *Goodfellas* (1990). It is notable that in each case his copy of the screenplay still shows very detailed analysis of the scenes on which he worked. There is, however, a change in how he approaches character and its representation, which becomes particularly clear if we contrast his methods for these later films with his work on *The Last Tycoon*. In preparing for the role of Irving Thalberg, much though by no means all of his research focused on questions of historical accuracy and the authentic reproduction of Thalberg's appearance, clothing and mannerisms. The roles he played in these two later films were also based on real-life characters, but the approach he takes is different. Al Capone is arguably the best-known and most persistently mediated and reproduced gangster in American history, while James 'Jimmy the Gent' Conway is based on another real gangster, the comparatively unknown James Burke.

In each case De Niro is working with a director with whom he has worked before, and both of whom, like De Niro, came from Italian-American backgrounds. In these films ethnicity is central to De Niro's characters: Capone was Italian, and a New Yorker who moved to Chicago; Conway was a New Yorker through and through, who because of his Irish background wasn't eligible to be a 'made man' in the Mafia. Placing *The Untouchables* and *Goodfellas* side by side allows us to explore the differences in his process in interpreting a known and an unknown historical figure. As we shall see, De Niro was still interested in verisimilitude, but this seems secondary to other considerations: understanding how the character has been mediated in previous representations, how to present the character in action, and how to expand his repertoire while also drawing on his previous experience in working on other films.

Character and Calligraphy

In amending the screenplay the actor is also preparing a performance. The performance to be inscribed on the film is also written on the screenplay; the inscriptions on the written work will exist in a different form in the film work to come. Acting can be seen as a kind of calligraphy, a form of writing which finds its meaning in gesture and balance as well as what it says. The word 'character' links these two forms of writing, and it is instructive to look at the etymology of this word and its various definitions in the *Oxford English Dictionary*.

What these definitions show is a continual to-and-fro between marks or writing, and the distinctive quality of a person. The word derives originally from the Greek verb *charassein*, which means to mark with a cut or furrow, coming to be used for writing in wet clay with a stylus or engraving on a stone surface. It then took on a metaphorical meaning, the way in which the human had been written by their creator, following which it started to acquire the meanings with which we are more familiar today: the 'character' of a human being, and what makes them both distinctively themselves and also like others. (In the fields of geology and biology 'character' is used to describe the distinguishing properties of a substance or distinguishing features of a species.) Finally, 'character' becomes applied to a person portrayed in a work of fiction, or a part played by an actor. This etymology shows that in portraying a character in a work of fiction the actor is bound up in a form of writing, using gesture and action to define the role they play: to establish their *characteristics*. The performer draws on all the other definitions of the word to produce a simulation of a human being who should be both recognisable yet fictional, unique and individual yet nonetheless clearly belonging to a type.

The word 'character', then, includes elements of both the written and the human, the distinctive and the universal, and the use of both of these elements in taxonomies and systems. It looks at 'characteristic' details and elements through which individual features are built up into larger structures: the ways in which characters combine to make a word or a sentence, or how characters combine in a drama. It is not surprising that embodiment of a character involves the written as well as the performed, and that building a character is a process of both holistic analysis and assembly. The character appears distinctive to the audience because of an imagined inner consistency but also because it remains interesting, intriguing, not entirely known.

Philip Drake remarks that '[i]n order to understand the distinctiveness of "performance," we can usefully examine some fundamental questions concerning its ontology and epistemology. The starting point is this: when does a performance come into "being," and what initiates the recognition that something is "a performance"?'.[2] Drake analyses a number of artists, including De Niro, and looks crucially at intentionality in performance. Such an approach returns agency to the film actor from the discourse of 'film studies', which has tended to see the actor chiefly as text or sign. Elia Kazan stressed De Niro's agency in describing him as a 'character actor': 'he's very imaginative. He's very precise. He figures everything out both inside and outside. He has good emotion. He's a character actor: everything he does he calculates. In a good way, but he calculates'.[3] An actor's performance is dependent on choice, as Stella Adler taught and as De Niro has often asserted. In order to express a character De Niro uses characters in all the ways we have described: we can see the iterative relationship between character as inscription, character as taxonomy and character as performance. In a performance character is both something fixed and changeable, and a great actor makes us feel both aspects in their rendition.

Drake tends to consider performance as something that only occurs on screen; and without the archive, of course, this is all that is available to study. Yet in other forms of cultural production the research, the practice, the exploration, the mistakes and blind alleys form just as much part of the practice as the final result, and in considering the history of a written text it would be negligent not to consider the various iterations of how it came to be. The paratexts and annotations which can be seen in De Niro's archive are not just preparations for a performance, they are in many ways performances in themselves. Examining the way De Niro approaches the development of our two selected character roles from the evidence in the archive tells us a great deal about how De Niro realises these two identities on screen, and from this we can postulate both what he considers character to be, and how we as members of the audience understand characters in screen drama and respond to them.

---

[2] Philip Drake, 'Reconceptualizing Screen Performance', *Journal of Film and Video*, Vol. 58, No. 1/2 (2006), p. 84.

[3] William Baer (ed.), *Elia Kazan: Interviews* (Jackson, MS: University Press of Mississippi, 2001), p. 210.

The Untouchables

In *The Untouchables* De Niro is playing the most iconic figure he would ever portray. Capone was a star in his own lifetime, who has been dramatised countless times in film: both under his own name and others; generically, in dramatisations of Chicago gangsters and the prohibition era; and as the character Tony Montana, better known as 'Scarface', as portrayed in two very well known yet radically different films of that name, by Paul Muni in 1932 and by Al Pacino in the remake/homage of 1983 that Brian De Palma directed just four years before *The Untouchables*. De Niro is once again playing a public figure whose mythologisation is dependent on his readiness to offer a performance: to his own men, to his enemies and to the wider public.

De Niro plays Capone as a star, and that is what he was. Even at the time Capone was being watched by actors,[4] including James Cagney and Edward G. Robinson, who between them largely defined the Warner Brothers gangster of the early talkies era in *Public Enemy* and *Little Caesar* (both 1931), respectively. According to Ken Burns, Cagney came to watch Capone's arrest, and Edward G. Robinson attended the Capone trial to get a sense of Capone's body language and his mannerisms.[5] Damon Runyon, author of *Guys and Dolls,* came from New York to report it: 'The testimony revealed Al as rather a busy and shrewd shopper. While he is usually pictured as a ruthless gang chieftain, he was today presented as a domesticated sort of a chap going around buying furniture, and silverware, and rugs, and knickknacks of one kind and another for the household'.[6] Capone would also have been watching his own representations, just as De Niro chose to watch his own gangster performances as part of his research for the role. Both De Niro and Capone, then, elided the boundary between character and performance. Capone decided to become a celebrity, and De Niro plays him as such.

Capone, then, is a figure who is at least in part knowable. Notably, there is a vast amount of evidence of what he wore, in part because his

[4] Jonathan Eig, 'What You Didn't Know About Gangster Al Capone' (interview), *WBUR*, 9 August 2010, https://www.wbur.org/npr/128872365/what-you-didnt-know-about-gangster-al-capone [Accessed 20 May 2020].

[5] Ken Burns, *Prohibition*, TV Mini-Series, US: PBS, 2011.

[6] Damon Runyon, *Trials and Other Tribulations* (Philadelphia; New York: J.B. Lippincott Company, 1974), p. 237.

expenses were documented so thoroughly for the Inland Revenue case, documented by Runyon among others, that put Capone behind bars and which forms the climax of *The Untouchables*. As we have already seen, De Niro has always paid meticulous attention to how his characters dress. For Mick McAloon,

> there are countless examples of De Niro's great costume choices: in *Good-fellas*, for example, when De Niro's Jimmy Conway is arrested. What struck me about De Niro's costume choice here—a yellow jersey, jeans—was the level of detail for such a seemingly offhanded moment that takes place within a montage of arrests. It can only be for a few seconds of screen time, but that yellow jersey speaks volumes.[7]

Talking about De Niro's wardrobe tests for *Falling in Love*, and how he finally decided on the type of jacket his character would wear, Meryl Streep recalled:

> He is relentless in his desire to find just the right detail, the little things that's gonna tell you everything about a man. […] I had the privilege of watching his process in a wardrobe test. For three hours, he tried on 37 identical little boxy jackets – windbreakers – that to me looked identical but he's checking the cuff, the collar, the zip […] until he found the right one. […] Details are important and Bob knows that. He changed everything for generations of actors.[8]

The real costumes and props that a character wore, then, offer not only historical accuracy but an insight into the decisions the character made, and therefore about their own self-image.

When De Niro decided to take the role, producer Art Linson estimated that the actor's meticulousness regarding costume would add $50,000 to the budget.[9] For the role of Capone De Niro worked with a team including Richard Bruno, costume designer on many other films De

---

[7] Mick McAloon, 'Robert De Niro: Detail in Service of the Truth', *Running From The Reels*, undated, https://runningfromthereels.com/2013/07/18/de-niro-detail-in-service-of-the-truth/ [Accessed 20 May 2020].

[8] Meryl Streep in tribute to Robert De Niro, 32nd annual Kennedy Center Honors held in Washington, D.C., 6 December 2009, https://www.youtube.com/watch?v=coC xLpWUz50 [Accessed 20 May 2020].

[9] Levy, *De Niro*, p. 325.

Niro worked on (including *Goodfellas*), and tailor Henry Stewart. He was playing a character who loved clothes, as indicated by the nickname 'Snorky' with which his close friends favoured him.[10] Capone's silk underwear, which was manufactured by the luxury menswear outfitters Sulka, forms part of the Internal Revenue case against him:

> There are submitted herewith as Exhibits Nos. 141 to 144, invoices covering purchases made by Al Capone from A. Sulka and Company on April 25, 1931, of ten pair of French model pajamas at $50.00, one pair of French model pajamas at $46.00 and eleven monograms at $3.10, or a total of $580.10. They were identified by Albert Nusbaum a salesman and he testified that he secured the orders from Al Capone at the Lexington Hotel. A transcript of his testimony is attached as Exhibit No. 148.[11]

De Niro's costumes with the Capone monogram in dark blue are in the archive. He acquired his own Sulka underwear; the shirts are made by New York shirtmaker Arthur Gluck, and the suits and the baseball bat in the HRC are still smeared with artificial blood.

De Niro is able to surround himself in the actual clothes that would have been worn by the character, but this is not just authenticity for its own sake; his body is better able to move as a gangster when wearing the gangster's clothes. De Niro knows the power of clothes on others, in a room and on screen, but he also uses Capone's costumes in a number of different ways: as external iconography and as a memory of transformation, to remind others of his wealth and power, but also to remind himself. There may be an element of testing his own power, and exploiting the situation, of proving that he can demand, and get, anything; but if so, this in itself offers useful character insight for an actor playing this particular character.

Before filming, De Niro repeated his *Raging Bull* exercise and visited Italy to eat himself out of shape for the role. On his return to Chicago he was, in Levy's description, 'plumped out and with his hairline altered,

---

[10] Elizabeth Nix. '8 Things You Should Know About Al Capone', *History*, 5 May 2015, https://www.history.com/news/8-things-you-should-know-about-al-capone [Accessed 20 May 2020].

[11] U.S. Treasury Department, Internal Revenue Service, SI-7085-F: Chief, Intelligence Unit, Bureau of Internal Revenue, Washington, D.C. In Re: Alphonse Capone, 21 December 1933, *IRIS*, https://www.irs.gov/pub/irs-utl/file-2-report-dated-12211933-in-re-alphonse-capone-by-sa-frank-wilson.pdf [Accessed 20 May 2020].

unrecognizable' from before; he then 'sat for the makeup department to give him a prosthetic nose, then went into the wardrobe trailer, put on his silk drawers and bespoke suit, donned a fedora, lit a cigar, and stepped out onto the set'. Linson remembers that 'It was like witnessing a grand magic trick performed by a maestro', with not just the appearance but the whole persona changed so that 'Capone–De Niro suddenly became sly, dangerous, confident, and even witty. [...] The character had been created'.[12] Yet again we find a fellow professional astonished by De Niro's powers of transformation.

Another means of bringing this about was through analysing previous representations of Capone, via documentary footage and possibly other dramatised versions of the gangster; and also, perhaps more strikingly, by carefully rewatching some of his own performances in other films, in what we might think of as a kind of review of his previous research. The archive does not reveal whether he looked again at his own extensive notes for, say *Once Upon a Time in America*, but we do know that he reviewed the film:

> *Look at old tapes*
> *'Raging Bull'? 'Once upon A Time'*
> *Remember study ?lips??*
> *Fat cigars*
> *Work with video*
> *Voice (work on)*
> *Clem and others that whole list*[13]

(Clem is De Niro's long term friend Clem 'Jimmy Whispers' Caserta, who knew De Niro from the Lower East Side and appears in many of his films in supporting roles.)

> *Listen to opera Rose OF PICARDY*
> *Need reason for baseball bat scene*
> *In final days rotten things and lots of water*
> *Any witness of baseball bat*
> *People in Chicago to talk to researcher*
> *Do nails*

---

[12] Quoted in Levy, *De Niro*, p. 325.

[13] *The Untouchables* (1987), Undated (early) and incomplete script, with RDN notes, Box 145.5, Robert De Niro Papers, Harry Ransom Center, Texas, Austin.

> *Purse lips. Looks right and a physicality based out of and reflected thru that physicality*
> *See Pinky Ring*
> *Think of what I wear in [illegible] indecipherable thought of this at Rocketts in white suit*
> *Try and say try to see all my movies!*

The exclamation mark suggests that '*my*' could be a reference to Capone, and not De Niro. A report for the thirtieth anniversary of the film records that '[t]o physically recreate Capone, De Niro says he watched footage of the gangster and "tried to gain as much weight as I could and shave my head more so I could look as round as I could in the time that I had to prepare for it"'.[14]

> *Gen Note*
> *Not too much if any head movement*
> *Be clear straightforward and forthright I am a King*
> *'There is violence in Chicago, of course, but not by me and not by anybody I employ'*

De Niro is preparing to produce the combination of extreme control and extreme spontaneity that he is building. As Drake observes, De Niro's performance as Capone

> draws upon specific elements of his earlier performances in mobster narratives and his history of acting roles; together, these elements convey the required authority of Capone in a short amount of screen time. This performance directly encourages intertextual referencing in order to establish the narrative significance of the character and his mythological status: the character of Capone gains its authority from De Niro's previous roles and the legitimacy that his image (rooted in a fetishism of his acting and the framing discourses of naturalism) can confer.[15]

---

[14] Quoted in Mary Sollosi, 'The Stars of *The Untouchables* Look Back, 30 Years Later', *Entertainment*, 5 June 2017, https://ew.com/movies/2017/06/05/the-untouchables-kevin-costner-robert-deniro-sean-connery-look-back/ [Accessed 20 May 2020].

[15] Drake, 'Reconceptualizing Screen Performance', p. 87.

More specifically, James Naremore suggests that in playing Capone, De Niro 'add[ed] a bit of [Rupert] Pupkin to his portrait of the gangster'.[16]

De Niro's screenplay annotations reveal an in-depth analysis of the motivations and physical gestures of the character, and these together with the line readings create a representation of the affect and energy of Capone. It is remarkable, too, how these annotations respond to the stylisation of screenwriter David Mamet's dialogue. Just as De Niro's notes on *The Last Tycoon* appear to channel the character of Stahr/Thalberg, his commentary here[17] seems to pick up the rhythms of the Runyonesque, non-naturalistic dialogue that Mamet has created for Capone. There is, for example, something reminiscent of *Guys and Dolls* in De Niro's delivery of the line: 'What is that which gives me joy?' De Niro is already enthusiastically preparing to enter the world Mamet has written. As an actor he doesn't just play the character, he also plays the writer—or the writing:

> *I was royally fucked.*
> *These men have betrayed me and I am now giving them a lesson in Respect.*
> *Loyalty! Loyalty & when there are certain times for some things and certain*
> *times for others and when those certain times are not abided by and can be*
> *a matter of life and death To the fuck-up and the fuckee!*

It is difficult to imagine anything more tonally dissimilar to the annotations on *The Last Tycoon*. When De Niro is performing a character written by Mamet his comments pick up on Mamet's speech patterns, and the Capone he will be performing is Mamet's Capone. As De Niro observed at an anniversary event for the film in Chicago in 2017, 'The rhythm of the dialogue [...] especially is so specific that you really have to know it so that it will work'.[18]

We can see something similar when he works with Quentin Tarantino on *Jackie Brown* (1997)[19]; once again, he picks up on the writer's

---

[16] James Naremore, *Acting in the Cinema* (Berkeley: University of California Press, 1988), p. 276.

[17] *The Untouchables* (1987), Box 145.5, HRC, Texas, Austin.

[18] Quoted in Sollosi, 'The Stars of *The Untouchables* Look Back'.

[19] *Jackie Brown* (1997), Screenplay by Quentin Tarantino; final draft, 16 April 1997, revised through May 1997, with RDN notes, Box, Robert De Niro Papers, Harry Ransom Center, Texas, Austin.

rhythms and speech patterns. When De Niro's character Louis shoots Melanie (Bridget Fonda) in the car park when she speaks after he has told her to keep her mouth shut, Tarantino writes:

> That did it! Louis whips out the Beretta Odell gave him... shoots her...
> BAM...in the belly.
> She bounces OFF one of the cars and goes down.
> BAM Louis shoots her again on the ground.
> One; to make sure. Two; cause it felt good.

De Niro has added in pen: '*& maybe one more!*' This seems to be a suggestion about what Louis might do, but it also engages with the rhythms and style of Tarantino's writing by picking up on his casual, half-comic, splatter-style representation of the act of killing. (In fact, in the released film there are only two shots fired, fewer than either Tarantino or De Niro suggested.)

When an actor is trying to create a character they can only interpret him or her through the words of the screenwriter. They may use material from other sources to decide how to read that text, or to amend it, but the text that is being interpreted always has the character of the writer, as well as of the actor and the role they are playing. When De Niro performs Mamet's Capone he is performing both Capone and Mamet, but he remains De Niro. Often he uses the text to find the way to the character, but here he seems to be using his understanding of the character of Capone to find the best way to speak Mamet's text. He needs to find a way to make the instrument of his body perform those lines in front of the camera.

To give the best performance he can, De Niro offers himself line readings for Capone in a way that differs from his normal practice. The last line of Capone's written dialogue is: 'But I get nowhere unless the team wins', to which De Niro adds: '*And if the team don't winnnnnnnn, Noooobodddy wins*'. Our transcription of the number of NNN's is an approximation because the line here is just a wobbly streak that goes up and down, rather than a clearly distinguishable number of letters. The annotation is not simply a verbal comment to indicate how the word should be spoken, but a graphic representation of a kind of physical energy. As we look at the word turning into the pure line we can see how the mark changes from a set of characters into something purely visual, preparing for the moment in the scene where De Niro's Capone will exhaust the elegant words of Mamet's speech as a form of expression, and resort to action instead.

He also offers a piece of advice to himself about how to deliver the stylised language of the scene: '*Don't push on voice. Only what can do and is right. The logic reality and believability are more IMP*'. There are other ways to get there, as De Niro has acknowledged, but perhaps because the language does unconsciously motivate behaviour De Niro needs to find a way to ensure that he remains in control—to find ideas of 'logic, reality and believability'. He thus explores the psychological motivations of Capone at this stage. In a Strasbergian moment, '*It's also personal what they did to me and Final! / Just think of self. Betrayals in life*'. One similarity between *The Untouchables* and *The Last Tycoon*, then, is that De Niro states the character's belief in the rightness of his cause. Just as, when describing Monroe Stahr's reaction to receiving the news that Kathleen has got married, De Niro writes: '*I'm sure of my priorities I know I'm right*', in *The Untouchables* a note on the baseball bat speech in large confident lettering states: '*I'm Right*'. Both characters are bosses of major enterprises carrying enormous responsibility, and neither can have room for doubt.

De Niro is also considering the physical expression of the actions, as well as the dialogue. In addition to a note that he needs to '*Work with baseball bat*', in another fascinating annotation at the top of the page he writes: '*remember: things a little tighter and shorter because I'm about to kill the motherfucker right here*'. This is another place where De Niro seems to pick up on Mamet's sentence structure; indeed it seems to distil the structure of the entire speech, technical description at the beginning with the dramatic energy of the vocabulary at the end. 'Tighter and shorter' is both a dialogue reading and also, perhaps, a note on embodiment.

Sometime before working on *The Untouchables* De Niro said in an interview, 'It's a lot of fun trying to make something stylised',[20] and we can see this commitment to stylisation in his annotations in the baseball bat scene. De Niro does more than just parse the text; he also finds ways to visually represent gesture. In the screenplay's sentence 'Capone raises the baseball bat above his head and brings it down viciously on the head of the very fat man', he slightly underlines the word 'down'. He

---

[20] Quoted in Bert Cardullo et al. (ed.), *Playing to the Camera: Film Actors Discuss Their Craft* (New Haven: Yale University Press, 1998), p. 288.

has also drawn a line from the white space outside the main text, which goes through the word 'heavyset' in the phrase 'large heavyset man', and provides a note: '*not necessarily crazy [...] but under pressure*'. The combination of verbal and visual anticipations of his screen performance on the page are becoming increasingly sophisticated and precise. De Niro is both describing points of emphasis and making a textual representation of what the scene will look like. We might see the block of text as being like the table Capone will walk around before delivering the killer blow. The annotations and lines surrounding it are not only suggestions for particular interpretations, but when taken as a whole echo the table shot from above, the image with which De Palma concludes the sequence.

In working with De Palma, De Niro was working again with the man with whom he made his first films, but also someone who shared his knowledge of artistic New York, having made documentaries about a Museum of Modern Art exhibition in 1965 featuring Josef Albers, and The Performance Group's adaptation of Euripides' *Dionysus in '69*. Perhaps this is why we can find more experimental and visual ways of representing performance in the *Untouchables* annotations. This also manifested itself during the shoot, with cinematographer Stephen H. Burum recalling that

> De Niro, as Capone, did some very interesting things with his hands, and used a lot of body language. He needed space, an area for the audience to see the body language work [...] you have to respect elements like De Niro's use of body language and gesture, and use those elements in framing shots. If you don't do that, you're cheating the actor and you're cheating the audience.[21]

De Niro's notes on a later scene, when an increasingly frustrated Capone calls for the death of his nemesis Eliot Ness, is full of writing and lines that connect the annotations to the text. But instead of the neat and measured observations of *The Last Tycoon*, the comments on *The Untouchables* are expressed with a violence and anger that better suits Capone, and the language of Mamet:

[21] Al Harrell, '*The Untouchables:* A Search for Period Flavor', *American Cinematographer*, 7 (1987), https://staging.ascmag.com/articles/flashback-the-untouchables [Accessed 30 May 2020].

> *This is real personal*
> *I want this real personal*
> *In order to get this angry*

Do this for my friend Moment [or possibly '*do this for my friend Mamet*']
NECK

That's it I finally made the decision
The commitment that's it.

Further idea? If he is an agent I'd lose my whole empire
Really take the time, the moment almost an imperceptible
double take what is it he (?) doing
maybe something

but I keep it altogether and how many people do I take care of
Worst thing is an 'I don't care'

This extract presents just half of the list of annotations embroidering the page, linked with arrows and looping lines which connect the threads of De Niro's analyses and reflections. Some offer specific line readings and suggestions for delivery, others think about the motivation or points of reference for the character or the actor. Taken together, however, they represent a three-dimensional set of connections on a flat plane. In the same way that costume is crucial to De Niro's construction of character, the annotations form a visual mapping that connects the chronological narrative of the scene, identifies points of energy, and makes connections within it. It is like an emotional cartography of the text, as well as a preparation for reconstruction in movement and gesture. As the film will reduce De Niro from three dimensions to two, the annotations seem to lift the flat page into contours and offer the illusion of substance and form in space, projecting from the page as the three-dimensional actions recorded on film will eventually be projected on a flat screen to an audience.

The paginated flat planes of the screenplay page indicate not just space but time. De Niro ends up performing the script as written, but he is included in the conversations between writer and director in a very different way from the *Last Tycoon*, as an archived note from Brian De

Palma shows: 'Bobby—this is the idea for Capone's final speech. Mamet would rewrite it but I think the attitude is just right. Brian'. Attached is a photocopy of what was a Capone interview with the *Chicago Tribune* in 1927 in which he threatened retirement: 'I am going to St. Petersburg, Florida, tomorrow. Let the worthy citizens of Chicago get their liquor the best they can. I'm sick of the job—it's a thankless one and full of grief. I've been spending the best years of my life as a public benefactor'. The speech was not ultimately included in the film, but De Niro is part of the conversation about both who the character is and how he should be written. Building a character is an iterative process of observation and modifications of narrative, text and behaviour. De Niro moves between the traces of the real Capone as far as he was knowable, the various mediatised renditions of him in documentary and fiction, Mamet's creation, and De Niro's own representations of gangsters.

This Capone is a knowing performance, which emphasises believability yet finds a mode of stylisation entirely appropriate to Mamet's version of the character. De Niro's techniques are revealed in the content of the notes, but also in how they are expressed and presented. In his portrayal of the historical person De Niro uses 'character' in its primary meanings, as inscription, ideogram and symbol, to realise his performance both as a distinctive representative of a human being and as the psychological manifestations of the 'character' of Alphonse Gabriel Capone, as written by David Mamet and directed by Brian De Palma. De Niro is able to synthesise all of these different ideas for, and sources of, character and to express them ultimately in his screen performance; but we can see their formation in the annotations, where his research meets Mamet's text. To understand how De Niro built the character, then, the evidence of the archive is essential. It shows the extent to which the actor is responding to an authored text with a performance designed to draw out the distinctive features of the historical Capone, but, just as important, to find ways to inhabit Mamet's highly stylised dialogue and to inscribe on screen the words Mamet wrote on paper.

GOODFELLAS

When De Niro plays the role of Jimmy Conway in what came to be known as *Goodfellas* (the screenplays in the Ransom Center are labelled *Wiseguy*), he is playing another historically grounded figure (whose real name was Jimmy Burke), but one who is far less well known than Capone, and different from any of the characters De Niro has played so far. Previously his gangster characters have been central to the narrative, but Conway is peripheral: he is one of the Goodfellas, a man thwarted by his ethnicity, which means he can never be a 'made' man in the Mafia. This is a film about 'Ordinary individuals who happen to be gangsters', as Scorsese put it, operating in a world where 'money governs everything'; a bourgeois gangster trapped by home life: 'It wasn't the fact that interested me, but the details of everyday life. How a family involved in organised crime lived. How they dressed. What they ate, what music they listened to', whereas for Scorsese the robbery itself 'didn't interest me; it would be another film. You just see them go in and come out'.[22]

De Niro isn't the star, but in some ways his role is the most remarkable. The character is not flamboyant, but he goes through the most interesting journey, from welcoming Henry Hill (Ray Liotta) to the gang to preparing to kill him and being betrayed by him at the end of the film. His character is complex and hard to read, and there are some fascinating moments, such as his heartbroken rage when he learns that his friend Tommy has been murdered instead of 'made', or his ruthless assassination spree to keep all the cash from the Lufthansa heist for himself. The real Jimmy Burke had a terrible history:

> Burke's early years were harsh by any standards. He never knew his real parents, and was taken into care at the age of two, a development that marked the beginning of over a decade of alternating violence, sexual abuse, kindness and pampering at the hands of dozens of foster parents. At the age of 13, an altercation with his latest foster parents while riding in a car resulted in a crash and the death of his foster father, an episode that earned him the enmity of his foster mother.[23]

And yet at no point did we discover any reference to the backstory or formation of Burke/Conway in De Niro's annotations. The HRC catalogue on *Goodfellas* contains the court documents,[24] and De Niro's

---

[22] Michael Henry Wilson, *Scorsese on Scorsese* (Cahiers du Cinéma) (Paris: Phaidon Press, 2011), p. 164.

[23] Dick Hobbs, *Obituary: Jimmy Burke, The Independent*, 29 April 1996, https://www.independent.co.uk/news/obituaries/obituary-jimmy-burke-1307376.html [Accessed 31 May 2020].

[24] Court Documents, research materials re James Burke, Henry Hill, and others, Box 72.4, Robert De Niro Papers, Harry Ransom Center, Texas, Austin.

annotations make reference to wiretaps where his character talks about the need to 'whack' Henry Hill. There is also research material on the Tampa Case in which Hill, Burke and three others (including two brothers from Tampa) were convicted by a Federal court jury of extortion and interstate gambling involving betting on baseball: 'The defendants were accused of abducting Mr. Ciaccio, beating him, threatening to stuff his children into a refrigerator, threatening to force his wife into prostitution, and threatening to blow up his bar if he went to the police'.[25] But there is no file on James Burke himself, and no correspondence with anyone who knew him. All that is mentioned is an annotated version of Nicholas Pileggi's *Wiseguy: Life in a Mafia Family*, with some loose items.[26] There is a remarkable contrast between this and, say, the research materials for *Raging Bull* or *The Untouchables*.

According to a report of an onstage Q&A to mark the film's 25th anniversary, De Niro was crucial in casting Ray Liotta as Henry Hill: 'Even though Liotta hadn't done too many films before landing the lead role in *Goodfellas*, he was the first person the filmmakers had met with, thanks to a recommendation from Robert De Niro'.[27] Chronologically the film's story stretches back to a time when Hill was still a boy (played by Christopher Serrone); his character develops over time, in marked contrast to De Niro's Conway, who seems unchanging, timeless. The real Henry Hill says that 'De Niro hammered me endlessly to get Jimmy's character down',[28] but it seems that in *Goodfellas* De Niro's idea of 'character' is different: he is less interested in how Burke/Conway became this person than in what it is like to be Jimmy Conway, what he represented, and what it felt like to live in his world. De Niro plays him over a period of almost thirty years, and yet he barely changes beyond some nods to modifications of hairstyle, even though during this time his

---

[25] 'Tampa case', research materials re James Burke, Henry Hill, and others, Box 72.6, Robert De Niro Papers, Harry Ransom Center, Texas, Austin.

[26] Nicholas Pileggi. *Wiseguy: Life in a Mafia Family* (1985), annotated by RDN; loose items withdrawn from BV135, BV. 135–136, Robert De Niro Papers, Harry Ransom Center, Texas, Austin.

[27] Bilge Ebiri, '11 Things We Learned About *Goodfellas* From Saturday's Tribeca Q&A', *Vulture*, 26 April 2015, https://www.vulture.com/2015/04/11-things-we-learned-about-goodfellas.html [Accessed 25 September 2019].

[28] Henry Hill and Bryon Schreckengost, *A Goodfella's Guide to New York: Your Personal Tour Through the Mob's Notorious Haunts, Hair-Raising Crime Scenes, and Infamous Hot Spots* (New York: Three Rivers Press, 2003), p. 169.

family grows up and his son Jesse James Burke is involved in the Lufthansa Robbery. As the screenplay says, 'he was already a legend'. De Niro notes on page 25, where Henry meets all the 'family' in the Bamboo bar and Tommy beckons Jimmy over to discuss the Air France heist with Frenchy, that '*I'm more of a wiseguy big shot than the actual wiseguy big shots. I got more style and knowhow than they do[.] maybe I over-compensate because I'm not Italian*'. And at the margin: '*Don't let the clothes wear me, I wear the clothes*'.[29]

Scorsese's stated aim for the film was that it should be 'like a staged documentary, the spirit of a documentary. As if you had a 16 mm camera with these guys for 20, 25 years; what you'd pick up. I can't say it's "like" any other film, but in my mind it [has] the freedom of a documentary'.[30] In keeping with this approach, De Niro throughout uses the wiretap material as annotation. In the aforementioned Bamboo bar scene, where Tommy threatens the restaurant owner who is trying to get his debt repaid, his annotations are boxed on either side of the text. On the left-hand side: '*"Make sure you wipe the car down real good. take it over to Jersey and have it chopped." or "get rid of it"*'. And on the right: '*"Burn the wrapper from the money and make sure you get rid of the suits" Tommy "Jesus but it's a fucking Brioni* [suit]*"*'. Both of these blocks of text feel like shadows, powerful presences that do not directly connect to the scene but instead are a reminder of the power of this character who has killed many times. The evidence is scattered throughout the annotations, as are reflections on his relationship with Henry and Tommy, and the logistics of the story: what happens, and in what order. If Scorsese is interested in the details of everyday life De Niro is interested in the work a gangster does, and how the work manifests itself in social relations and emotions.

Unlike with the Mamet/Capone dialogue for *The Untouchables*, De Niro's annotations for *Goodfellas* do not attempt to replicate an authorial style for the voice of the character; nor does he write the kind of lengthy character monologue, independent of any particular moment in the script, that are seen in the annotations for (say) *Taxi Driver*. The character seems

---

[29] *Goodfellas* (1990), Shooting script with extensive RDN notes, revised script pages, and production material laid in, Box 187, Robert De Niro Papers, Harry Ransom Center, Texas, Austin.

[30] Gavin Smith, 'Goodfellas: Martin Scorsese Interviewed (1990)', *Scraps From The Loft*, 15 February 2018, https://scrapsfromtheloft.com/2018/02/15/goodfellas-martin-scorsese-interview-1990-gavin-smith/ [Accessed 31 May 2020].

a given. Instead there are scrawled quotations, also presumably from wire-taps; and although the numbered lists seen on the reverse pages of other screenplays are still in evidence, for *Goodfellas* the lists are of incidents that haven't been filmed: what the sequence of events was when Billy Batts was murdered, and at what point he killed Marty. These events are absent from the screenplay itself because although Scorsese was not interested in the mechanics of the heist, De Niro has to recall what has happened, and in what order. So, for example, the annotations mention Burke/Conway having to go to Stacks' funeral:

> Henry 'Stacks was a sweet kind beautiful kid'
> Tony and Stacks best of friends.
> Usually Stacks brags about killing somebody but this time didn't say anything about it except to cry. Though Tony knew Henry knew. Didn't have to be said.
> I have to kill everyone and having other guys do it.
> I was moving fast [illegible] cocaine in case have to go to the can.
> Lot of pressure, front page of papers, on news. Bodies all around. Tony getting killed ... and all in a three week period. I have to cut all the ties.

This is bleak, factual and utterly impersonal. He describes the emotions of others but not those of his own character; nor does De Niro reference his own emotional state, as he did for example in *The Untouchables* when writing '*Just think of self. Betrayals in life*'.

After the Lufthansa job the script says that Jimmy puts a thick stack of bills in Henry's pocket. De Niro—again with a keen eye on a character's need to calculate money—estimates that this should be '*about $10,000*', calculates how many 50-dollar bills should be in the bundle in each jacket pocket, and observes: '*I'm really happy to share it with him*'. He then adds in the margin: '*That's it. The greed takes over from now on*'. He thereby marks a distinct turning point in the character through his physical rela-tionship with the bundles of cash. Apart from the decision not to share any more of the money there are no further changes in Jimmy Conway; only the logic of his position, and the ruthlessness with which he defends it. That is what the job, and therefore the character, entails. De Niro is focused on materiality and physicality, with an awareness of how it can be used to explore metaphor and produce emotion.

In another haunting scene, pivotal to the construction of the movie, Tommy DeVito's mother (played by Catherine Scorsese) cooks a meal in the middle of the night for Conway, Hill and Tommy (Joe Pesci) while the not-quite-dead body of Billy Batts lies in the trunk of their car. The moment is unforgettable in its juxtaposition of the horrific and the domestic, and in the combination of knowing and not knowing in Tommy's mother as she indulges her son and his associates, who have been up to something she would perhaps rather not know about. It is the moment when Hill is forced to swallow the pleasure in casual violence and heartlessness that is the mark of his profession, and it is fitting that it takes place in this most domestic of settings. The killing of Batts is what prevents Tommy becoming a made man, a privilege to which neither Jimmy nor Harry can aspire because they are not Italian.

According to Pileggi, it was specifically about this scene that De Niro sought information from Henry Hill about the character he was playing. Pileggi says that De Niro wanted to know how Jimmy would get ketchup out of a bottle: would he slam it on the bottom, hit it from the side, use a knife, or what? 'It's those little moments of insane authenticity that make Marty's movies work'.[31] De Niro ended up rolling the bottle between his palms so the ketchup floods out. He is eating ketchup with his food to underline his difference: he is a friend of Tommy, but is an Irishman not an Italian; as Scorsese says, 'Bob is playing an Irish guy, give him some potatoes and eggs with ketchup'.[32]

This may be natural, but it is also artificial in the best way. De Niro's flourish with the ketchup bottle covers the moment where Tommy begins his transparent lies to his mother. He picks the ketchup up as Tommy starts his story ('I been working nights'), and puts it down at the very moment that Tommy, his shirt smeared with the blood of the man he is just killed, mentions blood in the dialogue ('that's where the blood came from'). Ketchup is a metonym for blood, and theatrical blood in particular. De Niro's actions emphasise how matter-of-fact the act of killing is to his character: for him to kill a man is as mundane and as easy as putting ketchup on his food. It reminds us and Hill about the murder Hill has just been involved in, but it also draws attention to the artificiality of the cinematic concoction we are watching, which combines the stylisation of the avant-garde with a different kind of authenticity. Whether De Niro is reproducing the way Jimmy Conway actually handled a ketchup bottle is perhaps irrelevant, though something feels right about the skill and

---

[31] https://www.vulture.com/2015/04/11-things-we-learned-about-goodfellas.html.

[32] Ebiri, '11 Things We Learned About *Goodfellas*'.

dexterity, with just a touch of flamboyance, with which the ketchup flows on to the plate.

Ketchup is also mentioned in the very last scene of the film, when Hill has entered the witness protection scheme and complains: 'Can't even get decent food. Right after I got here, I ordered some spaghetti with marinara sauce, and I got egg noodles and ketchup. I'm an average nobody'. So De Niro's gesture with the ketchup bottle is also a way of connecting to Hill's disillusion: this is the moment when Hill sees what becoming a gangster entails, and when he finally escapes all that he will be able to retain is the ketchup, which therefore stands for both fakery and authenticity, and for both the pleasure in killing and the revulsion at it. Pileggi's comments show that making the ketchup bottle a part of the scene was something De Niro and Scorsese had been thinking about in advance, and there are many powerful ways in which De Niro's action with the bottle ties together the meanings and harmonics of both the scene and the film.

The moment provides yet another demonstration that De Niro is something other than a pure Method actor, and he has occasionally attracted criticism for this. As Lesley Stern observes, De Niro 'adopts some of the laconic, sardonic tropes of an earlier Hollywood masculinity and yet has leaned from the method boys a rhetoric of the body. Perhaps it is his more Catholic and inventive rhetorical ploys that incite an uneasiness, and sometimes hostility from those who seek to site him squarely within a Method tradition'.[33] In the ketchup scene De Niro is integrating the practices of performance, the original text and Pileggi's screenplay, and incorporating Jimmy Burke's gesture into his fictional Conway to produce something that blends the 'real' and the 'authentic' with the dramatic and the artistic. Everything was improvised in the scene except the exchange about the painting, which was made by Pileggi's mother. But the odd imagery draws attention to another form of illusion, at the moment where the film is closest to naturalism. The director Martin Scorsese's mother welcomes the actor Robert De Niro to her table just as she had done many times before, but she reaches down for a painting created by the writer Nicholas Pileggi's mother—a painting that just happens to be under the kitchen table in the middle of the night. The gesture is another element in an act of showing in which they are all

[33] Lesley Stern, *The Scorsese Connection* (Indianapolis: Indiana University Press, 1995), p. 210.

participating. *Goodfellas* is a collage: of the real, the remembered and the performed, and of the facts of the present situation, with a baroque emphasis on details of the lives of both the writer and the director, who in this scene are sharing these elements of their lives just as an actor does. De Niro's annotations are made in this vein.

If the notion of character has a very different quality in *Goodfellas* than it does in *The Untouchables*, so does his route to building his performance. In *Goodfellas* the complexity of the annotations is taken to another, often breathtaking level. In addition to annotations and lines De Niro adds colour, using a highlighter pen. This adds to the visual complexity of the image, which is also enhanced by blue ballpoint and black felt tip. Boxes, underlinings, arrows and other graphic techniques are used to connect moments and concepts in the script. He is doing something similar in the way he is assembling his performance. For example, there are two versions of the scene in which De Niro as Jimmy is sounding out Ray Liotta's Henry Hill and preparing to murder him, having just threatened and failed to kill Henry's wife Karen. In the first version, De Niro makes several different annotations, including variant line readings, analyses of subtext and motivation, and suggestions for action and gesture:

> *I been telling you your whole fucking life don't talk on the phone. Waving paper Now maybe you understand. But it's gonna be Ok we've been in worse situations.*

> *I had to feel him out test the fucking water*
> *They're our worst fucking enemy*
> *I know that we both know what I have to do*

There are other ways in which he uses various levels of text in the scene to represent what was and was not said. For example, he suggests and crosses out words and variant possibilities that are implied but not spoken: '*Down in that place where we had that* beef Trouble *where that thing happened*'. He suggests an alternate '*Would you have any problem going down there with Anthony. Would you?*' This, the version that was used in the finished film, is emphasised by a line surrounding the text, but instead of marking it off with a box, as he has done in some other annotations, here the line surrounding De Niro's suggested text twists and bends, making the text itself look like a snake, as De Niro finds a way for his character to invite Henry Hill to become complicit in his own murder.

Other lines that were not ultimately used suggest the tonal delivery. In the above-mentioned scene in the diner, immediately after he has threatened Karen and is trying to persuade Henry to come to Florida (to be killed), he changes the subject but with an implicit threat: '*How's Karen?*' acts like a flashback to the previous scene, in which he has probably tried to have her murdered. The entire layout of the page shows a complicated structure where the analytical thoughts of De Niro or his character Jimmy meet with interventions of a different kind. Individual words he adds to the text operate like words in a collage, scattered on the page of the screenplay, as interruptions that appear in the midst of the text, grammatically unconnected to sentences: '*The face*'; '*Eye contact*'. Again, this is not a technique that we have seen De Niro employ elsewhere. These laconic words-as-images, which function very much like cutaways in a film, become a way of textually representing his own face as it will appear visually in the scene. De Niro's techniques in the annotations, then, are similar to, and offer a textual representation of, the filmic techniques that Scorsese is planning to use in the finished film. This, after all, is a scene where freeze frame is specified in the screenplay De Niro is annotating. It is a reminder that De Niro is never just preparing a performance, he is preparing a *filmed* performance, and just as he has adapted to delivering performance to a camera, he also explores how performance can be adapted to other areas of the medium.

In this complicated form of representation the script becomes more provisional. De Niro chips away at the text, finding ways of blurring the clear boundary between what was written in the screenplay and what will be said or done on film, just as Scorsese wanted to break up traditional ways of shooting. The provisionality of the text is enhanced visually by the green highlighter pen, which underlines the moments when Jimmy has to speak and actions that mention him. Just as his annotations to *The Untouchables* show De Niro's attentiveness to representing Mamet's writing style, the annotations to *Goodfellas* can be seen to be finding modes of representing Scorsese's visual strategy for the film. If time is the medium of cinema, the notes on *Goodfellas* show De Niro's response to the complexity of Scorsese's use of flashback, multiple timelines and stylistic curlicues, including freeze frame and slow motion: 'all the basic tricks of the [French] New Wave from around 1961', as Scorsese remarked.[34]

Many of these 'tricks' are referenced in the screenplay, for which Scorsese received a credit as co-writer for the first time since *Mean Streets*.[35] 'I was interested in breaking up all the traditional ways of shooting the picture', he remarked in an interview in the year of the film's release, and 'the hell with the exposition'. Citing also Federico Fellini's *I Vitelloni* (1953) and Bernardo Bertolucci's *Before the Revolution* (1964), Scorsese notes that *Goodfellas* is characterised by jump cuts, voice-over, 'compressing time' and 'jump[ing] the scene together', so that '[t]he action is pulled out of the middle of the scene, but I know where I'm going to cut it [...] the style gave me the sense of going on a ride, some sort of crazed amusement-park ride, going through the Underworld, in a way'.[36] As we saw, De Niro employs his own analogous cut-up approach in his annotations to *Goodfellas*: time is interrupted; he flashes back.

There are other imaginative ways in which he uses his words on the page to connect to the printed dialogue of the screenplay, as seen in Fig. 7.1:

> JIMMY
> He's hiding, the son of a bitch, in Florida.
> HENRY
> Yeah.
> JIMMY
> I want you and Anthony to go down there and take care of that bastard. Without him, they've got no case.

In his annotations here, De Niro finds graphic ways to connect the printed text of the screenplay to the spoken word of the actor. After the printed words 'Without him they've', De Niro adds '*Got nothing*', extending the dialogue into the margin and rewriting it so that the attempt to convince Henry is now multiply present on the page: '*Me and you we gotta take care of that situation. Without that they got nothing*'.

---

[34] David Thomson and Ian Christie (ed.), *Scorsese on Scorsese* (London; Boston: Faber & Faber, 1989), p. 151.

[35] Wilson, p. 164.

[36] Kathleen Murphy, Martin Scorsese and Gavin Smith, 'Made Men', *Film Comment*, Vol. 26, No. 5 (1990), p. 69.

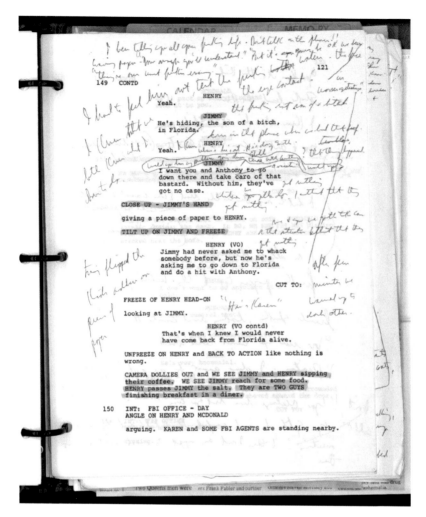

Fig. 7.1 *Goodfellas* (1990), Shooting script, Box 187, RDN, p. 121

The annotations, like the film itself, are a stylised collage. De Niro often places material from the wiretaps in quotation marks, but these are always about the facts:

On page 234 Henry says he doesn't think they have a case & then I could say 'yeah right and of course and don't worry while somewhere there being preoccupied with a million things like 'what's he saying, really?' 'he's bluffing, lying' How can I get him?' 'How?' etc.

Do some Improv here (see how Ray [Liotta] *is)*

And in response to Henry's voice-over describing the meeting—'If you're part of a crew nobody tells you that they're going to kill you'—and the stage direction 'Jimmy looks up', on the page is a laconic '*eh*'. The '*eh*' is a thought from the future, connecting Jimmy's look during Henry's voice-over to the moment when the other character is remembering this scene and what it means.

On the next page, during a long voice-over, De Niro writes in the left-hand margin '*What happens during this?*', while in the right suggests '*Maybe more here good— to cover up what we're both feeling*'. Further down the page is a laconic suggested addition in black felt tip: '*some shitty*' to precede 'Quaaludes'. De Niro ensures the whole dialogue is rethought in the light of the lines about what can be used in court. This maintains the dramatic irony in which his character Jimmy, who has guided Henry Hill on his journey to becoming a gangster, continues his teacherly tone. Jimmy's reiteration to Henry of his earlier advice about never speaking on the phone reminds us of the nature and intensity of their relationship, and in turn makes Henry's voice-over, in which he realises that Jimmy is planning to have his former apprentice whacked, more powerful and more shocking.

De Niro's notes to Scorsese ensure that this is not lost in the revisions. Hill's voice-over in the original screenplay reads:

HENRY

Jimmy had never asked me to whack anyone before. It was crazy. He said he wanted me to go down to Florida and do a hit with Anthony. If anything happened to me down there he and Mickey would be crying at my funeral with Karen. If he got rid of me in Florida he wouldn't even have to hit Karen.

Freeze of Henry head on, looking at JIMMY.

HENRY

That's when I knew I would never have come back from Florida alive.

De Niro's annotations propose a break after 'Anthony', with the following note to Scorsese: '_Marty Too long? You see here's he's saying it twice, in original went like from here_'—with a line to Anthony and a looping line that connects to 'That's when I knew I would never have come back from Florida alive'. But he also adds: '_Marty[.] What about when MacDonald_ [the Detective in the case] _plays that tape and Sepe and whoever else and me talk about whacking Henry good thing to have maybe!_' The dialogue in the finished film follows De Niro's suggested cut: 'Jimmy had never asked me to whack somebody before. But now he's asking me to go down to Florida and do a hit with Anthony? That's when I knew I would never have come back from Florida alive'.

De Niro's role here is as more than just an actor. He is not just curating his own role, he is curating the dramatic structure of the film, using the point of view of his character; indeed his advisory role to Scorsese on the script is not unlike his character's role in relation to the protagonist in the movie. De Niro's precision and commitment to team acting are visible in the way he dutifully sits in the background laughing at Tommy's jokes, and in the specifics of his gestures, from a tilt of the head to the opening of a ketchup bottle. The only relationships that De Niro explores are those with Henry Hill, who betrays him, and Tommy, who is betrayed. He lives vicariously through Henry and Tommy and is relying on both of them to achieve what he cannot. He finds ways to represent the complete inaccessibility of Jimmy Conway. He also finds a methodology to represent on the screenplay text the narrative techniques that Scorsese is using. The character De Niro creates in _Goodfellas_ is as much an absence as a presence, but the details of his observation and the control make it in many ways De Niro's finest and most shocking performance.

BIBLIOGRAPHY

ABBREVIATION

RDN: Robert De Niro Papers, Harry Ransom Center, University of Texas at Austin.

PRIMARY

Goodfellas (1990), Shooting script with extensive RDN notes, revised script pages, and production material laid in, Box 187, RDN.

Jackie Brown (1997), Screenplay by Quentin Tarantino; final draft, 16 April 1997, revised through May 1997, with RDN notes, Box, RDN.

The Untouchables (1987), Undated (early) and incomplete script, with RDN notes, Box 145.5, RDN.

Wiseguy: Life in a Mafia Family (1985), Pileggi, Nicholas. annotated by RDN; loose items withdrawn from BV135, BV. 135–136, RDN.

Secondary

Baer, William (ed.), *Elia Kazan: Interviews*, Jackson, MS: University Press of Mississippi, 2001.

Cardullo, Bert et al. (ed.), *Playing to the Camera: Film Actors Discuss Their Craft*, New Haven: Yale University Press, 1998.

Drake, Philip. 'Reconceptualizing Screen Performance', *Journal of Film and Video*, Vol. 58, No. 1/2 (2006), pp. 84–94.

Ebiri, Bilge. '11 Things We Learned About *Goodfellas* From Saturday's Tribeca Q&A', *Vulture*, 26 April 2015, https://www.vulture.com/2015/04/11-thi ngs-we-learned-about-goodfellas.html, [Accessed 25 September 2019].

Eig, Jonathan. 'What You Didn't Know About Gangster Al Capone' (interview), WBUR, 9 August 2010, https://www.wbur.org/npr/128872365/what-you-didnt-know-about-gangster-al-capone [Accessed 20 May 2020].

Harrell, Al. '*The Untouchables:* A Search for Period Flavor', *American Cinematographer*, Vol. 7 (1987), https://staging.ascmag.com/articles/flashback-the-untouchables [Accessed 30 May 2020].

Hill, Henry and Bryon Schreckengost. *A Goodfella's Guide to New York: Your Personal Tour Through the Mob's Notorious Haunts, Hair-Raising Crime Scenes, and Infamous Hot Spots*, New York: Three Rivers Press, 2003.

Hobbs, Dick. 'Obituary: Jimmy Burke', *The Independent*, 29 April 1996, https://www.independent.co.uk/news/obituaries/obituary-jimmy-burke-1307376.html [Accessed 31 May 2020].

Levy, Shawn. *De Niro: A Life*, New York: Three Rivers, 2014.

McAloon, Mick. 'Robert De Niro: Detail in Service of the Truth', *Running From The Reels*, undated, https://runningfromthereels.com/2013/07/18/de-niro-detail-in-service-of-the-truth/ [Accessed 20 May 2020].

Naremore, James. *Acting in the Cinema*. Berkeley: University of California Press, 1988.

Nix, Elizabeth. '8 Things You Should Know About Al Capone', *History*, 5 May 2015, https://www.history.com/news/8-things-you-should-know-about-al-capone [Accessed 20 May 2020].

Smith, Gavin. '*Goodfellas*: Martin Scorsese Interviewed (1990)', *Scraps from the Loft*, 15 February 2018, https://scrapsfromtheloft.com/2018/02/15/

goodfellas-martin-scorsese-interview-1990-gavin-smith/ [Accessed 31 May 2020].

Sollosi, Mary. 'The Stars of *The Untouchables* Look Back, 30 Years Later', *Entertainment*, 5 June 2017, https://ew.com/movies/2017/06/05/the-untouchables-kevin-costner-robert-deniro-sean-connery-look-back/ [Accessed 20 May 2020].

Wilson, Michael Henry. *Scorsese on Scorsese* (Cahiers du Cinéma), Paris: Phaidon Press, 2011.

CHAPTER 8

Conclusion

This book has been dedicated to exploring the acting of Robert De Niro via the materials preserved in his archive. It hopes to emphasise the value of primary research: bringing to public attention material that is otherwise unavailable, so that a critical understanding of the work—in this case, the films, and what is required to bring them into being—is enhanced or reoriented.

This means that we have to think differently about De Niro's more recent performances, for which his script materials are not yet available. There is a danger of reverting to the pre-archival situation we described in our introduction, in which critical commentary was too often restricted to a description of affect, speculation about what might occasion it, and an over-reliance on reviews and second-hand anecdote. Nevertheless, we can start to use what we know about the archive, and about De Niro's performance history, in looking at a film like Todd Phillips' *Joker* (2019), already the most successful R-rated film in history. De Niro plays a talk show host whose show is invaded by Joaquin Phoenix' Joker character, just as De Niro's Rupert Pupkin plotted to invade Jerry Lewis' *Jerry Langford Show* in *The King of Comedy*. As Christina Newland observes, 'Todd Phillips has stolen wholesale chunks from the work of Martin Scorsese, especially *Taxi Driver* (1976) and *The King of Comedy* (1984).

© The Author(s) 2020
A. Ganz and S. Price, *Robert De Niro at Work*,
Palgrave Studies in Screenwriting,
https://doi.org/10.1007/978-3-030-47960-2_8

The former inflects the whole cityscape and the visual elements of the film'.[1]

De Niro was only on set for a week, and neither actor, each with a good case to be considered the defining male performer of his generation, felt the need to maintain significant contact with the other.[2] There had previously been conflict about their different methodologies of performance. Phoenix's process appears not to involve the meticulous planning of De Niro, and is something far more unstructured, as Paul Thomas Anderson describes: 'Working with Joaquin kind of requires looseness, it requires an ability to improvise, instinctually, where he might go […] inevitably if you feel that he should sit on the couch, he's going to find a way to sit over there on the chair. That probably contributes to this idea of things having been loose'.[3] De Niro reportedly wanted to have his habitual cast read-through, which conflicted with Phoenix's more serendipitous approach.[4] Ultimately the stand-off was resolved by a recognition of hierarchies that ensured sufficient respect was shown to De Niro, whose presence was so crucial for the film. After Phoenix finally 'mumbled his way through the script […] De Niro turned to Phoenix, took his face in his hands, and kissed him on the cheek. "It's going to be okay, *bubbeleh*," he said'.[5]

This is anecdotal, but greater knowledge of De Niro's working methods as revealed in the archive, especially concerning his approaches to different kinds of improvisation, and the creative potential of developing a character or persona that has previously been embodied by another performer, can enhance our understanding of the reported tensions between the two actors. Perhaps it was Phoenix that De Niro had in mind when he paid tribute to Marlon Brando in an interview for *GQ* to promote Scorsese's *The Irishman*, also released in 2019: 'He was so great.

[1] Christina Newland, '*Joker* Review: Joaquin Phoenix's Alienated Antihero Is No Laughing Matter', *Sight and Sound*, 14 November 2019, https://www.bfi.org.uk/news-opinion/sight-sound-magazine/reviews-recommendations/joker-todd-phillips-joaquin-phoenix [Accessed 23 April 2020].

[2] Joe Hagan, '"I Fucking Love My Life": Joaquin Phoenix on *Joker*, Why River Is His Rosebud, His Rooney Research, and His "Prenatal" Gift for Dark Characters', *Vanity Fair*, 1 October 2019, https://www.vanityfair.com/hollywood/2019/10/joaquin-phoenix-cover-story [Accessed 23 April 2020].

[3] Pierre Sauvage, 'Beware the Golden Fang! An Interview with Paul Thomas Anderson', *Cineaste*, Vol. 40, No. 2 (Spring 2015), p. 21.

[4] Hagan, ibid.

[5] Hagan, ibid.

Actors of my generation all loved him. He was so smart. But then you ask kids today in terms of those actors [...] Some know. Some don't. And nothing, nothing lasts forever'.[6] Ultimately, though, until his script materials for *Joker* are archived, we cannot see clearly how De Niro approached working with Phoenix, or how he felt about watching another actor play a character so influenced by a performance of his own, just as he had been influenced by Brando.

The archive, then, has fundamentally transformed our understanding of De Niro's practice and the role of the actor more generally. Paul Schrader remarks that De Niro 'doesn't feel the need to establish an identity apart from his screen persona. He doesn't want to. The only thing he desires to be public about himself is his work. That's the only thing he estimates has any real value'.[7] For many others, though, the actor's resolute determination to avoid self-revelation presents an interpretive difficulty in responding to the work itself. In 2002 Greg M. Smith published a chapter entitled 'Choosing Silence: Robert De Niro and the Celebrity Interview'. At this point, seven years before the archive opened, Smith could legitimately propose that '[w]hether De Niro's methods actually affect his on-screen performance is open to question'. For example, '[w]e are told that he prepares for a part by asking real people incessant questions, but we never learn what kinds of questions he asks', and De Niro thereby 'further imbues his acting with "realness" while simultaneously mystifying the process'.[8] De Niro's archiving of that process has now answered these questions: it reveals the extent of his dedication, astonishing sensitivity, attention to detail and articulacy of a very particular kind, all of which manifests itself on screen.

[6] Stuart McGurk (Interview), 'Robert De Niro on Martin Scorsese's Ultimate Mafia Masterpiece', *GQ*, 25 November 2019, https://www.gq-magazine.co.uk/culture/article/robert-de-niro-interview [Accessed 15 April 2020].

[7] Quoted in Lorraine York, 'Robert De Niro's (In)articulate Reluctance', in *Reluctant Celebrity: Affect and Privilege in Contemporary Stardom* (Basingstoke: Palgrave, 2018) (pp. 67–100), p. 77.

[8] Greg M. Smith, 'Choosing Silence: Robert De Niro and the Celebrity Interview', in Angela Ndalianis and Charlotte Henry (eds.), *Stars in Our Eyes: The Star Phenomenon in the Contemporary Era* (Westport, CT: Praeger, 2002), (pp. 45–58), p. 50.

We know more about De Niro than we did before, and this means that even in the absence of archival materials pertaining to *Joker*, we can find more informed ways of discussing his performance. As Lorraine York puts it,

> I would not divide De Niro's reluctance into willing embodiment and unwilling verbalization. In the De Niro archives […] there is plenty of evidence of De Niro's capacity to verbalize his acting choices; his generously annotated screenplays challenge the romantic notion of the non-verbal hyper-embodied actor. The reading of De Niro as the inarticulate genius needs this corrective of archival evidence; what looks like simple refusal is, instead, a reluctance that marries intellectual articulateness and a disinclination to produce it on public, promotional occasions.[9]

Moreover, even since York published this article in 2016, De Niro himself has changed. He still avoids gossip, but as an interviewee he has become more forthcoming: he is no longer 'choosing silence'. If the interviews inevitably provide none of the detail of the archival annotations, what they do offer is perhaps De Niro's most sustained public articulation of his philosophy of performance, and this seems to have been directly prompted by the intensification of a war of words with Donald Trump in which he has been engaged since 2011.[10] A recent interview that was set-up ostensibly to discuss *The Irishman* prompted the interviewer to remark that when De Niro talks about Trump, 'his natural reticence evaporates and anger […] drives an eloquence that can otherwise elude him'.[11]

In so doing he has begun to articulate more publicly his own ideas of what performance is and should be, and to explore more openly the moral and ethical considerations involved in bringing a character to the screen. For De Niro performance is an intensely moral activity, a form of research and expression which has as its heart exploring the human condition, just as dramatist Terence wrote over two thousand years ago: '*Homo sum, humani nihil a me alienum puto*' ('I am human and nothing human is

---

[9] Lorraine York, '"You (Not) Talkin' to Me?": Robert De Niro and the Affective Paradox of Reluctant Celebrity', *The Smart Set*, 25 April 2016, https://www.thesmartset.com/you-not-talkin-to-me-2/ [Accessed 29 June 2020].

[10] Palash Ghosh, 'Trump and DeNiro Engage in War of Words Over Obama', *International Business Times*, 25 April 2011, https://www.ibtimes.com/trump-deniro-engage-war-words-over-obama-281171 [Accessed 23 April 2020].

[11] McGurk, ibid.

alien to me'). Paradoxically, his repeated attacks on the current President appear to be connected to De Niro's perception that Trump lacks an essential human quality—the possibility for redemption—that makes him unperformable.

The two men are in many ways polar opposites, but they have much in common: they are both media stars, property developers with interests in hospitality and iconic New Yorkers. And if De Niro is a performer who has often played a gangster, Trump is a performer who sometimes claimed to have gangster connections, explaining in 2004 that he could never be in a reality show because 'mobsters don't like, as they're talking to me, having cameras all over the room'.[12] He may of course have already been performing,[13] but this connection between the two men even reached the floor of the House of Representatives when House Speaker Nancy Pelosi, before signing the articles of impeachment against Trump for requesting that the Ukrainian President 'Do us a favor', mockingly reframed him as De Niro's character in *The Irishman*: 'Do you paint houses too? What is this? "Do me a favor"?'[14]

It is the notion of Trump as being in any way 'authentic' above all that De Niro finds unacceptable. He considers him 'a mutt who doesn't know what he's talking about, doesn't do his homework, doesn't care'.[15] De Niro's own focus in building a performance—on doing his homework—is on a process of transformation, centred around the notion of honesty or believability on screen. In his annotations on *Casino*, for example (a film based on real events written by Nicolas Pileggi, author of the book

[12] Quoted in Patrick Radden Keefe, 'How Mark Burnett Resurrected Donald Trump as an Icon of American Success', *The New Yorker*, 27 December 2018, https://www.new yorker.com/magazine/2019/01/07/how-mark-burnett-resurrected-donald-trump-as-an-icon-of-american-success [Accessed 23 April 2020].

[13] But see David Cay Johnston, 'Just What Were Donald Trump's Ties to the Mob?', *Politico Magazine*, 22 May 2016, https://www.politico.com/magazine/story/2016/05/donald-trump-2016-mob-organized-crime-213910 [Accessed 23 April 2020].

[14] Aaron Feis, 'Pelosi Quotes *Irishman* Before Signing Impeachment Articles Against Trump', *York New Post*, 15 January 2020, https://nypost.com/2020/01/15/pelosi-quo tes-irishman-after-signing-impeachment-articles-against-trump/ [Accessed 23 April 2020].

[15] Daniel Kreps, 'See Robert De Niro Eviscerate Trump: "I'd Like to Punch Him in the Face"', *Rolling Stone*, 8 October 2016, https://www.rollingstone.com/politics/pol itics-news/see-robert-de-niro-eviscerate-trump-id-like-to-punch-him-in-the-face-111689/ [Accessed 23 April 2020].

on which *Goodfellas* was based), he sometimes just adds laconically in the margin: '*True?*'

In contrast to De Niro's investment of his performance with research-based understanding, Mark Burnett, who devised *The Apprentice*, reveals how the Trump on-screen persona was manufactured in the editing, especially by the use of reaction shots, to retrospectively structure a narrative and make him seem more acute than he was.[16] Shortly after a gunman had killed 22 people in El Paso, De Niro told *GQ* that Trump is 'dangerous. That stupid show *The Apprentice*, people bought it. They buy into it. […] They created a monster'.[17] James Poniewozik has argued that the key to Trump's persona is that 'he did not consider whether his words were kind or responsible or pleasing—or true—but simply whether he wanted to say them. That was being real, which was better than being honest, more liberating than being tethered to fact'.[18]

De Niro has responded not just as a citizen, but as an actor. As he told Stephen Colbert: 'As an actor, I watch this, and I say: "This is like Shakespeare." […] What could be worth it to them [Trump's Republican enablers], to sacrifice their souls? To make this deal with the devil to work with this guy?'[19] It was De Niro who proposed to *Saturday Night Live* producer Lorne Michaels the idea that he could take on the recurrent role of Robert Mueller, who as Special Counsel for the Department of Justice oversaw the investigation into alleged Russian interference in the 2016 Presidential election[20]; when asked why, he said he considered it his 'civic duty'.[21] He has said that Trump is the only character he could never play because 'There's nothing redeemable about him, and I never

[16] Keefe, ibid.

[17] McGurk, ibid.

[18] James Poniewozik, *Audience of One: Donald Trump, Television, and the Fracturing of America* (New York: Liveright, 2019), p. 251.

[19] Louis Chilton, 'Robert De Niro slams Trump Associates' *Independent*, 7 May 2020, https://www.independent.co.uk/arts-entertainment/films/news/robert-de-niro-trump-stephen-colbert-interview-shakespeare-president-a9503241.html [Accessed 6 June 2020].

[20] *Late Night with Seth Meyers*, Show 0928, NBC, aired 17 December 2019, https://www.youtube.com/watch?v=1d7vZmrl2oY [Accessed 23 April 2020].

[21] 'De Niro Says It's His "Civic Duty" to Play Mueller on SNL', *Reuters*, 4 April 2019, https://www.reuters.com/video/watch/de-niro-says-its-his-civic-duty-to-play-id533905347 [Accessed 28 June 2020].

say that about any character'.[22] Or even more simply: 'He's not even evil [...] He's mundane'.[23]

Whatever Trump's intentions in characterising De Niro as having 'received too many shots to the head by real boxers in movies. I watched him last night and truly believe he may be "punch-drunk"',[24] it suggests he is trying to establish a binary opposition between actors and 'real' boxers, one that contrasts tellingly with his own polarised erosion of difference between performance and self. By contrast, in another interview to mark the launch of *The Irishman*, De Niro connected the need to maintain the boundary between reality and fiction to the responsibilities of the actor: 'What we're doing in film, it's like a dream. We know it's not real. There are people who will take anything to be real and that we have no control over'.[25] It was a reminder that De Niro has always seen performance as both an artistic and an ethical activity. He knows all too well the responsibility he faces as a creator of illusions: in March 1981 John Hinckley tried to assassinate President Reagan, inspired by De Niro's portrayal of Travis Bickle in *Taxi Driver* and obsessed by the character Jodie Foster played. Hinckley remarked of the shooting: 'I felt like I was walking into a movie',[26] and when asked why he bought so many handguns he replied: 'because Travis bought so many handguns. Ask him. Not me'.[27]

As a performer De Niro's talent has been devoted to making audiences understand the character he is performing through inspiring a kind of critical sympathy, achieved through the techniques revealed by the archive.

---

[22] David Marchese (Interview), 'Great Performers: Robert De Niro', *New York Times Magazine*, 9 December 2019, https://www.nytimes.com/interactive/2019/12/09/magazine/robert-deniro-interview.html [Accessed 15 April 2020].

[23] David Smith, 'Robert De Niro: "Trump Is a Real Racist, a White Supremacist"', *The Guardian*, 6 January 2019, https://www.theguardian.com/film/2019/jan/06/robert-de-niro-trump-is-a-real-racist-a-white-supremacist [Accessed 15th June 2020].

[24] Donald J. Trump, Twitter Post, 13 June 2018, 10:40 a.m. https://twitter.com/realDonaldTrump/status/1006833565022031873?s=20 [Accessed 23 April 2020].

[25] Marchese, ibid.

[26] Michael Newton, 'Assassination at the Movies', *The Guardian*, 4 October 2012, https://www.theguardian.com/books/2012/oct/04/assassination-movies-michael-newton [Accessed 23 April 2020].

[27] '*Taxi Driver* Inspires Real Sequel—With A Frightening End', *Chicago Tribune*, 23 May 1985, https://www.chicagotribune.com/news/ct-xpm-1985-05-23-8502010882-story.html [Accessed 23 April 2020].

This extraordinary quality in De Niro was described by Scorsese in 1995: 'He takes characters that ordinarily are your villains—and in my pictures I like to make them heroes, in a way—and there's something about him that's very compassionate and the audience feels for him. And so there's no character he plays that's irredeemable. They can do anything'.[28] De Niro discussed this approach in explaining one way in which he went about creating the character of Frank Sheehan in *The Irishman*:

> The rule in acting is you never make a judgment about your character. The characters have their reasons, and you understand them. You're trying to look at their point of view. I mean, in *The Irishman*, Frank has a problem with his daughter. He has problems that anybody can relate to. I never thought of him as being amoral or immoral. He lives in a world where the penalties are harsh if you don't do what you're supposed to do. He says he's going to do something, he does it.[29]

For *The Irishman* De Niro resumed his partnership with Scorsese, perhaps the most significant actor/director partnership since Akira Kurosawa and Toshiro Mifune, revisiting the world of the New York gangster that De Niro had made his own since his breakthrough role in *The Godfather, Part II*. As De Niro points out in an interview with David Marchese, 'The fact that me, Joe [Pesci] and Al [Pacino] were doing this film is something in and of itself [...] Marty directing it says something. It all sets a tone. The audience's perception of each character, us actors being together and what the story is—the film is all those things'.[30] In the same interview he expands on his process:

> In acting they say: Make it your own. Personalize it. It's the same thing with these stories. There has to be some — I don't like to say poetic license, because that has a negative connotation when it shouldn't — but it's a way of expressing how you see it. It doesn't mean it's right. But it's how you see yourself.[31]

---

[28] McGurk, ibid.

[29] Marchese, ibid.

[30] Marchese, ibid.

[31] Marchese, ibid.

In response to Marchese's direct question 'What did you see in yourself that you put into Frank Sheeran?', De Niro initially deflects ('Aha! *That* is the question'), before putting the focus on his working methods, not his personal life:

> the answer is personal. I mean, when I talked to Marty about certain things about the film — sometimes he's like a priest. We talk, and I have to be honest with him in order to get stuff in the film that we need to say. But it's personal stuff that I would express through the character. It's not stuff I'd tell other people.[32]

While happy to reveal that he uses his personal life in shaping his performance, then, De Niro is silent about the specifics of 'certain things'; he maintains a clear distinction between discussion of his process and gossip. The intimate material has value precisely because it is not 'stuff I'd tell other people', and how those weighty silences are used in shaping the role remains a matter for him.

We have argued that De Niro writes (on) the film with his body, and described in some detail the attention he pays to ensure that every aspect is as precise as it can be. In *The Irishman*, digital technology was used to alter the image and de-age his character, producing a kind of hybrid imagery in which he is responsible for his movements and expression, but only to a degree. Marchese asks how this embodiment works when the actor is not 'able to feel those changes physically', in comparison to (for example) *Raging Bull*, to which De Niro responds that 'it's harder to act younger than it is the other way round [...] some people felt [...] they could see my real age. O.K., fine, that's interesting. I should've taken steroids or something'.[33]

De Niro might have used his conversations with Scorsese and his own emotional memory to evoke an emotion, but it was harder to retain the delicacy in his performance once the images were digitally treated. We have noted earlier the emotional affect created by the extended close-ups on De Niro's eyes in many of his most celebrated performances, and it is surely significant that De Niro gave an expansive response to Marchese in focusing on how the new digital technology created a problem regarding this particular aspect of his work:

[32] Marchese, ibid.
[33] Marchese, ibid.

Marty would see, and I saw it, too, that there would be an expression in my eyes during a scene, but after they youth-ified me, my eyes had a different emotional expression. Marty was concerned about that. I had the right emotional intention, the right attitude, but when that de-aging came, the expression in the eye changed. So they had to figure out a way to make sure that after I was youth-ified it would not alter the intention of the scene as we acted it. It was an interesting problem.[34]

De Niro and the director had to ensure that the digitised figure of Frank Sheeran retained what Marchese called 'soul'.

Ironically, 'soul' was precisely what De Niro was accused of lacking by many critics, including Pauline Kael, who appeared to confuse his taciturnity with absence in remarking that 'De Niro in disguise denies his characters a soul. It's not merely that he hollows himself out and becomes Jake La Motta, or Des the priest in *True Confessions*, or Rupert Pupkin (in *King of Comedy*)— he makes them hollow, too, and merges with the characters' emptiness'.[35] As Lorraine York observes in her 2018 book chapter discussing 'Robert De Niro's (In)articulate Reluctance', 'Kael does not stop to consider that in the case of Rupert Pupkin, his lack of a "soul" has everything to do with that film's caustic critique of the desire for fame: the two-dimensionality of the cardboard cutouts of stars that Rupert "interviews" in his basement fantasy sessions are very much to the point'.[36]

In York's acute analysis, journalists and critics are too often trapped in their own myths of performance and expectations of how an actor 'should' perform off-screen. Unlike Smith, York had access to the Ransom Center archive, and puts it to excellent use, analysing the articulacy of his script annotations and the depth of his research but also looking at the extensive correspondence to reveal his generosity and warmth. She quotes, for example, 'a lovely note from the British director Michael Powell in 1984, thanking De Niro for offering his thoughts on a script: "Thank you for reading the draft script. It was just like you: very deliberate before making a move and very generous when you do"'. As York suggests, '[w]e have, it would seem, made much of Robert De Niro's

---

[34] Marchese, ibid.

[35] Quoted in York, 'Robert De Niro's (In)articulate Reluctance', p. 75.

[36] York, 'Robert De Niro's (In)articulate Reluctance', p. 96, fn. 1.

deliberation, to the exclusion of his generosity'.[37] She traces his readiness to speak about things he cares about, and how this has increased as he has grown older and more confident, and observes that '[w]hen there is a sense of commitment, then, to a cause, whether a professional one, such as Tribeca's support for filmmakers, or a personal one, growing out of his own experience, De Niro reveals, even if for a moment, his affectively open, communicative side'.[38]

This side of the actor has in recent years emerged particularly strongly in his greater willingness to talk about his father, including in the documentary *Remembering the Artist: Robert De Niro, Sr.*, which the son made for HBO in 2014. Strikingly, in this film, as York notes, 'the actor is openly emotional when he speaks of his father's life and career, his struggles with lack of recognition, and with being gay'.[39] In 2019 De Niro helped to consolidate his father's place in an art world that had often rejected him in life when Rizzoli Electa published a beautiful monograph *Robert De Niro Senior: Paintings, Writing and Drawings, 1942–1993*. The book highlights Robert De Niro Senior's work as a painter, and reprints some of his poetry and extracts from his diaries. It discusses his formation and struggle for success, and comments on his work. Above all it reproduces his pictures, his life's work of powerful imagery rooted in art history.

In his introduction, Robert De Niro Jr observes that 'art is made to be seen and experienced. Throughout his life my father believed his work would outlast him [...] This book is my way of making that happen'.[40] The son acknowledges that 'I am not an art historian or a documentarian and I know that I cannot alone be the curator of my father's legacy. With this volume I turn to art historians and curators Robert Storr, Charles Stuckey Susan Davidson and the artist Robert Kushner to view my father's work through the lens of their expertise'.[41] We cannot help thinking

---

[37] York, 'Robert De Niro's (In)articulate Reluctance', p. 81.

[38] York, 'Robert De Niro's (In)articulate Reluctance', p. 84.

[39] York, 'Robert De Niro's (In)articulate Reluctance', p. 84.

[40] Robert De Niro Jr., 'Introduction', in Robert Storr, Charles Stuckey, Robert Kushner and Susan Davidson, *Robert De Niro, Sr.: Paintings, Drawings, and Writings: 1942–1993* (New York, NY: Rizzoli, 2019), p. 9.

[41] De Niro Jr., p. 9.

about the similarities between the way he has made his father's work available to scholars and the way he has made it possible for researchers to study his own process as an actor. We and those others who have taken advantage of the astonishing resource of the Robert De Niro collection have only touched on the possibilities of what the archives reveal, about his own practice, and about the cinema in the second half of the twentieth century. They offer an extraordinary record of some of the greatest films ever made, and the working practices of some of the greatest writers and directors at a particular historical moment. They will contain the life's work of an actor from his first student films to the films we have discussed here, and every other project he makes or tries to make. In making these accessible he is continuing in the spirit of his father's quest for the truth in art among everything, and his own battle to protect the context in which making art was possible.

Critic Irving Sandler, interviewed for the HBO documentary, says that Robert De Niro Sr 'just had to paint [...] Piero della Francesca, Velazquez, these are your gods. You're painting for the greater glory of art, not for anybody out there, really'.[42] Although the son received success on a scale that the father could not even dream of, they are united in homage to the work itself and its place in human understanding. A screen performance, Stanley Cavell observed, 'requires not so much training as planning'.[43] De Niro's planning both for each moment within every individual role and for the execution of the entire project is meticulous, and he is able to combine this extraordinary attention to detail while retaining the possibility for improvisation and for others to express themselves as well as himself. His attention is on the story and the work, and he is always interested in exploration rather than repeating what he already knows.

When asked what he might hope to see if he were to review all of his own films, De Niro replied: 'I would probably be apprehensive, because I'm critical about what I did. But the other thing is what I could learn if I looked at all my stuff and got an idea of what I've done, what the pattern is. Because I'd like to do something that's really different from

[42] Robert Storr, in Storr et al., p. 23.

[43] Stanley Cavell, *The World Viewed: Reflections on the Ontology of Film* (Cambridge, MA: Harvard University Press, 1979), p. 28.

what I've done or been known to do'.[44] Even in his seventies he is still thinking about what he could do differently. De Niro has devoted a career to study how a text appears on a film, and he knows that he has not yet exhausted the possibilities. As Cavell observes, 'It is an incontestable fact that in a motion picture no live human being is up there. But a human *something* is, and something unlike anything else we know'.[45] No-one has done more than Robert De Niro find that 'human something' from a text and find ways to put it up on screen, drawing on analysis, embodied performance, and a grace in motion which still has a capacity to astonish. It is not surprising that he is now battling to protect the values that he has lived by for over half a century.

BIBLIOGRAPHY

Cavell, Stanley. *The World Viewed: Reflections on the Ontology of Film*, Cambridge, MA: Harvard University Press, 1979.

Cay Johnston, David. 'Just What Were Donald Trump's Ties to the Mob?', *Politico Magazine*, 22 May 2016, https://www.politico.com/mag azine/story/2016/05/donald-trump-2016-mob-organized-crime-213910 [Accessed 23 April 2020].

Chilton, Louis, 'Robert De Niro slams Trump Associates' *Independent*, 7 May 2020 https://www.independent.co.uk/arts-entertainment/films/news/ robert-de-niro-trump-stephen-colbert-interview-shakespeare-president-a95 03241.html [Accessed 6 June 2020].

'De Niro Says It's His "Civic Duty" to Play Mueller on SNL', *Reuters*, 4 April 2019, https://www.reuters.com/video/watch/de-niro-says-its-his-civic-duty-to-play-id533905347 [Accessed 28 June 2020].

De Niro, Robert. 'Introduction', in Robert Storr, Charles Stuckey, Robert Kushner and Susan Davidson, *Robert De Niro, Sr.: Paintings, Drawings, and Writings: 1942–1993* (New York, NY: Rizzoli, 2019), p. 9.

Feis, Aaron. 'Pelosi Quotes *Irishman* Before Signing Impeachment Articles Against Trump', *York New Post*, 15 January 2020, https://nypost.com/ 2020/01/15/pelosi-quotes-irishman-after-signing-impeachment-articles-aga inst-trump/ [Accessed 23 April 2020].

Ghosh, Palash. 'Trump and DeNiro Engage in War of Words Over Obama', *International Business Times*, 25 April 2011, https://www.

---

[44] Marchese, ibid.

[45] Cavell, p. 26, italics in the original.

ibtimes.com/trump-deniro-engage-war-words-over-obama-281171 [Accessed 23 April 2020].

Hagan, Joe. '"I Fucking Love My Life": Joaquin Phoenix on *Joker*, Why River Is His Rosebud, His Rooney Research, and His "Prenatal" Gift for Dark Characters'. *Vanity Fair*, 1 October 2019, https://www.vanityfair.com/hol lywood/2019/10/joaquin-phoenix-cover-story [Accessed 23 April 2020].

Kreps, Daniel. 'See Robert De Niro Eviscerate Trump: "I'd Like to Punch Him in the Face"', *Rolling Stone*, 8 October 2016, https://www.rollingst one.com/politics/politics-news/see-robert-de-niro-eviscerate-trump-id-like-to-punch-him-in-the-face-111689/ [Accessed 23 April 2020].

Late Night with Seth Meyers, Show 0928, NBC, aired 17 December 2019, https://www.youtube.com/watch?v=1d7vZmr12oY [Accessed 23 April 2020].

Marchese, David (Interview). 'Great Performers: Robert De Niro', *New York Times Magazine*, 9 December 2019, https://www.nytimes.com/int eractive/2019/12/09/magazine/robert-deniro-interview.html [Accessed 15 April 2020].

McGurk, Stuart (Interview). 'Robert De Niro on Martin Scorsese's Ultimate Mafia Masterpiece', *GQ*, 25 November 2019, https://www.gq-magazine.co. uk/culture/article/robert-de-niro-interview [Accessed 15 April 2020].

Newland, Christina. '*Joker* Review: Joaquin Phoenix's Alienated Antihero Is No Laughing Matter', *Sight and Sound*, 14 November 2019, https://www. bfi.org.uk/news-opinion/sight-sound-magazine/reviews-recommendations/joker-todd-phillips-joaquin-phoenix [Accessed 23 April 2020].

Newton, Michael. 'Assassination at the movies', *The Guardian*, 4 October 2012, https://www.theguardian.com/books/2012/oct/04/assassination-movies-michael-newton [Accessed 23 April 2020].

Poniewozik, James. *Audience of One: Donald Trump, Television, and the Fracturing of America*, New York: Liveright, 2019.

Radden Keefe, Patrick. 'How Mark Burnett Resurrected Donald Trump as an Icon of American Success', *The New Yorker*, 27 December 2018, https://www.newyorker.com/magazine/2019/01/07/how-mark-bur nett-resurrected-donald-trump-as-an-icon-of-american-success [Accessed 23 April 2020].

Sauvage, Pierre. 'Beware the Golden Fang! An Interview with Paul Thomas Anderson', *Cineaste*, Vol. 40, No. 2 (Spring 2015), p. 21.

Smith, David. 'Robert De Niro: "Trump Is a Real Racist, a White Supremacist"', *The Guardian*, 6 January 2019, https://www.theguardian.com/film/2019/jan/06/robert-de-niro-trump-is-a-real-racist-a-white-supremacist [Accessed 15 June 2020].

Smith, Greg M. 'Choosing Silence: Robert De Niro and the Celebrity Interview', in Angela Ndalianis and Charlotte Henry (Eds.), *Stars in Our Eyes: The Star*

Phenomenon in the Contemporary Era (Westport, CT: Praeger, 2002), pp. 45–58.

Storr, Robert, Charles Stuckey, Robert Kushner and Susan Davidson, *Robert De Niro, Sr.: Paintings, Drawings, and Writings: 1942–1993* (New York, NY: Rizzoli, 2019).

'*Taxi Driver* Inspires Real Sequel—With A Frightening End', *Chicago Tribune*, 23 May 1985, https://www.chicagotribune.com/news/ct-xpm-1985-05-23-8502010882-story.html [Accessed 23 April 2020].

Trump, Donald J. Twitter Post, 13 June 2018, 10:40 a.m. https://twitter.com/realDonaldTrump/status/1006833565022031873?s=20 [Accessed 23 April 2020].

York, Lorraine '"You (Not) Talkin' to Me?": Robert De Niro and the Affective Paradox of Reluctant Celebrity', *The Smart Set*, 25 April 2016, https://www.thesmartset.com/you-not-talkin-to-me-2/ [Accessed 29 June 2020].

York, Lorraine. 'Robert De Niro's (In)articulate Reluctance', in *Reluctant Celebrity: Affect and Privilege in Contemporary Stardom* (Basingstoke: Palgrave, 2018), pp. 67–100.

Bibliography

Abbreviation

RDN: Robert De Niro Papers, Harry Ransom Center, University of Texas at Austin.

Primary

A Tree Is a Tree (1953), Vidor, King, annotated by RDN, BV 201, RDN.

Arthur (1981), by Steve Gordon, with John Gielgud notes, ADD MS 81370, John Gielgud Archive, British Library, London.

Bloody Mama (1970), Screenplay by Robert Thom, Shooting script; final draft with shooting schedules, photographs of RDN, research photographs, and song lyrics inserted; extensive RDN notes, Box 178, RDN.

Brazil (1985), Screenplay by Terry Gilliam, Tom Stoppard, and Charles McKeown, undated, Box 20.2, RDN.

The Godfather, Part II (1974), Shooting script, with RDN notes, lacks title page; contains 'old script' and 'new script' pages, with additional script pages and extensive RDN notes re character development, undated, Box 182, RDN.

Goodfellas (1990), Shooting script with extensive RDN notes, revised script pages, and production material laid in, Box 187, RDN.

The Hoods. Novel by Harry Gray (photocopy), with RDN notes, Box 120.1, RDN.

Jackie Brown (1997), Screenplay by Quentin Tarantino; final draft, 16 April 1997, revised through May 1997, with RDN notes, Box, RDN.

The King of Comedy (1983), Production materials (Character and script notes, list of scenes, lyrics for 'Come Rain or Come Shine', and script fragments), Box 88.1, RDN.

The King of Comedy (1983), Undated script, with RDN notes, Box 235.2, RDN.

The Last Tycoon (1976), 11 August 1975, Script Copy 20, with extensive RDN notes, additional mimeo and RDN notes in pocket at front, Box 191, RDN.

The Last Tycoon (1976), Production materials, notes and correspondence from Elia Kazan re Stahr character, Box 89.2, RDN.

Mayer and Thalberg: The Make-Believe Saints (1975), by Marx, Samuel, annotated by RDN, BV 193, RDN.

Mean Streets (1973), Screenplay by Martin Scorsese, with RDN notes, Folder 93.10, RDN.

Meet the Parents (2000), Revised script, with RDN notes, bound script with inserted re-shoot pages, Box 101.5, RDN.

New York, New York (1977), Shooting script, with script revisions and RDN notes; production material laid in, Box 215, RDN.

Once Upon a Time in America (1984), Script in 151 scenes (291 pages); extra scenes laid in, with RDN notes, undated, Box 120.4, RDN.

Raging Bull (1980), 'Final Script', Box 126.4, RDN.

Raging Bull (1980), Shooting script, with RDN notes, Box 229, RDN.

Raging Bull (1980), undated screenplay by Paul Schrader; with RDN notes, Box 125.3, RDN.

Raging Bull (1980), untitled, undated, rough first draft in three acts; typescript with notes by RDN and Mardik Martin, Box 124.6, RDN.

Raging Bull: My Story (1970), LaMotta, Jake, with Joseph Carter and Peter Savage. inscribed by LaMotta to RDN, and annotated by RDN, BV 235, RDN.

Ronin, Typescript draft by David Mamet, with typed and handwritten revisions, 25 October 1997, Container 176.1, David Mamet Papers, Harry Ransom Center, Texas, Austin.

Rosenthal, Jane to David Mamet (correspondence), 25 October 1977, Container 176.2-4, David Mamet Papers, Harry Ransom Center, Texas, Austin.

Taxi Driver (1976), Screenplay by Paul Schrader, 29 April 1975, Shooting script with revisions to 29 May 1975; shooting schedule and extensive RDN notes throughout; one page of RDN notes re wolves in back pocket, Box 221, RDN.

Thalberg: Life and Legend (1969), Thomas, Bob, annotated by RDN, BV 199, RDN.

The Untouchables (1987), Undated (early) and incomplete script, with RDN notes, Box 145.5, RDN.

Wiseguy: Life in a Mafia Family (1985), Pileggi, Nicholas. annotated by RDN; loose items withdrawn from BV135, BV. 135–136, RDN.

SECONDARY

Abel, Marco. 'Becoming-Violent, Becoming-DeNiro', in *Violent Affect: Literature, Cinema, and Critique After Representation* (Lincoln: University of Nebraska Press, 2007), pp. 133–181.

Auslander, Philip. *Liveness: Performance in a Mediatized Culture*, 2nd ed., London: Routledge, 2008.

Austin, J. L. *How to Do Things with Words*, Oxford: Oxford University Press, 1962.

Baer, William (ed.), *Elia Kazan: Interviews*, Jackson, MS: University Press of Mississippi, 2001.

Balcerzak, Scott. *Beyond Method: Stella Adler and the Male Actor*, Detroit: Wayne State University Press, 2019.

Beale, Simon Russell. 'Without Memory or Desire: Acting Shakespeare', Ernest Jones Lecture organised by the Scientific Committee of the British Psychoanalytical Society, 21 June 2009. The British Psychoanalytical Society Archives, London, UK.

Belgrad, Daniel. The *Culture of Spontaneity: Improvisation and the Arts in Postwar America*, Chicago and London: The University of Chicago Press, 1998.

Benjamin, Walter. 'The Work of Art in the Age of Mechanical Reproduction', in Hannah Arendt (ed.), *Illuminations*, trans. Harry Zohn (New York: Schocken, 1969).

Billington, Michael. *Harold Pinter*, London: Faber, 2007.

Black, Louis. 'Down We Go: Revisiting Renaissance Man Robert Thom's prolific and Hellish Hollywood Visions', *The Austin Chronicle*, 10 August 2007, https://www.austinchronicle.com/screens/2007-08-10/517929/ [Accessed: 15 May 2020].

Bordwell, David. 'How to Tell a Movie Story: Mr. Stahr Will See You Now', *Observations on Film Art* (website), 5 January 2014, http://www.davidbordwell.net/blog/2014/01/05/how-to-tell-a-movie-story-mr-stahr-will-see-you-now/ [Accessed 24 May 2020].

Brant, Peter, Colleen Kelsey and Ingrid Sischy, 'A Walk and a Talk with Robert De Niro', *Interview*, 21 March 2012, https://www.interviewmagazine.com/film/new-again-robert-de-niro [Accessed 15 May 2020].

Braudy, Leo. *The World in a Frame: What We See in Films*, Chicago: University of Chicago Press, 1984.

Braudy, Susan. 'Robert De Niro—The Return of the Silent Star', *The New York Times*, 6 March 1977, https://www.nytimes.com/1977/03/06/archives/robert-de-niro-the-return-of-the-silent-screen-star-robert-de-niro.html [Accessed 20 May 2020].

Brewer, John. 'Microhistory and the Histories of Everyday Life', *CAS-LMU eSeries*, No. 5 (2010), pp. 1–16.

Brown, Mark. 'British Library's £1.1m Saves Pinter's Papers for Nation', *The Guardian*, 12 December 2007, https://www.theguardian.com/uk/2007/dec/12/books.theatrenews [Accessed 29 September 2019].

Bruccoli, Matthew J. (ed.). *The Love of the Last Tycoon: A Western*, ed. Matthew J. Bruccoli, Cambridge: Cambridge University Press, 1993.

Bruner, Jerome. 'The Narrative Construction of Reality', *Critical Inquiry*, Vol. 18, No. 1 (Autumn 1991), pp. 1–21.

Cardullo, Bert et al. (ed.), *Playing to the Camera: Film Actors Discuss Their Craft*, New Haven: Yale University Press, 1998.

Cavell, Stanley, *The World Viewed: Reflections on the Ontology of Film* (Cambridge, MA: Harvard University Press, 1979).

Cay Johnston, David, 'Just What Were Donald Trump's Ties to the Mob?', *Politico Magazine*, 22 May 2016, https://www.politico.com/magazine/story/2016/05/donald-trump-2016-mob-organized-crime-213910 [Accessed 23 April 2020].

Chilton, Louis, 'Robert De Niro Slams Trump Associates' *Independent*, 7 May 2020, https://www.independent.co.uk/arts-entertainment/films/news/robert-de-niro-trump-stephen-colbert-interview-shakespeare-president-a9503241.html [Accessed 6 June 2020].

Conrad, Andreas. 'Wie Robert De Niro per Anhalter durch die DDR reiste', *Die Tagesspiegel*, 11 February 2007, https://www.tagesspiegel.de/kultur/wie-robert-de-niro-per-anhalter-durch-die-ddr-reiste/809516.html [Accessed 15 May 2020].

Coppola, Francis Ford. *Live Cinema and Its Techniques*, New York: Liveright Publishing Corporation, 2017.

Davies, Gail. 'Science, Observation and Entertainment: Competing Visions of Post-war British Natural History Television, 1946–1967', *Ecumene*, Vol. 7, No. 4 (2000), pp. 432–460.

Davies, Rosamund. 'The Screenplay as Boundary Object', *Journal of Screenwriting*, Vol. 10, No. 2 (2019), pp. 149–164.

Davies, Rosamund and Ryan Flynn, 'Explicit and Implicit Narratives in the Co-design of Videogames', in Anastastions Maragiannis (ed.), *Proceedings of the Digital Research in the Humanities and Arts Conference, DRHA2014* (London: University of Greenwich, 2015), pp. 73–80.

Davis, Gary. 'Rejected Offspring: The Screenplay as a Literary Genre', *New Orleans Review*, Vol. 11, No. 2 (1984), pp. 90–94.

de Balzac, Honore. *Cousin Pons: Part Two of Poor Relations*, trans. Herbert J. Hunt, Harmondsworth: Penguin, 1978.

De Curtis, Anthony. 'Martin Scorsese: The Rolling Stone Interview', *Rolling Stone*, 1 November 1990, https://www.rollingstone.com/movies/movie-features/martin-scorsese-the-rolling-stone-interview-192568/ [Accessed 20 May 2020].

'De Niro's Film Materials Collection Opens at Ransom Center' (Press Release), *Harry Ransom Center*, 27 April 2009, https://www.hrc.utexas.edu/press/rel eases/2009/robert-de-niro-collection.html [Accessed 16 June 2019].

'De Niro Says It's His "Civic Duty" to Play Mueller on SNL', *Reuters*, 4 April 2019, https://www.reuters.com/video/watch/de-niro-says-its-his-civic-duty-to-play-id533905347 [Accessed 28 June 2020].

De Niro, Robert, 'Introduction', in Robert Storr, Charles Stuckey, Robert Kushner and Susan Davidson, *Robert De Niro, Sr.: Paintings, Drawings, and Writings: 1942–1993* (New York, NY: Rizzoli, 2019), p. 9.

De Niro, Robert and Xan Brooks, 'I'd Like to See Where Travis Bickle Is Today' (interview), *The Guardian*, 14 November 2013, https://www.theguardian.com/film/2013/nov/14/robert-de-niro-travis-bickle-taxi-driver [Accessed 20 May 2020].

Denby, David. 'Review: *Bang the Drum Slowly* by John Hancock', *Film Quarterly*, Vol. 27, No. 2 (1973), pp. 49–52.

Derrida, Jacques. 'Structure, Sign, and Play in the Discourse of the Human Sciences', in *Writing and Difference*, trans. Alan Bass (London: Routledge, 1978), pp. 278–294.

Derrida, Jacques. *Margins of Philosophy*, trans. Alan Bass, Brighton: Harvester, 1982.

'Dialogue on Film: Robert De Niro' (interview), *American Film*, Vol. VI, No. 5 (1981), p. 40.

Dickey, Tina and Helmut Friedel. *Hans Hofmann: Wunder Des Rhythmus und Schönheit Des Raumes* [Catalogue for Exhibition at the Städtische Galerie Im Lenbachaus in Munich, from 23 April to 29 June 1997, Schirn Kunsthalle, Frankfurt, from 12 September to 2 November 1997], New York: Hudson Hills Press, 1998.

Dietz, Howard. 'A Positive Personal Force, Says Dietz', *Motion Picture Herald*, Vol. 124 (1936).

Drake, Philip. 'Reconceptualizing Screen Performance', *Journal of Film and Video*, Vol. 58, No. 1/2 (2006), pp. 84–94.

Ebert, Roger. 'Interview with Theresa Russell', *Roger Ebert*, 21 September 1988, https://www.rogerebert.com/interviews/interview-with-theresa-rus sell [Accessed 22 September 2019].

Ebert, Roger. 'Reviews: *Bang the Drum Slowly*', *Roger Ebert*, 26 August 1973, https://www.rogerebert.com/reviews/bang-the-drum-slowly-1973 [Accessed 15 May 2020].

Ebert, Roger. 'Reviews: *Mean Streets*', *Roget Ebert*, 2 October 1973, https://www.rogerebert.com/reviews/mean-streets-1973 [Accessed 20 May 2020].

Ebiri, Bilge. '11 Things We Learned About *Goodfellas* From Saturday's Tribeca Q&A', *Vulture*, 26 April 2015, https://www.vulture.com/2015/04/11-thi ngs-we-learned-about-goodfellas.html [Accessed 25 September 2019].

Eig, Jonathan. 'What You Didn't Know About Gangster Al Capone' (interview), *WBUR*, 9 August 2010, https://www.wbur.org/npr/128872365/what-you-didnt-know-about-gangster-al-capone [Accessed 20 May 2020].

Eisenstein, Sergei. 'The Form of the Script', in *Selected Works, Vol. 1: Writings, 1922–34*, trans. and ed. Richard Taylor (London: BFI, 1988).

Ellis, John. 'The Performance on Television of Sincerely Felt Emotion', *The Annals of the American Academy of Political and Social Science*, Vol. 625, The End of Television? Its Impact on the World (So Far) (2009), pp. 103–115.

Esch, Kevin. '"I Don't See Any Method at All": The Problem of Actorly Transformation', *Journal of Film and Video*, Vol. 58, No. 1–2 (2006), pp. 95–107.

Feis, Aaron, 'Pelosi Quotes *Irishman* Before Signing Impeachment Articles Against Trump', *York New Post*, 15 January 2020, https://nypost.com/2020/01/15/pelosi-quotes-irishman-after-signing-impeachment-articles-aga inst-trump/ [Accessed 23 April 2020].

Field, Syd. *Screenplay: The Foundations of Screenwriting*, New York: Dell, 1979.

Fitzgerald, F. Scott. *The Last Tycoon*, ed. Edmund Wilson, Harmondsworth: Penguin, 1974.

Fitzgerald, F. Scott. *The Great Gatsby*, ed. Ruth Prigozy, Oxford: Oxford University Press, 1998.

Flamini, Roland. *Thalberg: The Last Tycoon and the World of M-G-M*, New York: Crown, 1994.

Fraser-Cavassoni, Natasha. *Sam Spiegel*, New York: Little, Brown, 2003.

Fussman, Cal. 'Robert De Niro: What I've Learned', *Esquire*, 14 December 2010, https://www.esquire.com/entertainment/interviews/a9087/robert-de-niro-quotes-0111/ [Accessed 22 May 2020].

Ghosh, Palash, 'Trump and DeNiro Engage in War of Words Over Obama', *International Business Times*, 25 April 2011, https://www.ibtimes.com/trump-deniro-engage-war-words-over-obama-281171 [Accessed 23 April 2020].

Giarrusso, Vincent. 'An Insider Perspective on the Script in Practice', *Journal of Screenwriting*, Vol. 10, No. 1 (2019), pp. 41–61.

Ginzburg, Carlo. 'Microhistory: Two or Three Things That I Know About It', trans. John Tedeschi and Anne C. Tedeschi, *Critical Inquiry*, Vol. 20, No. 1 (1993), pp. 10–35.

Goldfarb Marquis, Alice. *Hopes and Ashes: Birth of Modern Times, 1929–39*, New York: Macmillan, 1987.

Grist, Leigh. *The Films of Martin Scorsese, 1963–77: Authorship and Context*, New York: Palgrave Macmillan, 2013.

Grobel, Lawrence. '*Playboy* Interview: Robert De Niro', *Playboy*, Vol. 36, No. 1 (1989), pp. 69–90, 326.

Gropius, Walter and Arthur S. Wensinger (ed.), *The Theater of the Bauhaus: Oskar Schlemmer, Laszlo Moholy-Nagy, Farkas Molnár*, Middleton, CT: Wesleyan University Press, 1971.

Grossberg, Josh. 'Robert De Niro, Martin Scorsese, Jodie Foster on making *Taxi Driver*' (Interview from Tribeca Film Festival 2016, edited and condensed), *New York Vulture*, 25 April 2016, https://www.vulture.com/2016/04/de-niro-scorsese-foster-talk-taxi-Driver-At-40.html [Accessed 30 September 2019].

Guerrasio, Jason. 'What It Means to Be "Method"', *Tribeca Film Institute*, 19 December 2014, https://www.tfiny.org/blog/detail/what_it_means_to_be_method [Accessed 20 May 2020].

Hagan, Joe, '"I Fucking Love My Life": Joaquin Phoenix on *Joker*, Why River Is His Rosebud, His Rooney Research, and His "Prenatal" Gift for Dark Characters', *Vanity Fair*, 1 October 2019, https://www.vanityfair.com/hollywood/2019/10/joaquin-phoenix-cover-story [Accessed 23 April 2020].

Harrell, Al. '*The Untouchables*: A Search for Period Flavor', *American Cinematographer*, Vol. 7 (1987), https://staging.ascmag.com/articles/flashback-the-untouchables [Accessed 30 May 2020].

Hill, Henry and Bryon Schreckengost. *A Goodfella's Guide to New York: Your Personal Tour Through the Mob's Notorious Haunts, Hair-Raising Crime Scenes, and Infamous Hot Spots*, New York: Three Rivers Press, 2003.

Hirsch, Foster. *A Method to their Madness: A History of the Actors Studio*, New York: Norton, 1984.

Hobbs, Dick. 'Obituary: Jimmy Burke', *The Independent*, 29 April 1996, https://www.independent.co.uk/news/obituaries/obituary-jimmy-burke-1307376.html [Accessed 31 May 2020].

Holden, Stephen. 'The Movies That Inspired Martin Scorsese', *The New York Times*, 21 May 1993, https://www.nytimes.com/1993/05/21/movies/the-movies-that-inspired-martin-scorsese.html [Accessed 20 May 2020].

Horowitz, Frederick A. 'What Josef Albers Taught at Black Mountain College, and What Black Mountain College Taught Albers', *Journal of Black Mountain College Studies*, Vol. 11 (2011), http://www.blackmountainstudiesjournal.org/volume1/1-9-frederick-a-horowitz/ [Accessed 20 May 2020].

Horowitz, Frederick A. and Brenda Danilowitz, *Josef Albers: To Open Eyes*, London: Phaidon Press, 2006.

Jarnot, Lisa. *Robert Duncan, The Ambassador from Venus: A Biography*, Berkeley, Los Angeles, and London: University of California Press, 2012.

Jones, Kimberley. 'HRC Opens the Doors on De Niro: The Harry Ransom Center Bulks Up Its Movie Holdings', *The Austin Chronicle*, 28 April 2009, https://www.austinchronicle.com/daily/screens/2009-04-28/hrc-opens-the-doors-on-de-niro/ [Accessed 29 September 2019].

Kael, Pauline. 'Everyday Inferno', *The New Yorker*, October 1973, https://www.newyorker.com/magazine/1973/10/08/everyday-inferno [Accessed 20 May 2020].

Kael, Pauline. '*Mean Streets*: Everyday Inferno', *Scraps from the Loft*, 11 January 2018, https://scrapsfromtheloft.com/2018/01/11/mean-streets-pauline-kael/ [Accessed 20 May 2020].

Kael, Pauline. 'Underground Man: Martin Scorsese's *Taxi Driver*', *The New Yorker*, 2 February 1976, https://www.newyorker.com/magazine/1976/02/09/underground-man [Accessed 20 May 2020].

Kazan, Elia. *Elia Kazan: A Life*, New York: Da Capo, 1997.

Kazan, Elia. *Kazan on Directing*, New York: Knopf, 2009.

Kilday, Gregg. 'Taxi Driver Oral History: De Niro, Scorsese, Foster, Schrader Spill All on 40th Anniversary', *The Hollywood Reporter*, 7 April 2016, https://www.hollywoodreporter.com/features/taxi-driver-oral-history-de-881032 [Accessed 30 September 2019].

Knopf, R. (ed.), *Theater and Film: A Comparative Anthology*, New York: Yale University Press, 2005.

Kreps, Daniel, 'See Robert De Niro Eviscerate Trump: "I'd Like to Punch Him in the Face"', *Rolling Stone*, 8 October 2016, https://www.rollingstone.com/politics/politics-news/see-robert-de-niro-eviscerate-trump-id-like-to-punch-him-in-the-face-111689/ [Accessed 23 April 2020].

'*The Last Tycoon*' (review), *Variety*, 31 December 1975, https://variety.com/1975/film/reviews/the-last-tycoon-2-1200423612/ [Accessed 20 May 2020].

Late Night with Seth Meyers, Show 0928, NBC, aired 17 December 2019, https://www.youtube.com/watch?v=1d7vZmr12oY [Accessed 23 April 2020].

Leitch, Thomas. 'Adaptation and Intertextuality, or, What Isn't an Adaptation, and What Does It Matter?', in Deborah Cartmell (ed.), *A Companion to Literature, Film, and Adaptation* (West Sussex: Blackwell, 2012), pp. 87–104.

Levy, Shawn. *De Niro: A Life*, New York: Three Rivers, 2014.

Linson, Art. *What Just Happened. Bitter Hollywood Tales from the Front Line*, New York: Bloomsbury, 2003.

Lowe, Vicky. 'Acting with Feeling: Robert Donat, the "Emotion Chart" and *The Citadel* (1938)', *Film History: An International Journal*, Vol. 19, No. 1 (2007), pp. 73–85.

Macaulay, Scott. 'Scorsese, De Niro, Lewis and Bernhard recall *The King of Comedy*', *Filmmaker*, 1 May 2013, https://filmmakermagazine.com/69894-scorsese-de-niro-lewis-and-bernhard-recall-king-of-comedy/#.XtPISlB7mYV [Accessed 31 May 2020].

Macdonald, Ian. *Screenwriting Poetics and the Screen Idea*, Basingstoke: Palgrave Macmillan, 2013.

Malone, Aubrey. *The Defiant One: A Biography of Tony Curtis*, Jefferson, NC: McFarland, 2013.

Mamet, David. *Bambi vs Godzilla: On the Nature Purpose and Practice of the Movie Business*, New York: Simon and Schuster, 2007.

Maras, Steven. *Screenwriting: History, Theory and Practice*, London: Wallflower, 2009.

Marchese, David (interview), 'Great Performers: Robert De Niro', *New York Times Magazine*, 9 December 2019, https://www.nytimes.com/int eractive/2019/12/09/magazine/robert-deniro-interview.html [Accessed 15 April 2020].

McAloon, Mick. 'Robert De Niro: Detail in Service of the Truth', *Running From The Reels*, undated, https://runningfromthereels.com/2013/07/18/ de-niro-detail-in-service-of-the-truth/ [Accessed 20 May 2020].

McDonald, Paul. 'Supplementary Chapter: Reconceptualising Stardom', in Richard Dyer, *Stars*, 2nd ed. (London: BFI, 1998), pp. 177–200.

McGurk, Stuart (interview), 'Robert De Niro on Martin Scorsese's Ultimate Mafia Masterpiece', *GQ*, 25 November 2019, https://www.gq-magazine.co. uk/culture/article/robert-de-niro-interview [Accessed 15 April 2020].

Merleau-Ponty, Maurice. *The World of Perception*, trans. Oliver Davies, London and New York: Routledge, 2002.

Millard, Kathryn. *Screenwriting in a Digital Era*, Basingstoke: Palgrave, 2014.

MoMA Documentation for 'An Exhibition of Recent Acquisitions', Held February 14 through March 18, 1945, *MoMA*, https://www.moma.org/doc uments/moma_master-checklist_325455.pdf [Accessed 15 May 2020].

Monkhouse, Bob. 'They're Not Laughing Now…', *The Guardian*, 29 December 2003, https://www.theguardian.com/uk/2003/dec/29/arts.art snews1 [Accessed 30 May 2020].

Murphy, J. J. *Rewriting Indie Cinema: Improvisation, Psychodrama, and the Screenplay*, New York: Columbia University Press, 2019.

Murphy, Kathleen. Martin Scorsese and Gavin Smith, 'Made Men', *Film Comment*, Vol. 26, No. 5 (1993).

Naremore, James. *Acting in the Cinema*, Berkeley: University of California Press, 1988.

Newland, Christina, '*Joker* Review: Joaquin Phoenix's Alienated Antihero Is No Laughing Matter', *Sight and Sound*, 14 November 2019, https://www. bfi.org.uk/news-opinion/sight-sound-magazine/reviews-recommendations/ joker-todd-phillips-joaquin-phoenix [Accessed 23 April 2020].

Newton, Michael, 'Assassination at the Movies', *The Guardian*, 4 October 2012, https://www.theguardian.com/books/2012/oct/04/assassination-movies- michael-newton [Accessed 23 April 2020].

Nix, Elizabeth. '8 Things You Should Know About Al Capone', *History*, 5 May 2015, https://www.history.com/news/8-things-you-should-know-about-al-capone [Accessed 20 May 2020].

'Oral History Interview with John Jr.', September 28–October 3 2017. Archives of American Art, Smithsonian Institution, https://www.aaa.si.edu/col lections/interviews/oral-history-interview-john-held-jr-17514 [Accessed: 15 May 2020].

Paris, Barry. 'Maximum Expression', *American Film*, Vol. 36, No. 5 (October 1989), pp. 34–35.

Pasolini, Pier Paolo. 'The Screenplay as a "Structure That Wants to Be Another Structure"', *American Journal of Semiotics*, Vol. 4, No. 1–2 (1986), pp. 53–72.

Pauline Kael, *For Keeps: 30 Years at the Movies*, New York: Dutton, 1994.

Phipps, Keith. 'Sandra Bernhardt Remembers *The King of Comedy*', *The Dissolve*, 30 January 2014, https://thedissolve.com/features/movie-of-the-week/389-sandra-bernhard-remembers-the-king-of-comedy/ [Accessed 31 May 2020].

Pinter, Harold. *Collected Screenplays One*, London: Faber, 2000.

Poniewozik, James, *Audience of One: Donald Trump, Television, and the Fracturing of America*, New York: Liveright, 2019.

Price, Steven. *The Screenplay: Authorship, Theory and Criticism*, Basingstoke: Palgrave, 2010.

Quigley, Austin E. *The Pinter Problem*, Princeton: Princeton University Press, 1975.

Radden Keefe, Patrick, 'How Mark Burnett Resurrected Donald Trump as an Icon of American Success', *The New Yorker*, 27 December 2018, https://www.newyorker.com/magazine/2019/01/07/how-mark-bur nett-resurrected-donald-trump-as-an-icon-of-american-success [Accessed 23 April 2020].

Richards, Jeffrey. *The Age of the Dream Palace: Cinema and Society in 1930s Britain*, London and New York: I. B. Tauris, 2010.

'Robert De Niro: A Preliminary Inventory of His Papers at the Harry Ransom Center', https://norman.hrc.utexas.edu/fasearch/findingAid.cfm? kw=ronin&x=42&y=8&eadid=00481&showrequest=1 [Accessed 18 May 2020].

Romanelli, Claudia. 'From Dialogue Writer to Screenwriter: Pier Paolo Pasolini at Work for Federico Fellini', *Journal of Screenwriting*, Vol. 10, No. 3 (2019), pp. 323–337.

Rowin, Michael Joshua. 'Free Radical', *Reverse Shot*, 3 November 2006, http://reverseshot.org/archive/entry/906/hi_mom_depalma [Accessed 31 May 2020].

Rutherford, Anne. 'Cinema and Embodied Affect', *Senses of Cinema*, 25 March 2003, http://sensesofcinema.com/2003/feature-articles/embodied_ affect/ [Accessed 15 August 2019].

Sauvage, Pierre, 'Beware the Golden Fang! An Interview with Paul Thomas Anderson', *Cineaste*, Vol. 40, No. 2 (Spring 2015), p. 21.

Schrader, Paul. *Transcendental Style in Film: Ozu, Bresson, Dreyer*, Berkeley, CA: University of California, 2018.

Schrader, Paul and Richard Thompson, 'Screen writer: *Taxi Driver*'s Paul Schrader' (interview), *Film Comment*, Vol. 12, No. 2 (1976), pp. 6–19.

Schruers, Fred. 'De Niro' (interview), *Rolling Stone*, 25 August 1988, https:// www.rollingstone.com/movies/movie-news/a-rare-talk-with-robert-de-niro-242940/ [Accessed 15 May 2020].

Scorsese, Martin. 'Martin Scorsese on Jerry Lewis: "It Was Like Watching a Virtuoso Pianist at the Keyboard"', *The Guardian*, 1 September 2017, https://www.theguardian.com/film/2017/sep/01/jerry-lewis-martin-sco rsese-king-comedy-nutty-professor [Accessed 31 May 2020].

Shone, Tom. 'How *Taxi Driver* Ruined Acting', *The Economist 1843*, 6 May 2016, https://www.1843magazine.com/culture/the-daily/how-taxi-dri ver-ruined-acting [Accessed 20 May 2020].

Sklar, Robert. 'Filming an Unfinished Novel: *The Last Tycoon*', in R. Barton Palmer (ed.), *Twentieth-Century American Fiction on Screen* (Cambridge: Cambridge University Press, 2010), pp. 8–25.

Smith, David, 'Robert De Niro: "Trump Is a Real Racist, a White Supremacist"', *The Guardian*, 6 January 2019, https://www.theguardian.com/film/2019/ jan/06/robert-de-niro-trump-is-a-real-racist-a-white-supremacist [Accessed 15 June 2020].

Smith, Gavin. '*Goodfellas*: Martin Scorsese Interviewed (1990)', *Scraps from the Loft*, 15 February 2018, https://scrapsfromtheloft.com/2018/02/15/ goodfellas-martin-scorsese-interview-1990-gavin-smith/ [Accessed 31 May 2020].

Smith, Greg M., 'Choosing Silence: Robert De Niro and the Celebrity Interview', in Angela Ndalianis and Charlotte Henry (ed.), *Stars in Our Eyes: The Star Phenomenon in the Contemporary Era* (Westport, CT: Praeger, 2002), pp. 45–58.

Sobchack, Vivian. *Carnal Thoughts: Embodiment and Moving Image Culture*, Berkeley: University of California Press, 2004.

Sollosi, Mary. 'The Stars of *The Untouchables* Look Back, 30 Years Later', *Entertainment*, 5 June 2017, https://ew.com/movies/2017/06/05/the-unt ouchables-kevin-costner-robert-deniro-sean-connery-look-back/ [Accessed 20 May 2020].

Sontag, Susan. 'Film and Theatre', *The Tulane Drama Review*, Vol. 11, No. 1 (1966), pp. 24–37.

Star, Susan Leigh. 'This Is Not a Boundary Object: Reflections on the Origin of a Concept', *Science, Technology, & Human Values*, Vol. 35, No. 5 (2010), pp. 601–617.

Star, Susan Leigh and James R. Griesemer. 'Institutional Ecology, "Translations" and Boundary Objects: Amateurs and Professionals in Berkeley's Museum of Vertebrate Zoology, 1907–39', *Social Studies of Science*, Vol. 19 (1989), pp. 387–420.

Stern, Lesley. *The Scorsese Connection*, Indianapolis: Indiana University Press, 1995.

Sternberg, Claudia. *Written for the Screen: The American Motion-Picture Screenplay as Text*, Tübingen: Stauffenburg, 1997.

Storr, Robert, Charles Stuckey, Robert Kushner and Susan Davidson, *Robert De Niro, Sr.: Paintings, Drawings, and Writings: 1942–1993*, New York, NY: Rizzoli, 2019.

Tait, R. Colin. 'Robert De Niro's *Raging Bull*: The History of a Performance and a Performance of History', *Canadian Journal of Film Studies*, Vol. 20, No. 1 (2011), pp. 20–40.

Tait, R. Colin. 'De Niro and Scorsese: Director-Actor Collaboration in *Mean Streets* (1973) and the Hollywood Renaissance', in Yannis Tzioumakis and Peter Krämer (ed.), *The Hollywood Renaissance: Revisiting American Cinema's Most Celebrated Era* (London: Bloomsbury, 2018), pp. 204–220.

'*Taxi Driver* Inspires Real Sequel—With a Frightening End', *Chicago Tribune*, 23 May 1985, https://www.chicagotribune.com/news/ct-xpm-1985-05-23-8502010882-story.html [Accessed 23 April 2020].

Thomson, David. 'The Director as Ranging Bull: Why Can't a Woman Be More Like a Photograph?', *Film Comment*, Vol. 17, No. 1 (1981), pp. 9–15.

Thomson, David. *The Whole Equation: A History of Hollywood*, London: Abacus, 2006.

Thomson, David and Ian Christie (ed.), *Scorsese on Scorsese*, London and Boston: Faber & Faber, 1989.

Thompson, Kristin. *Storytelling in the New Hollywood: Understanding Classical Narrative Technique*, Cambridge, MA: Harvard University Press, 1999.

Trompette, Pascale and Dominique Vinck, 'Revisiting the Notion of Boundary Object', *Revue d'anthropologie des connaissances*, Vol. 3, No. 1 (2009), pp. 3–25.

Trump, Donald J., Twitter Post, 13 June 2018, 10:40 a.m., https://twitter.com/realDonaldTrump/status/1006833565022031873?s=20 [Accessed 23 April 2020].

Vertuno, Jim. 'De Niro Donates to Texas' Ransom Center', *AP News*, 7 June 2006, https://apnews.com/677908d9d6406ff5bfe41daef7a72bfb [Accessed 29 September 2019].

Wille, Jacob Ion and Anne Marit Waade, 'Production Design and Location in the Danish Television Drama Series *The Legacy*', *Kosmorama #263*, 16 May 2016, https://www.kosmorama.org/en/kosmorama/artikler/produc tion-design-and-location-danish-television-drama-series-legacy [Accessed 20 May 2020].

Wilson, Michael Henry. *Scorsese on Scorsese* [Cahiers Du Cinema], Paris: Phaidon Press, 2011.

Wilson, Steven. 'You Talkin' to Me?', *Ransom Center Magazine*, 13 October 2016, https://sites.utexas.edu/ransomcentermagazine/2016/10/ 13/you-talkin-to-me/ [Accessed 20 May 2020].

York, Lorraine '"You (Not) Talkin' to Me?": Robert De Niro and the Affective Paradox of Reluctant Celebrity', *The Smart Set*, 25 April 2016, https://www. thesmartset.com/you-not-talkin-to-me-2/ [Accessed 29 June 2020].

York, Lorraine, 'Robert De Niro's (In)Articulate Reluctance', in *Reluctant Celebrity: Affect and Privilege in Contemporary Stardom* (Basingstoke: Palgrave, 2018), pp. 67–100.

INDEX

© The Editor(s) (if applicable) and The Author(s) 2020   241
A. Ganz and S. Price, *Robert De Niro at Work*,
Palgrave Studies in Screenwriting,
https://doi.org/10.1007/978-3-030-47960-2

Direction and movement

focus on the big transitions
in the scene... Can take
more time here

Contrasting energies
What's the Brechtian moment?
↳ I have a choice. To
continue, or retreat

Made in United States
Orlando, FL
23 December 2021

12402471R00146